Advance Praise for *Trans*

"This provocative and perceptive book argues that the current 'trans moment' presents an unparalleled opportunity for exploring vernacular classification systems and political claims about identities. Transposing and generalizing to the arena of race and ethnicity insights developed by transgender and feminist analysts, *Trans* reveals the paradoxical deployment of social construction, contingency, and biology."
—**Ann Shola Orloff**, Northwestern University

"Taking up Caitlyn Jenner's gender transition and Rachel Dolezal's status as a self-proclaimed black person, Brubaker sheds light on the paradoxes of choice and constraint that swirl around conceptions of identity at a time when our cultural understandings of gender and race are very much in flux. This is a timely, judicious, and tremendously thoughtful and learned investigation into present-day debates. Everyone will want to read this book."
—**Steven Epstein**, author of *Inclusion: The Politics of Difference in Medical Research*

"*Trans* provides an exceptionally lucid, insightful account of the contemporary discussion on 'trans' and an extremely useful investigation of the directions that 'transgenderism' and 'transracialism' might take. Offering original thinking about gender to prod us to consider race in new ways, this dauntingly good book will garner a great deal of attention."
—**Ann Morning**, author of *The Nature of Race: How Scientists Think and Teach about Human Difference*

"*Trans* provides a strong, nuanced perspective on the rapidly shifting cultural imaginary of transgender identities and the emerging questions about possibilities for transracial identification. In its analysis of how popular thinking on race aligns and diverges from beliefs about gender, this timely book will engender much discussion and perhaps some controversy—but it will definitely be read."
—**Kristen Schilt**, University of Chicago

trans

——

Gender and Race
in an Age of
Unsettled Identities

——

Rogers Brubaker

Princeton University Press
Princeton and Oxford

press.princeton.edu

ISBN 978-0-691-17235-4
Library of Congress Control Number: 2016936750
British Library Cataloging-in-Publication Data is available

This book has been composed in Sabon Next LT Pro
Printed on acid-free paper. ∞
Printed in the United States of America
1 3 5 7 9 10 8 6 4 2

In memory of
Allan Silver

Contents

Preface

This is a book that took me by surprise. In June 2015, as UCLA's spring quarter was drawing to a close, I was settling in for a summer's work on a longstanding book project on the politics of religious and linguistic pluralism when my attention was drawn to the pairing of "transgender" and "transracial" in debates about whether Caitlyn Jenner could legitimately identify as a woman and Rachel Dolezal as black. The provocative pairing generated an unusual moment of vernacular sociology: a contentious, sprawling, multi-stranded public seminar about the contemporary meanings and workings of gender and racial identities. For a week, until the fickle spotlight of public attention moved on, the mainstream media, the blogosphere, and social media were abuzz with discussions not only about Jenner and Dolezal but about the similarities and differences between gender and race, the ways in which gender and racial identities were naturally given or socially constructed, and the possibilities for choosing and changing gender and racial identities.

I found these debates interesting, revealing, and—surprisingly often—moving (though of course much of the online commentary was crude, narrow-minded, and riddled with sarcasm and invective). Contributors brought a wide range of personal experience to bear, sometimes in fresh and unexpected ways, on larger social and political questions. Still, discussion was fundamentally limited by what Loïc Wacquant, in a different context, has called the "logic of the trial," oriented to adjudication rather than understanding.[1] Analysis was largely subordinated to efforts to validate or invalidate the identities claimed by Jenner and Dolezal.

Reflecting on the initial round of commentary, Susan Stryker, a leading figure in transgender studies, urged scholars to "hold open a space for real intellectual curiosity, for investigations that deepen our understanding of how identity claims and processes function, rather than rushing to offer well-formed opinions based on what we already think we know."[2] It is in this spirit that I have written this book. The controversy that swirled around Jenner and Dolezal serves as a useful point of entry into my subject. But I step back from that controversy in order to analyze the deep tensions—between chosenness and givenness, self-transformation and social constraint—that structure contemporary understandings of gender and race.

This is an essay, not a monograph, and it has (I hope) some of the virtues as well as the limitations of that genre. An essay is by definition exploratory, tentative, and incomplete. It is a "means of thinking on paper, of trying things out in writing," as Carl Klaus has observed. Even when it is more disciplined than Samuel Johnson's "loose sally of the mind, an irregular indigested piece," the essay remains—as suggested by the original meaning of the word, a "process of trying or testing"—an open-ended experiment, a means of trying out new ideas and exploring new territory.[3] The essay offers a degree of freedom that the monograph does not.

The limitations of the essay form—limitations of depth, systematicity, and definitiveness—are evident enough. To these must be added the limitations of the author. The book is not just an essay; it is an "essay in trespassing," to borrow Albert Hirschman's wonderful title. My previous work has touched only glancingly on gender and not at all on transgender issues. And while I have written at length on ethnicity, argued for an integrated analysis of race, ethnicity, and nationalism, and analyzed the "return of biology" in the theory and practice of race and ethnicity, my work has not been centrally concerned with race per se.

An outsider who wades into conceptual and political thickets as densely controversial as these can scarcely hope to emerge unscathed. Yet writing as an outsider may offer certain advantages. As a comparativist with broad interests in the workings of identity categories and the politics of difference, I hope that the intellectual friction generated by thinking about sex and gender in relation to race and ethnicity may prove productive rather than reductive: I hope that it may suggest ways of going beyond misleading equivalencies and ready-at-hand analogies to a richer and more nuanced understanding of both similarities and differences.

I am an outsider not only to the fields of gender and transgender studies but also to the experience of crossing gender or racial boundaries. My analysis is no doubt shaped and limited by my own identity as a white cisgender male. But my primary interest in the book is not in the lived experience of those who move between gender or racial categories or position themselves between or beyond such categories. It is rather in the contemporary transformations of, and struggles over, gender and race as systems of social classification. An ample literature describes the experiences of those engaged in these transformations and struggles; I have learned a great deal from it. But I seek in this book to provide a broader account, one that is necessarily more distant from lived experience.

The book is addressed to all who are interested in contemporary transformations of identity, not simply those with a special interest in race or gender. To make the argument accessible to a wide readership, I have sought to avoid academic jargon as much as possible. At the same time, however, I have tried not to oversimplify complex issues. I have made ample use of notes—for the most part endnotes, but a handful of footnotes as well—to qualify, illustrate, and extend the argument without encumbering the main text. Sources are cited in the notes by author and date only; full publication details can be found in the bibliography.

Two matters of terminology require brief comment. The first concerns sex and gender. For much of the second half of the twentieth century, the distinction between them seemed relatively clear and stable. "Sex" denoted biological differences, "gender" the varied and complex systems of cultural meanings, norms, and expectations attached to sex differences. In recent decades, the distinction has been challenged by those who argue that sex is just as socially and culturally constructed as gender, and that it is therefore misleading to treat sex as biological and gender as cultural. Others, however, continue to see the sex-gender distinction as indispensable, even as they acknowledge that sex is socially and culturally co-constructed.[4] Independently of this theoretical dispute, the distinction between the terms has been eroded in everyday life, popular culture, and the media by the expansive use of "gender" to denote both biologically based differences and cultural codes and expectations. In the face of these terminological complexities and controversies—not to mention the additional complexities associated with transgender phenomena—I have opted to speak most often of gender, since that is the language in which most claims are articulated, though I sometimes refer to "sex/gender," "sex or gender," or "sex and gender."

Paralleling the encompassing use of "gender" is the encompassing use of "transgender"—by transgender people themselves and by scholars—to designate a broad range of gender-variant identifications, presentations, and trajectories. In the public eye, the paradigmatic transgender experience remains that of the transsexual, who moves permanently from one clearly defined sex/gender category to another, often by surgically and hormonally remolding the body. Transgender scholars and activists, however, decenter the transsexual experience; some even implicitly or explicitly devalue that experience, especially the experience of transsexuals who seek to "pass," which some see as reproducing rather than subverting gender norms. Constructed as a self-consciously inclusive category, designed to embrace all forms of gender variance, "transgender" includes a wide range of people and practices, and scholars and activists have given increasing attention to those who situate themselves between or beyond established categories without seeking to move definitively from one to the other. I follow the practice of using "transgender" as the more general term and "transsexual" only in certain specific contexts.

The second terminological issue concerns race and ethnicity. The line between the categories we call "racial" and those we call "ethnic" is not a sharp one, and neither scholarly nor popular usage is consistent. I speak of "racial" categories when I am concerned with the distinctive American history of race, particularly with the unique experience of African Americans, and more particularly still with the peculiar classification system that long defined a person with any identifiable African ancestry as black. In other contexts, where I cast a broader analytical net, I refer more inclusively to "racial and ethnic" or "ethnoracial" categories.

This brings me to a final observation, which concerns the scope of my argument. While some strands of the discussion

pertain specifically to the United States, others are relevant
to a broader range of societies in which prevailing understandings of ethnoracial and sex/gender difference have been
unsettled in recent decades by demographic, cultural, and
political changes. For the most part, shifts in the sex/gender
domain are similar across a wide range of liberal demo-
cratic contexts, while it is harder to generalize about shifts
in the domain of race and ethnicity. The scope of different
parts of the argument should be clear from the context.

Acknowledgments

Venturing into new territory makes one more than usually dependent on others, and it is a pleasure to acknowledge the abundant help I have received along the way. I am especially grateful to Susan Ossman, who encouraged me to take on the project, talked through the argument with me, and read draft after draft with a keen critical eye. Conversations with Sébastien Chauvin helped prepare me for this book before I knew I was writing it. Jacob Foster and Jaeeun Kim provided extensive and penetrating comments on an early statement of the argument; Matías Fernández did the same for the manuscript as a whole. I was fortunate to receive exceptionally rich and detailed comments from Steven Epstein, Ann Morning, and Kristen Schilt, the reviewers for Princeton University Press. My sister, Elizabeth Brubaker, generously went through the manuscript with a fine-tooth comb, prompting me to weed out overly academic language. In the home stretch, Neil Gong provided helpful comments.

I have benefited from several opportunities to present the work-in-progress to audiences of friendly critics. An invitation from Julia Adams and Adria Lawrence enabled me to present drafts of two chapters to a joint meeting of the Comparative Research Workshop and the Comparative Politics

Workshop at Yale; I thank discussant Elisabeth Becker and participants for their comments. Mária Kovács invited me to discuss parts of the book with students in the Nationalism Studies program at the Central European University in Budapest; I thank Mária, her colleagues Michael Miller and Szabolcs Pogonyi, and the students for their comments and questions. Gail Kligman encouraged me throughout, provided helpful written comments, and generously organized and hosted a delightful dinner at which a set of friends and colleagues discussed a draft of the complete manuscript; I thank Jacob Foster, Lynn Hunt, Marcus Hunter, Sherry Ortner, Abigail Saguy, Roger Waldinger, and Juliet Williams for taking part.

Chapters 1 and 2 develop an argument made in "The Dolezal Affair: Race, Gender, and the Micropolitics of Identity," *Ethnic and Racial Studies* 39, no. 3 (2016): 414–48 © Taylor and Francis, available online: http://www.tandfonline.com /doi/pdf/10.1080/01419870.2015.1084430. I am grateful to *ERS* editors John Solomos and Martin Bulmer for encouraging me to work on the subject and for publishing the article so expeditiously. For their comments on the article, which proved helpful as I worked on the book, I would like to thank Zsuzsa Berend, Sarah Boxer, Ben Brubaker, Daniel Brubaker, Nitsan Chorev, Harry Cooper, Erica Davis, Kevan Harris, Micheline Ishay, Richard Jenkins, Mara Loveman, Kausar Mohammed, László Neményi, Richard Owens, Kay Schlozman, John Skrentny, Ben Spangler, and, last but not least, my mother, Elizabeth Brubaker senior, who, in her ninety-first year, continues to serve as an inspiration.

I have benefited greatly from the experienced editorial eye of Katya Rice and from her impeccable judgment on matters substantive as well as stylistic. And I am grateful to Meagan Levinson, my editor at Princeton University Press, and to Peter Dougherty, the Press's director, for their support and encouragement. I was fortunate to have the help of two superb research assistants, Matías Fernández and Melissa Tay. A precious gift of unencumbered time in a surpassingly beautiful place—a four-week residency at the Rockefeller Foundation's Bellagio Center on Lake Como—enabled me to meet a very tight deadline for drafting the manuscript.

In the midst of my work on this book, I was greatly saddened by the death of my teacher and friend Allan Silver. Allan was a scholar of the deepest learning, a teacher and mentor of the highest order, and a person of consummate integrity and extraordinary delicacy of feeling and insight. After completing my dissertation in 1990, I wrote to Allan about the problem of "irredeemable" gratitude that is generated by the experience of working with a generous mentor: a form of gratitude, as Georg Simmel observed, that consists "not in the return of a gift, but in the consciousness that it cannot be returned." Allan replied that the only solution consists in doing for those who follow what has been done for oneself: "That this is the only reciprocation possible is not an imperfection, but in the nature of these matters, where gratitude consists in the giver's certainty that the receiver will pass on knowledge, value, and sentiment, contending with darkness, contingency, and time." I know of no finer description of the calling of the teacher, and of no more shining example of devotion to this calling than Allan. I dedicate the book to his memory.

trans

Introduction

On June 11, 2015, Rachel Dolezal, the thirty-seven-year-old president of the Spokane chapter of the NAACP, who had presented herself as black for a number of years, was "outed" as white by her parents. A reporter for a newspaper in Coeur d'Alene, Idaho, where Dolezal had lived for a time, had been investigating her many claims—in Coeur d'Alene and later in Spokane—to have been the victim of hate crimes and harassment; when the investigation raised questions about Dolezal's identity, the reporter contacted her parents.[1]

Dolezal had long been immersed in African American culture, networks, and institutions.[2] Her fundamentalist Christian parents had adopted four black children in quick succession when Rachel was a teenager; she played a significant role in caring for them and later became the legal guardian of one.[3] Dolezal left her native Montana, where she had been home-schooled in a Christian curriculum, to study art at Belhaven College, a Christian liberal arts college in Jackson, Mississippi. She was drawn to Jackson by a book about a small interracial religious community there that was devoted to "racial reconciliation."[4] The chair of the Art Department at the time Rachel was at Belhaven later recalled her "interest [in] and, as I suppose she would frame it now, her 'identification' with black culture," adding that while she did not represent herself as black, "it was clear where her heart was." Another teacher remembered her as a "white woman with a black soul" and an unusually sophisticated social awareness.[5] Her friends at Belhaven and at the Voice of Calvary, the church she attended, were black, and she was active in the Black Students Association. After college, she received an MFA from historically black Howard University;[6] much of her artwork features African and African American themes and subjects.[7] Dolezal was married for several years to an African American man and had one child with him.

After her divorce, Dolezal began to alter her appearance, darkening her skin and styling her hair in a virtuosic succession of braids, weaves, and dreadlocks.[8] The conspicuously "authentic" and "natural" hair—in 2013, she posted photos of her latest style on her Facebook page with the caption "going with the natural look as I start my 36th year"— would later win grudging admiration from her black critics.[9] With her new look—a striking contrast with the straight blond hair and pale skin shown in old photographs— Dolezal was easily taken for black, especially since the look fit well with her social relations, cultural knowledge, and political interests. She taught part-time for several years in the Africana Studies program at Eastern Washington University; joined Spokane's police ombudsman commission as an advocate for black interests; and in 2014 was elected president of the Spokane chapter of the NAACP, where she organized Black Lives Matter protests and hosted a weekly online video show to raise awareness of black issues. But Dolezal apparently felt the need to reconstruct her biography as well as her appearance: she publicly identified an African American man as her father, discussed his life experiences, and announced on the Facebook page of the Spokane NAACP chapter, where she posted a photograph of them together, that he would be coming to town to speak at an NAACP event.

Dolezal resigned a few days after her parents' revelations became national news. But she insisted in a series of interviews that she was "definitely not white" and that she "identif[ied] as black" (though not as African American), a stance she has continued to maintain.[10] The story prompted a flurry of commentary about passing, choice, authenticity, privilege, and appropriation. Dolezal was widely condemned—and ridiculed—for identity fraud, "cultural theft," and a racial "masquerade" that was the contemporary equivalent of blackface. Others, however, defended her right to identify as black, praised her commitment to racial justice, and underscored the fictitious nature of race.

Just ten days before the Dolezal story broke, Annie Leibovitz's photograph of a corseted Caitlyn Jenner for the cover of *Vanity Fair* had marked a new stage in the mainstreaming of transgender identity. Having been—as Bruce Jenner—an Olympic gold medalist in the decathlon in 1976, a figure on the front of the iconic Wheaties "Breakfast of Champions" cereal box, and, more recently, a regular on *Keeping Up with the Kardashians* (as the husband of the matriarch of the hugely popular reality TV show), Jenner was no stranger to publicity. The carefully orchestrated coverage of her transition—which included an April 2015 interview with Diane Sawyer, the glamorous *Vanity Fair* rollout of her new name and look, and the eight-part TV series *I Am Cait*—received massive public attention, making her easily the world's most famous publicly transgender person. Mainstream media commentary was strikingly positive, applauding her courage and validating her identity as a woman; even President Obama tweeted his support.

Given the timing, it's no surprise that the Jenner story, and the transgender phenomenon more generally, served as a key point of reference in public discussion of the Dolezal case. If Caitlyn Jenner could legitimately identify, and be accepted, as a woman, could Rachel Dolezal legitimately identify, and be accepted, as black? If Jenner could be recognized as transgender, could Dolezal be recognized as transracial? The pairing of transgender and transracial was deployed in the debates mainly by the cultural right; it was intended as a provocation, designed to embarrass the cultural left for embracing Jenner while censuring Dolezal. And the pairing was taken as a provocation by the cultural left, which categorically rejected the "if Jenner, then Dolezal" syllogism and proclaimed that transracial was "not a thing."

In this book, I treat the pairing of transgender and transracial not as a political provocation but as an intellectual opportunity. Participants in the debates about Jenner and Dolezal were not just thinking *about* trans; they were thinking *with* trans. As Susan Stryker observed, they were using transgender narratives as a cultural model for thinking about "other kinds of bodily transformations that similarly pose problems regarding the social classification of persons."[11] Yet they were doing so in a generally narrow and partisan way. Stepping back from the controversy allows us to think with trans in a broader and more fruitful way about the complexities, tensions, and contradictions in the contemporary politics of identity.

Reflecting in October 2015 on "the year we obsessed over identity," the *New York Times* critic-at-large Wesley Morris situated the Jenner and Dolezal debates in the context of developments in popular culture that have shown us "how trans and bi and poly-ambi-omni- we are." Morris pointed to video games and social media platforms that enable us to "create alternate or auxiliary personae" and to the ubiquity of makeover shows.[12] But the "sense of fluidity and permissiveness and a smashing of binaries" he described has deeper roots. It is part of a much broader moment of cultural flux, mixture, and interpenetration, as suggested by the burgeoning discussions of hybridity, syncretism, creolization, and transnationalism in the last quarter century.[13]

In this landscape of unsettled identities, sex/gender and ethnoracial categories have ceased to be taken for granted and have become the focus of self-conscious choices and political claims. These choices and claims in turn have given rise to a series of questions. Who has access to what categories, and to the social spaces reserved for their members? Who controls—and patrols—the boundaries of categories? How do new categories—and new kinds of people named by those categories—come into being? Can one choose to become a member of a category that is generally understood as biologically based and fixed at birth? In a world crisscrossed by dense classificatory grids, is it possible to live between or beyond categories? These are not simply questions for scholars; they are questions for us all.

It is in the domain of sex and gender that these questions have been raised most urgently. Here, challenges to established categories have been spectacular, as indicated by the stunningly rapid shift toward social and legal recognition of gay marriage, the mainstreaming of transgender options and identities, and the gathering challenges to the binary regime of sex itself. But racial and ethnic categories have also been profoundly unsettled: by demands for the recognition of multiracial identities, by the increasing fluidity and fragmentation of the ethnoracial landscape, and by the proliferation of crossover forms of racial identification.

The unsettling of identities has substantially enlarged the scope for choice and self-transformation. The enlargement of choice, however, is itself unsettling. It has given rise to anxieties about unnatural, opportunistic, or fraudulent identity claims, and it has prompted challenges to questionable claims in the name of authentic and unchosen identities. In the face of actual or anticipated challenges, many of those who advance unorthodox identity claims have themselves sought to justify the claims by appealing to nature rather than to choice. The language of "born that way" has been deployed to legitimize claims to nonconforming gender and sexual identities, the language of DNA to fortify unorthodox claims to racial and ethnic identities. Thus instead of a straightforward enlargement in the scope for choice and self-fashioning, we see a sharpened tension—evident in everyday identity talk, public discourse, and even academic analysis—between the language of choice, autonomy, subjectivity, and self-fashioning and that of givenness, essence, objectivity, and nature.

As I will show, this tension plays out in different ways in the two domains. Paradoxically, while sex is a biological category in a way that race is not, sex and gender are understood to be more open to choice and change than are race and ethnicity. The distinction between sex and gender—and the irrelevance of ancestry to definitions of sex and gender—has made it possible to construe gender identity as a subjective individual property that is uncoupled from the body. Racial identity, however, is understood to be tightly coupled to the body and to be grounded in social relations, specifically in family and ancestry. This holds even more strongly in North America, where racial classification has historically depended not only on phenotype but also, crucially, on ancestry.

Prevailing understandings of gender and racial identity thus make changing sex or gender much more thinkable than changing race.† Changing one's gender need not be understood as changing one's gender *identity*; it can

† Sex, of course, is a legally regulated identity, while race, in liberal contexts, is not. Yet race remains a *socially* regulated identity, and as the debates about Dolezal and Jenner showed, changing sex or gender is understood by a broad segment of the public to be possible and legitimate, while changing race is not.

be understood as bringing one's gender presentation—including, often, one's bodily shape and secondary sex characteristics—into alignment with that identity. (For this reason, some trans men and women, as well as medical practitioners and scholars, prefer to speak of gender or sex *confirmation* surgery than of gender or sex *reassignment* surgery.)[14] Changing one's gender also entails changing the way one is identified by others. There is no established vocabulary for thinking about changing race in this way, not least because there are no widely available cultural tools for thinking of racial identity in subjectivist and individualist terms.

But what makes subjective gender identity a socially legitimate basis for demands to reconstitute the body and change the way one is identified by others? After all, there is a history of characterizing subjective identifications that are radically at variance with prevailing classifications of sexed bodies as a sign of mental illness and as grounds for treating the mind rather than altering the body.[15] If subjective gender identity is today endowed with credibility and authority, this is in large part because it is widely understood to be grounded in a deep, stable, innate disposition. Thus while the sex-gender distinction allows gender identity to be disembodied and denaturalized, the "born that way" story allows it to be re-embodied and renaturalized. It is this asserted *objectivity of subjective identity* that makes it possible to defend choice in the name of the unchosen and change in the name of the unchanging.

The authority of ancestry over racial classification in North America explains why racial identity is not easily or legitimately changed or chosen. Passing as white is an old theme in American history, and the case of Rachel Dolezal, along with a few others, has shown that it is possible to pass as black as well. But passing is not understood as changing one's race; it is understood as getting others to *misperceive* that race. And while passing might be justified as a response to oppression, Dolezal's "reverse passing" was condemned for appropriating a culture, history, and social position that legitimately belonged to others.

Yet today the authority of ancestry over racial classification is declining. The multiracial movement, increasing rates of interracial marriage, the erosion of the one-drop rule, and even the growing popularity of genetic ancestry tests all highlight the mixedness of racial and ethnic ancestry. For a broadening circle of people, ancestry no longer determines identity. Mixed ancestry licenses choice and facilitates change; it authorizes people to selectively identify with different ancestral lines in different contexts. Identity options are of course unequally distributed, but many people with racially mixed ancestry—including President Obama—can and do choose and change their racial identities.[16]

Identity options have expanded in other ways as well. The condemnation of Dolezal for her "imitation" or "impersonation" of blackness is part of a long tradition of criticizing—as a form of appropriation, domination, or stigmatization—the enactment of a subordinate racial or ethnic identity that is not legitimately one's own. The critique often extends to the adoption of cultural forms and practices—styles of music, dress, hair, or speech, for example—that are construed as belonging to a subordinate group. In the last decade or so, however, as crossover practices and identifications have proliferated, they have come to be seen in more nuanced ways: as potentially affiliative rather than appropriative, as sites of sympathy and alignment rather than modes of domination, even as ways of subverting rather than reinforcing racial hierarchies.[17]

———

To the countless millions who are otherwise unfamiliar with transgender matters, Caitlyn Jenner has come to represent the possibility of changing sex or gender. And to the broad public that understands race as inborn and immutable, Rachel Dolezal has come to represent the absurdity of changing race. Neither story, however, is representative in a sociological sense. Jenner's conventional performance of femininity—not to mention her wealth and celebrity—did not resonate with many transgender people. And the idiosyncratic features of Dolezal's story—especially the role of deception, which turned the story into a morality play that ensured broad public rejection of her claims—distracted attention from the increasing fluidity of racial and ethnic identifications and the limited but growing space for choice and change.[18]

Yet if neither story is representative, the intertwining of the two affords an unusual opportunity to analyze gender and race in relation to each other. Gender and race are of course "different differences," but both are being reimagined, reconstructed, and newly contested in ways that are in some respects strikingly similar.[19] And the twinned debates about Jenner and Dolezal can be understood as a distinctive "trans moment" that provides a convenient point of entry into the subject.

Part One sketches the contours and contexts of this trans moment. Chapter 1 shows how the pairing of transgender and transracial in the discussions of Jenner and Dolezal was deployed to stake out positions in a field of argument defined by two questions: Can one legitimately change one's gender? And can one legitimately change one's race? I analyze the discourse of *essentialists*, who see gender and racial identities as grounded in nature or in a lifelong lived history and therefore as identities that cannot legitimately be changed; of *voluntarists*, for whom both gender and racial identities can legitimately be changed; and of those who combine *gender voluntarism* with *racial essentialism*. While essentialists and voluntarists stressed the similarities between

changing gender and changing race, advocates of gender voluntarism and racial essentialism sought to distinguish the
(legitimate) phenomenon of changing one's gender from
the (illegitimate) phenomenon of changing one's race.

Chapter 2 situates the Dolezal affair in its broader cultural
and political contexts. I take as my point of departure the profound unsettling of the ways we think about cultural and
bodily differences and the massive enlargement in the scope
for choice and self-transformation. I show how anxieties
about unregulated choice have generated efforts to police unorthodox choices—as well as to defend such choices *against*
policing—in the name of authentic and unchosen identities.

Part Two starts from the premise that "trans" is good to
think with: that we can fruitfully use the transgender experience as a lens through which to think about the fluidity of
racial identifications. But what does it mean to "think with
trans"? The sheer variety of transgender experience precludes
a univocal answer. I distinguish what I call the trans of migration, the trans of between, and the trans of beyond, taken
up in turn in chapters 3, 4, and 5.

The *trans of migration* involves moving from one established sex/gender category to another, often by surgically
and hormonally transforming one's body and formally
changing one's legal identity. The *trans of between* involves
defining oneself with reference to the two established categories, without belonging entirely or unambiguously to
either one, and without moving definitively from one to
the other. The *trans of beyond* involves positioning oneself
in a space that is not defined with reference to established
categories. It is characterized by the claim to transcend existing categories—or to transcend categorization altogether.

Each form of transgender, I argue, can help us think about
race and ethnicity in fruitful ways. Racial passing (including "reverse passing" like Dolezal's) exemplifies the trans of

migration, the multiracial movement illustrates the trans of between, and indifference or opposition to racial or ethnic categorization is an instance of the trans of beyond.

The concluding chapter ties together the strands of the argument about gender and race as embodied and enacted identities that are increasingly—yet in differing ways and to differing degrees—understood as open to choice and change. It seeks to explain why changing sex or gender is understood as more legitimate than changing race or ethnicity, even though biological differences between the sexes are deeper and more socially consequential than the superficial biological differences between socially defined racial and ethnic groups.

Analyzing race and ethnicity in relation to sex and gender is not without its risks and difficulties. Analogical reasoning has been criticized for neglecting the ways in which race and ethnicity intersect with sex and gender and other forms of difference.[20] Such intersections are obviously important. The transgender experience of Caitlyn Jenner, a wealthy, white Republican celebrity, has very little in common with that of Kricket Nimmons, a poor, HIV-positive African American ex-convict from the rural South, whose path to one of the first Medicaid-financed genital reconstruction surgeries was chronicled in a lengthy *New York Times* piece.[21] As theorists of "intersectionality" have argued, gender, race, class, and other dimensions of difference do not exist in isolation; they are mutually constitutive.[22] But gender and race are not simply intersecting differences; they are also systems of social classification with distinctive yet in some ways converging logics that can fruitfully be compared. Long understood as inborn, stable, and rigorously categorical, gender and race are increasingly open to choice, change, and blurring. The intertwined debates about Jenner and Dolezal afford a unique opportunity to explore both their similarities and their differences.[23]

Part One

———

The Trans Moment

Chapter 1

Transgender,
Transracial?

From the beginning, the story of Rachel Dolezal's identification as black was intertwined in public debate with that of Caitlyn Jenner's identification as a woman. Within hours of the breaking of the Dolezal story, the hashtag #transracial had started to trend on Twitter. Deployed by some to provoke, by others to persuade, by still others simply to amuse, the pairing of transgender and transracial generated wide-ranging public discussion about the possibilities and limits of choosing or changing racial and gender identities.

Before transgender and transracial were joined in the Dolezal affair, the terms had been juxtaposed only occasionally. One set of juxtapositions was initiated by the radical feminist Janice Raymond in her critique of the medical construction of transsexualism. In the introduction to the 1994 reissue of her book *The Transsexual Empire*, Raymond asked rhetorically, "Does a Black person who wants to be white suffer from the 'disease' of being a 'transracial'?" She went on to observe that "there is no demand for transracial medical intervention precisely *because* most Blacks recognize that it is their society, not their skin, that needs changing."[1]

While Raymond used the pairing dismissively, other feminist philosophers, more sympathetic to transsexual or transgender claims, have taken the analogy more seriously. Christine Overall argued that if one accepts the legitimacy of transsexual surgery, one should accept, in principle, the legitimacy of "transracial" surgery as well.[2] And Cressida Heyes—noting that there is in fact a demand for medical intervention to alter ethnically or racially marked bodies—analyzed the similarities and differences between changing sex and changing race as projects of self-transformation.[3] More recently, Jess Row's 2014 satirical novel *Your Face in Mine* turned on a white protagonist who becomes black through "racial reassignment surgery" in response to what he construes as "racial identity dysphoria syndrome."[4]

In the decade or so before the Dolezal affair, juxtapositions of transgender and transracial were occasionally picked up by journalists and others. A few conservative journalists sought to ridicule transgender by associating it with what they took to be the obviously absurd idea of choosing or changing one's race. And in the vast archive of ephemera that is the Web, one can find scattered—mainly humorous—uses of "transracial" (and "cisracial") that are paired with or play on "transgender" or "cisgender."†

Yet these earlier pairings of transgender and transracial had no public resonance. It was the Dolezal debates themselves that joined the terms in the public realm. I begin this chapter by characterizing the field of meanings associated

---

† "Cisgender" or "cis"—constructed by analogy to "transgender" or "trans," from the Latin preposition meaning "on this side of"—designates a person whose "gender corresponds to his or her sex at birth" (*Oxford English Dictionary*).

with transgender and transracial individually and then show how the Dolezal story brought the terms together to generate an unprecedented public discussion.

"Transgender" and "Transracial" before the Dolezal Affair

The term "transgender" has enjoyed a spectacularly successful career in the last two decades. As deployed by social movement activists to embrace all forms of gender variance, the term not only gained traction among activists but rapidly found broader public resonance, acquiring institutional recognition, legal weight, academic gravitas, media exposure, and popular currency.[5]

As an umbrella term, "transgender" conceals a key tension between *changing* gender (by moving from one established category to another) and *challenging* gender (whether implicitly, through gender-variant behavior or presentation, or expressly, through political claims-making). Those who seek to change their gender presentation and publicly recognized gender—whether or not they alter their bodies through surgery or hormones—do not necessarily challenge the binary gender regime; they may even reinforce it by subscribing to stories about unalterable, inborn identities. The difference between trans as a one-way trajectory from one established category to another and trans as a positioning of the self between or beyond established categories will be taken up and elaborated in the second part of the book. Here I simply note that while activist and academic discussions have highlighted the transgressive and disruptive potential of transgender and have addressed the full spectrum of gender-variant individuals—"encompassing transsexuals, drag queens, butches, hermaphrodites, cross-dressers, masculine women, effeminate men, sissies, tomboys," and others—broader public discussions have focused on transitions from one clearly and often stereotypically defined gender to the other, especially those that involve surgical or hormonal remolding of the body.[6]

Claims for recognition associated with binary transitions like Jenner's have greater public resonance, legitimacy, and visibility than claims that more directly challenge the gender binary. Transitions like Jenner's are more easily cast in a culturally consecrated narrative form. They can be narrated as stories of a tragic mismatch between an authentic personal identity, located in the deepest recesses of the self, and a social identity mistakenly assigned at birth—a mismatch overcome through an odyssey of self-awakening and self-transformation, culminating in the public validation of one's true self. It helps that these are framed as stories of individual alienation and redemption, not of systemic injustice, and that they are compatible with prevailing essentialist understandings of gender.

While the term "transgender" has come to enjoy broad public currency in recent years, the same cannot be said for "transracial." A common reaction to the pairing of the terms in the Dolezal affair was that transracial, unlike transgender, was "not a thing"; the word was treated as a pointless or pernicious neologism. In fact, the term "transracial" has a longer history than "transgender." But it has been used primarily in the specialized context of interracial adoption, where the prefix "trans" has had a quite different meaning and valence.

The formation of transracial families through adoption—in particular the placement of black children with white adoptive families—has been deeply controversial for nearly half a century.[7] The most radical and consistent opposition has come from the National Association of Black Social

Workers (NABSW). The association's 1972 position paper proposed a strict form of racial matching of adoptees and adoptive families; it rejected transracial adoption as an "unnatural" practice that prevents the "healthy development [of adoptees] as Black people."[8] In testimony to a Senate committee, the association's president denounced the practice as a "blatant form of race and cultural genocide." Black children raised in white homes, according to other NABSW presidents, would develop "white psyches" or "European minds" or would otherwise have severe identity problems and be lost to the black community.[9]

The argument for strict racial matching failed to gain broad political or legal support, but weaker forms of matching continue to be practiced by adoption agencies. Even where racial matching per se is not at issue, parents seeking to adopt transracially may be scrutinized for their "cultural competency" and for their commitment to "racially appropriate modes of parenting."[10]

Thus while the "trans" in transgender has signaled an *opportunity* for transgender people, the "trans" in transracial has signaled a *threat* to transracial adoptees. The transgender community has celebrated the crossing of gender boundaries. But the transracial adoption community—adoptees, adoptive families, and institutional intermediaries such as adoption agencies and social workers—has problematized the crossing of racial boundaries, seeing it as portending the loss, weakening, or confusion of racial identity.

Both the scholarly literature on transracial adoption and the vernacular literature—memoirs by adoptees and adoptive families, advice by psychologists and social workers, and websites produced by and for adoptive families and adoptees—emphasize the importance of cultivating and strengthening the (endangered) racial identity of transracial adoptees. While transgender activists have sought to destabilize and even subvert the gender order, transracial adoption activists have sought to restabilize and affirm the racial order. The transgender community is invested in a project of cultural transformation, the transracial adoption community in a project of cultural preservation.

The Dolezal affair wrenched "transracial" out of the adoption context and brought it into conversation with "transgender." Given the antithetical commitments and concerns of the transracial adoption and transgender communities, it should come as no surprise that an open letter from "members of the adoption community" declared the description of Dolezal as "transracial" to be "erroneous, ahistorical, and dangerous."[11] The idea that Dolezal could change her race by inserting herself in black networks and immersing herself in black culture suggested that transracial adoptees could change *their* race—a possibility the transracial adoption community strenuously rejected. Their rejection of the idea of changing race, to be sure, was more philosophical than empirical. It was precisely their concern that transracial adoption *could* lead to changes in racial identity—in particular to the loss of one's authentic identity for want of social support for it—that underlay their commitment to strengthening and stabilizing racial identity. In a sense, Dolezal embodied precisely the danger they wished to avert.

One prominent scholar and activist in the transracial adoption field regarded Dolezal with greater sympathy. John Raible had earlier argued that transracial adoption may indeed involve a process of "transracialization," insofar as white adoptive parents and siblings, for example, may "become immersed in wider social networks populated by people of color."[12] As he suggested in an open letter to Dolezal, much of her own experience would seem to illustrate this process.[13] Like others in the transracial adoption field, however, Raible insisted that Dolezal was confused when she claimed to identify as black. Identifying *with* black people and black culture was one thing; identifying *as* black was another.

Members of the transracial adoption community, which had owned the term "transracial," were offended by what they considered its misuse to refer to Dolezal's experience. But they were not especially concerned with Jenner or transgender matters. They were responding specifically to the description of Dolezal as transracial, not to the pairing of transgender and transracial. Their response to Dolezal therefore stands apart from the main body of commentary.

The Field of Argument

In the broader discussion of Jenner and Dolezal, the pairing of transgender and transracial was deployed to stake out positions—and to attack competing positions—in a field of argument defined by two questions: Can one legitimately change one's gender? And can one legitimately change one's race?

Combining the two questions yields four positions, which are depicted in the diagram on p. 22. (The positions—the diagram's quadrants—are numbered counterclockwise.) Quadrant 1, at the top left, represents the essentialist position that gender and racial identities cannot legitimately be changed. Quadrant 3, at the bottom right, represents the diametrically opposed voluntarist position, according to which both gender and racial identities *can* legitimately be changed. While essentialists and voluntarists emphasized the similarities between Jenner and Dolezal, and more broadly between gender and racial identities, others highlighted the differences. Quadrant 2, at the lower left, represents the combination of gender voluntarism and racial essentialism, and quadrant 4, in the upper right, the inverse combination of gender essentialism and racial voluntarism (which, for reasons I discuss below, was conspicuously missing from the Dolezal debates).

Can one legitimately change one's race?

		No	Yes
Can one legitimately change one's gender?	No	1. Essentialism	4. Gender essentialism, racial voluntarism
	Yes	2. Gender voluntarism, racial essentialism	3. Voluntarism

The labels are shorthand simplifications. "Essentialist" stances include both the view that gender and/or racial identities are grounded in nature and the view that they are grounded in history. "Voluntarist" stances include those that assert that gender and/or racial identities can be chosen, as well as those that assert (particularly with respect to gender) that public, socially validated identities can be changed even if—on some level—the core personal identity is understood as unchosen. In either case, "voluntarism" highlights choice and agency: even where the core identity is understood as unchosen, voluntarist stances emphasize the choice of self-presentation and public identification.[14]

"If Jenner, Then Dolezal": The Argument from Similarity

Essentialists and voluntarists used quasi-syllogistic reasoning to underscore the similarities between changing gender and changing race. If we accept that Caitlyn Jenner is a woman, they argued, then we must accept that Rachel Dolezal is black. The syllogism cut both ways. Addressed to an audience inclined to accept the legitimacy of transgender claims, it could be used to legitimize Dolezal's claim to identify as black, or at least to argue that her claim deserved a respectful hearing, not a derisive dismissal. But when it was addressed to an audience inclined to dismiss changing race out of hand, the syllogism worked in reverse; it served to undercut the legitimacy of Jenner's claim (and of transgender claims more generally).

The latter, reverse working of the syllogism was much more common than the former. "If Bruce Jenner Is a Woman, Then Rachel Dolezal Is Black," read the headline of a blog post on the site of the American Family Association of Pennsylvania, a branch of a national association devoted to "standing up for traditional Judeo-Christian values."[15] From the perspective of the association and others on the cultural right, Dolezal's claim to be black was so palpably absurd that it needed no refutation; this assumed absurdity was then used to assert or imply that Jenner—and by extension others following similar trajectories—could therefore not be legitimately recognized as a woman.

Much of the essentialist commentary was expressly partisan. Commentators on the cultural right gleefully seized on the Dolezal revelations as a weapon in the culture wars; they lambasted the mainstream media, "liberals," or "the left" for embracing Jenner while censuring Dolezal. Some added that Dolezal's claim might well be considered more reasonable than Jenner's, since differences of race are much more superficial than those of sex or gender. The conservative commentator Steven Crowder, for example, argued that "as opposed to sex, which differentiates humans by their organs, reproductive functions, hormonal profiles, bone-density, neuropsychiatry and physical capabilities, many of the delineations surrounding race are merely cosmetic." And a contributor to Glenn Beck's website observed, "My whiteness is far less hardwired and far more difficult to define than my maleness."[16] If one rejects racial reidentification out of hand, these commentators suggested, one has an even stronger case for rejecting transgender claims.

Essentialists assailed the cultural left not only for its inconsistency and hypocrisy but also, more fundamentally, for its subjectivism—for letting "self-identification trump objective truth,"[17] according to the *National Review*, or, more colorfully, for "solipsism" and the "end of reality," as a website devoted to "traditional Anglicanism" put it.[18] It was this climate of subjectivism that enabled both Jenner's and Dolezal's claims. To this anything-goes subjectivism essentialists counterposed a seemingly no-nonsense acceptance of "objective reality." An article on the culturally conservative Charisma News and Christian Post sites, for example, argued that "skin color is verifiable. It is not based on perception. It is not based on feelings. It is based on provable data. The same is true when it comes to gender (. . . putting aside the question of how to best help those with biological or genetic abnormalities)."[19]

Everyday essentialism was even more prevalent outside the professional commentariat and the blogosphere. In response to a Spokane newspaper's reporting of the Dolezal revelations, one commenter—among more than a thousand—wrote: "If we (not I) feel gender choice/identification is up for grabs, allowing anyone to choose and declare their gender (note, the current number of supposed genders is now over 50) . . . then why not allow one to chose [*sic*] their color/ethnicity? How can our society have it both ways? We either look for truth . . . , or we allow anything goes and deal with the fall out . . . which can be very destabilizing and tension producing."[20] A similar sense of the destabilization of the cognitive and moral order was expressed on a Catholic message board: "The world is upside down. If Bruce Jenner can claim he is female, regardless of the fact that he is not, then I don't see why a white person can't be black."[21]

Some conservative Christian commentaries appealed directly to the order of creation. God "made us the way we are ... for His purposes and His glory," argued the evangelical pastor Scott Crook; self-identification in terms at variance with this created order—as in the cases of Jenner and Dolezal—is therefore "nothing more than self-deception."[22] A post on an evangelical website urged readers to "embrace the fact that a master craftsman has chosen both our ethnicities and our genders for his glory."[23] And a reader comment on a conservative website observed that Jenner and Dolezal are "telling their Creator He mad[e] a mistake, and God being perfect, it is impossible for Him to make mistakes.... Why can't we all be ourselves as God made us? Why are we always trying to be someone else?"[24]

Conservative Christian churches and organizations made a few comments about Dolezal, but they were much more concerned with Jenner. The imbalance reflects their much deeper investment in preserving sex and gender boundaries than racial and ethnic boundaries. For conservative Christians, sex and gender are utterly central to the created order in a way that race and ethnicity are not. Dolezal was a mere sideshow; Jenner—and the mainstreaming of transgender more generally—commanded sustained attention.

In addressing Jenner's claim to have always known herself to be a woman, some conservative Christian commentaries added a theological dimension to the cultural right's critique of subjectivism. They interpreted Jenner's claim, and analogous transgender claims, as a contemporary form of Gnosticism. A dualistic current of thought of the early

Christian era, Gnosticism denigrated the body and the material world and privileged a form of intuitive knowledge (*gnosis*) that would enable men and women to achieve salvation by transcending the prison of the body and the imperfections of the material world. Conservative Christian commentaries challenged the neo-Gnostic idea that gender identity is intuitively knowable independently of the sexual constitution of the body and, more broadly, the "idea that the 'real' self is separate from who one is as an embodied, material being."[25] To divorce gender identity from the body is to turn one's back on nature and the created order; in the words of the Catholic natural-law blogger Andrew Greenwell, it is to rebel "against creation and against creation's God."[26]

The essentialists were mainly cultural conservatives, but they were joined by some liberal and radical feminists. Just five days before the Dolezal news broke, the *New York Times* published a critical reflection on the Jenner affair and transgender politics by the historian and liberal feminist writer Elinor Burkett, objecting to Jenner's claim to have a "female brain" and to the reactionary ideal of womanhood suggested by the *Vanity Fair* debut.[27] Unlike some radical feminists, Burkett did not expressly deny the legitimacy of Jenner's claim to be a woman, and she referred to Jenner using a female honorific and female pronouns. But she criticized attacks by trans activists on "women's right to define ourselves": "People who haven't lived their whole lives as women shouldn't get to define us. . . . They haven't traveled through the world as women and been shaped by all this entails."

Burkett's appeal to lifelong history and experience as a criterion of authentic womanhood exactly parallels a prominent strand of the self-consciously progressive critiques of Dolezal's claim to identify as black. And Burkett's essay strikingly anticipated the Dolezal affair: "The 'I was born in the wrong body' rhetoric favored by other trans people . . . is just as offensive, reducing us to our collective breasts and vaginas. Imagine the reaction if a young white man suddenly declared that he was trapped in the wrong body and, after using chemicals to change his skin pigmentation and crocheting his hair into twists, expected to be embraced by the black community."[28] Burkett and radical feminists of course espouse positions antithetical to those of the cultural conservatives, and their "historical essentialism," as it might be called, differs sharply from the naturalist essentialism of the cultural conservatives. Yet both articulate an objectivist critique of self-identification, voluntarism, and subjectivism.

Writing after the Dolezal revelations, the radical feminist journalist Megan Murphy made a similar argument. Like Burkett, she professed respect for Jenner's identity choices. But she noted that many of the arguments raised against Dolezal could be applied to Jenner as well; she mentioned specifically Alicia Waters's claim that Dolezal "presented to the world the trappings of black womanhood without the burden of having to have lived them for most of her life" and Zeba Blay's claim that she "play[ed] into racial stereotypes and perpetuate[d] the false idea that it is possible to 'feel' a race." Like Burkett, Murphy insisted that "those of us who were born and raised as female have the right to define and discuss that experience and our movement, as we have done for over a century now, as we see fit."[29]

The gender and racial essentialists, I have noted, were mainly cultural conservatives; conversely, most cultural conservatives adopted an essentialist stance. One might therefore have expected to find the cultural left defending the opposite stance of gender and racial voluntarism. The cultural right made this expectation explicit: given its attachment to a language of individual autonomy and social construction, the cultural left *ought* to adopt a consistently voluntarist stance. And indeed a few representatives of the cultural left (as well as others on the left) defended gender and racial voluntarism. But the overwhelming majority accepted Jenner's claim while rejecting Dolezal's; they combined gender voluntarism with racial essentialism. Before considering this stance, however, I sketch the main lines of argument developed by the small set of gender and racial voluntarists (who occupied quadrant 3 in the diagram).

The "if Jenner, then Dolezal" syllogism, as noted above, worked primarily in reverse. If one starts from the unquestionable assumption that Dolezal could *not* be black, the syllogism led ineluctably to the conclusion that Jenner could not be a woman—and, by extension, to the delegitimation of transgender more generally. This is why the syllogism was wielded so gleefully by the cultural right. And it explains why the cultural left, committed to both gender voluntarism and racial essentialism, rejected the terms of the syllogism and denied that the Jenner and Dolezal cases were comparable.

A few contrarian voices, however, accepted the terms of the syllogism. Addressing those who acknowledged that Jenner was a woman, they argued that, by a similar logic, one should acknowledge, or at least entertain seriously, Dolezal's claim to be black. Writing as a black transgender man and as a scholar of race, gender, and sexuality, Kai Green challenged prevailing black and transgender commentary by defending the legitimacy of asking about the relation between "transgender" and "transracial." "It is not a stupid question," he wrote. "It is a perplexing question," one that is "important [to] wrestle with." Labeling the question "transphobic" or simply asserting that race and gender "aren't the same thing" is "not a good answer."[30]

The legal scholar Camille Gear Rich, who has studied the cultural, institutional, and legal shift toward racial self-identification, challenged the prevailing framing in terms of "deceit" or "appropriation." In a CNN opinion piece Rich wrote: "I admire the way [Dolezal] chose to live her life as a black person.... I will not indict her for her choice to link herself to this community, and I would consider her claim no greater if she identified a long lost African ancestor."[31] The sociologist Ann Morning, who has studied the identification and classification of multiracial individuals, endorsed the transgender-transracial analogy in a CBS interview: "We're getting more and more used to the idea that people's racial affiliation and identity and sense of belonging can change."[32] And when the historian Allyson Hobbs, author of a book on racial passing, was asked by MSNBC's Melissa Harris-Perry whether, by analogy to the transgender experience, there might be "a different category of blackness, that is about the *achievement* of blackness, despite one's parentage," Hobbs replied that it was "absolutely possible.... Why not? ... There certainly is a chance that she identifies as a black woman, and that there could be authenticity to that."[33]

The anarchist philosopher Crispin Sartwell, while acknowledging others' discomfort with the prospect of gender and racial categories breaking down, envisioned the "wild and liberating possibilities [that] might open up" at this "excruciating and beautiful moment."[34] And from the perspective of queer theory, the sociologist Angela Jones celebrated Dolezal's "queering of race," stressing the possibility that Dolezal "*has* become a black woman," and that "maybe the only livable life [for her] is a black one." "Subjectivities are ours to craft," Jones wrote, and it is "an exercise of agency, empowerment, and queerness" to challenge the "hegemonic discursive power regimes that imprison our bodies." Dolezal's "choice to fulfill her own racial destiny is her choice, not ours."[35]

The most sustained argument for embracing racial along with gender voluntarism was developed by the political scientist and left intellectual Adolph Reed Jr.[36] Like the conservative essentialists, Reed criticized the inconsistency of the cultural left for embracing Jenner while repudiating Dolezal. But rather than deploy this critique in defense of gender essentialism, he used it in opposition to racial essentialism. That essentialism, he suggested, rests ultimately on biology: it depends on the argument that Dolezal simply couldn't be black because she had no known African ancestry, which implies that she *could* be black if she *did* have some African ancestry. As Reed and others observed, this troublingly mirrors the essentialist logic of the one-drop rule.[37]

Reed also challenged nonbiological, historical forms of essentialism that claim that Dolezal was "raised outside of 'authentic' black idiom or cultural experience." Such arguments pose the question of "whose black idiom or cultural experience" would count as definitive. Nor does authenticity enable us to distinguish between Jenner and Dolezal: "How do we know that Dolezal may not sense that she is 'really' black in the same, involuntary way that many transgender people feel that they are 'really' transgender?" Reed rejected, finally, the condemnation of Dolezal for engaging in "cultural appropriation." Following Walter Benn Michaels, he argued that this critique has force "only if 'culture' is essentialized as the property of what is in effect a 'race.'"[38] Reed concluded that there is "no coherent, principled defense of the stance that transgender identity is legitimate but transracial is not."[39]

Why were there so few consistent voluntarists in the Dolezal debates? (As will be noted below, a similar question can be asked about the complete absence of voices defending the combination of gender essentialism and racial voluntarism). Does this point to the robustness of essentialist understandings of race and to their imperviousness to decades of academic theorizing about race as a social construction? There is something to this, but it is not the whole story. The particularities of the Dolezal case in effect stacked the deck against voluntarism. Framed by the media in terms of deception and misrepresentation, her story was unlikely to elicit broad sympathy. Other developments, which I consider in subsequent chapters, reveal greater public appreciation of the openness of racial identities to change and choice.

Boundary Work:
The Argument from Difference

Essentialists and voluntarists held antithetical views, but both embraced the terms of the "if Jenner, then Dolezal" syllogism and underscored the similarities between gender transitions and racial reidentification. Other voices in the debate, however, rejected any kind of equivalence between Jenner and Dolezal and underscored the fundamental differences between "transgender" and "transracial." They did so, overwhelmingly, by accepting the legitimacy of changing one's gender while denying the legitimacy of changing one's race. In the terms of the diagram, they crowded into quadrant 2, defined by gender voluntarism and racial essentialism, while shunning altogether quadrant 4, defined by the inverse combination of gender essentialism and racial voluntarism.

The absence of advocates for gender essentialism and racial voluntarism is in one sense puzzling, given the widely shared sense that differences of sex and gender are deeper and more fundamental than differences of race.[40] The avoidance of this quadrant—as of the consistent voluntarism of quadrant 3—no doubt reflects the fact that Jenner had a "good" identity narrative while Dolezal's story was tainted by deception and misrepresentation.

Yet there are deeper patterns that go beyond Jenner and Dolezal. On the cultural left, race remains a much more closely policed category than gender: while gender voluntarism can fairly be said to be hegemonic, racial voluntarism is heretical or at best suspect. Transgender claims have been framed as a civil rights issue: as a response to exclusion, oppression, and violence. Claims to choose or change one's racial identity—such as those advanced by the multiracial movement—have been much more difficult to frame in this way; they have even been criticized for weakening and fragmenting the black community and undermining the civil rights and racial justice agendas.[41] This helps explain why the cultural left has endorsed gender voluntarism and racial essentialism rather than the inverse combination.

On the cultural right, by contrast, sex and gender—as categories central to both cognitive and social order—are much more closely policed than race and ethnicity. The destabilization of the sex/gender order is much more threatening than the destabilization of racial and ethnic categories to the core agenda of the cultural right, which is centered on the defense of the family. (This holds even more strongly, as noted above, for religious cultural conservatives.) Criticisms of multiculturalism, to be sure, are central to the message of the cultural right. But the perceived threat to nationhood from multiculturalism does not come from the unsettling of racial and ethnic categories; indeed, multiculturalism in a sense presupposes the stability of those categories. To the extent that the cultural right is invested in the ideology of color blindness or in the notion of a post-racial society, it would welcome rather than resist the destabilization of racial categories.

One might have expected, then, to find commentators from the cultural right endorsing racial voluntarism along with gender essentialism. As I noted above, some did observe that Dolezal's claim seemed on its face more plausible than Jenner's, since differences of sex and gender are deeper than those of race. But this did not lead these commentators to argue expressly for racial voluntarism, at least not in connection with Dolezal, whose politics were antithetical to their own.

The flood of commentary defending the combination of gender voluntarism and racial essentialism can best be understood as a kind of *boundary work*. This concept was introduced in the sociology of science by Thomas Gieryn to highlight the efforts undertaken to demarcate science—as a prestigious form of activity commanding certain privileges, resources, respect, and authority—from non-science or pseudoscience.[42] As Gieryn noted, the concept is easily applied to analogous attempts to distinguish medicine from quackery, religion from non-religion, art from crafts, disciplines and professional jurisdictions from one another, and so on; and it has since come to be used in a wide variety of contexts.[43] Here I extend the concept to the quasi-sociological rhetorical work undertaken to distinguish the (legitimate) practice of changing gender from the (illegitimate) practice of changing race.

The boundary work undertaken by defenders of gender voluntarism and racial essentialism rejected any equivalence between Dolezal's identification as black and Jenner's identification as a woman. Dolezal *chose* to identify as black; Jenner simply *was* a woman. Dolezal was living a lie; Jenner was being true to her innermost self. Dolezal was opportunistic; Jenner was authentic. Dolezal gained material benefits from her imposture; Jenner gained only the satisfaction of being true to herself. Dolezal was guilty of appropriation and "cultural theft," taking what rightfully belonged to others; Jenner harmed no one. But it was not simply the two cases that were distinguished; it was two orders of phenomena. Boundary work drew a more general, quasi-sociological line between changing sex or gender and changing race.

Boundary work in the Dolezal affair took two forms. Both sought to distinguish transgender claims as a socially legitimate form of identity change from transracial claims as a socially illegitimate form. But they were oriented to different threats and inscribed in different projects. Gender voluntarists—committed to institutionalizing and legitimizing transgender claims and identities—sought to prevent the policing of racial identities that was triggered by the Dolezal affair from strengthening the policing of gender identities. Racial essentialists—committed to preserving the integrity of racial categories—sought to prevent gender voluntarism (which had been strengthened by the Jenner debut) from licensing racial voluntarism and thereby encouraging fraudulent or opportunistic racial identity claims.

Gender voluntarist boundary work sought to protect Jenner—and the still-fragile public legitimacy of transgender claims—from "contamination" by association with Dolezal. The Jenner debut had marked an extraordinary moment in the mainstreaming of transgender identities. Writing in the *Economist*, the essayist Will Wilkinson declared the "social forces that brought us to the Caitlyn Jenner moment" to be "irreversibly ascendant."[44] Two days later, however, the Dolezal affair—with its discourse of deception, fraud, and pathology—threatened to undo the gains made by the broad public acceptance of Jenner. As the writer, television host, and prominent transgender activist Janet Mock tweeted, "Trans folks' lives should not be part of the Dolezal conversation. It's dangerous."[45] "To conflate trans folks with Dolezal," the media studies scholar Khadijah White wrote, "gives credence to the deepest, most malicious lie there is about transgender identity and queer sexuality—that they are deceitful."[46] For Samantha Allen, a scholar of gender and sexuality, "Dolezal's domination of public conversations around identity comes at a particularly inopportune time. . . . This lone woman from Idaho has the potential to do real damage to public perceptions and conceptions of transgender identity."[47]

Jenner thus risked being tainted by association with Dolezal, "transgender" by association with "transracial"— not to mention "transspecies" and other purported fruits of liberal solipsism and anything-goes social constructivism, conjured up by gleeful cultural conservatives. Faced with this attempted *reductio ad absurdum*, those who had cautiously embraced gender voluntarism as a result of the mainstreaming of transgender identities in the last few years might now revert to gender essentialism. Gender voluntarist boundary work was an effort to prevent such backsliding.

To forestall the delegitimation of Jenner and transgender by association with Dolezal and transracial, it was necessary to challenge the "if Jenner, then Dolezal" logic. This is the context for the oft-repeated assertion that transracial is "not a thing."[48] The Dolezal story was cordoned off, marked as pathological, and treated as a case unto itself, rather than as an instance of the broader phenomenon of racial reidentification. This quarantining of the Dolezal case facilitated the contrast between the "non-thingness" of transracial and the legitimate, institutionalized social reality of transgender.

Gender voluntarist boundary work underscored the objective foundations of transgender identities, which were characterized as deep, stable, lifelong, unchosen, and probably grounded in biology. "Caitlyn Jenner is not pretending," wrote Dana Beyer, the head of a Maryland gender rights association. "Jenner has been a woman since birth—or more likely, before birth—like many, if not most, trans women.... And while there are variations in trans biology ... it really is pretty clear cut: your sense of self as a sexual being, your gender identity, is rooted in your brain."[49] Without appealing to brain differences, Meredith Talusan, a writer and transgender activist, made a similar point: "The fundamental difference between Dolezal's actions and trans people's is that her decision to identify as black was an active choice, whereas transgender people's decision to transition is almost always involuntary.... Dolezal identified as black, but I *am* a woman, and other trans people *are* the gender they feel themselves to be."[50]

On accounts such as these, gender identity is at once subjective and objective. It is *defined* by one's subjective "sense of self," but that sense of self is understood as *grounded* in some objective—if at present still unknown—aspect of one's biological being. The sources of subjectivity are situated outside the realm of choice and reflexive self-transformation, outside the realm of culture, and even, paradoxically, outside the self. In this way the defense of gender voluntarism is pushed onto essentialist terrain. This is of course not new. The claim to a deep, unchosen, biologically grounded gender identity at variance with the sexed body has long been a prominent strand of transsexual and transgender discourse, just as the claim that sexual identity and orientation are innate and unchosen has long been a prominent strand of gay and lesbian discourse.[51]

Gender voluntarist boundary work thus presumed the illegitimacy of Dolezal's change of race and sought to explain the legitimacy of Jenner or others changing their gender. Racial essentialist boundary work, by contrast, presumed the legitimacy of changing one's gender and sought to explain the illegitimacy of Dolezal's change of race. And while gender voluntarists faced an acute threat of contamination from the Dolezal affair, racial essentialists were oriented to a more diffuse threat: that the growing legitimacy of gender voluntarism—dramatized by the broad public embrace of Jenner—might cross over into the racial domain and encourage "racial fraud" and cultural appropriation. The ubiquitous "if Jenner, then Dolezal" trope—and the suspicion that Dolezal herself was seeking to ride the transgender wave—seemed to make this threat more concrete.[52]

Racial essentialists' explanation of the illegitimacy of Dolezal's identification as black—in contrast to the presumed legitimacy of Jenner's identification as a woman—pivoted on two themes: objectivity and appropriation. The term "objectivity," unlike "appropriation," was not used by participants in the debate. But it enables me to bring together a set of ideas sounded repeatedly in the Dolezal debates. The underlying argument of racial essentialists was that racial identity, unlike gender identity, is constituted by an ensemble of supra-individual facts: the biogenetic and genealogical facts of ancestry; the social facts of classification systems and categorization practices; and the historical facts of enslavement, oppression, and discrimination. Subjectivity is constitutive of gender: the "truth" of gender is found in the innermost feelings of an individual, and those feelings must be recognized and respected. But as many commentators emphasized, how one *feels* about race is irrelevant. Subjectivity is understood as an *expression* of racial identity, not as its ground.

The supra-individual objectivity of race, on this account, explains why it cannot legitimately be changed or chosen. Dolezal could change her appearance, style, and self-presentation; she could change her networks of social relations and activities; she could "feel" black and identify, no doubt sincerely, with black culture and history; and she could exploit contemporary versions of the one-drop rule to pass as black. But passing, on the objectivist understanding of race, does not involve changing one's race; it involves successfully pretending to be something one is not. Passing intrinsically involves deception—justifiable deception, perhaps, for the many light-skinned blacks who have successfully passed as white, but deception nonetheless.[53] Passing is always trespassing.[54]

The deception involved in performing an identity to which one has no legitimate claim underwrites the charges of appropriation and cultural theft.[55] In a context in which *who is what* can determine not only *who* (legitimately) *gets what* but also *who* (legitimately) *gets to do what*, Dolezal was accused of selectively indulging in "blackness as a commodity," of "donning blackness" in order to "negotiate black spaces," while retaining the privilege of removing her "costume" at will.[56] While gender transitions are understood to be undertaken at great personal cost and to bring no extrinsic benefits, Dolezal was asserted to have "capitalized on her fake blackness," "building a career and persona off it": she selectively "appropriated aspects of blackness" for her "personal benefit" and "occupied and dominated spaces ostensibly reserved for people who had life-long experiences of racial marginalization and disenfranchisement."[57]

The viscerally negative reaction to Dolezal's "reverse passing" that informed racial essentialist boundary work drew on a politically and morally charged contrast between the optional and reversible donning of blackness by Dolezal and the involuntary and (for most) inescapable reality of the black body, understood as *the* or at least *a* primary meaning of blackness for black Americans.[58] Dolezal could "pick and choose [her] blackness." But "those of us born into black bodies can't do that. We can't take our blackness off when the situation doesn't suit us."[59] This contrast was all the more poignant in the context of the Black Lives Matter movement, focused on police violence against black bodies.[60] "Michael Brown couldn't be transracial," the legal scholar Jody Armour noted. "When you walk into prisons and jail cells, you see cellblocks brimming with bodies that are conspicuously black. Those black bodies had no choice in how they were perceived."[61]

The contrast became more poignant still on June 17, when Dylann Roof killed nine parishioners during a prayer service at a historic black church in Charleston. This marked the end of the Dolezal affair; further discussion seemed frivolous. As Jelani Cobb wrote in the *New Yorker* the day after the massacre: "A week that began with public grappling with race as absurdity has concluded . . . with race as the catalyst for tragedy. The existential question of who is black has been answered in the most concussive way possible."[62]

It is tempting to dismiss the Dolezal affair as an inconsequential, Internet-driven summer diversion, and on one level it was no doubt just that. At the same time, however, the affair revealed with striking clarity the tensions and contradictions in the contemporary politics of sex/gender and ethnoracial identity. It is to a broader analysis of these tensions and contradictions that I turn in chapter 2.

Chapter 2

Categories
in Flux

The pairing of transracial and transgender in the Dolezal debates points to an underlying shift in the landscape of identities. Prevailing understandings of cultural and bodily difference have been rocked by a series of challenges, and longstanding assumptions about the stability of basic identity categories have been called into question. This has vastly enlarged the scope for choice and self-transformation.

The enlargement of choice seems at first glance to conform to certain classical narratives of modernity, which underscore the shift from given to chosen identities. Yet matters are not so simple. The expansion of the space for choice has fostered anxieties about the exercise of unregulated choice; the idea that basic identities are not given but chosen has provoked concerns about unnatural, opportunistic, or fraudulent identity claims. This, in turn, has prompted efforts to police questionable claims in the name of authentic and unchosen identities, as well as attempts to justify unorthodox claims in the name of such identities. Instead of a shift from given to chosen identities, we see a sharpened tension—in everyday identity talk, public discourse, and even academic analysis—between the language of choice, autonomy, subjectivity, and self-fashioning on the one hand and the language of givenness, essence, objectivity, and nature on the other. It is this fundamental tension between chosenness and givenness that I analyze in this chapter.

Unsettled Identities

In recent decades, identity categories of all kinds have come to seem fragile and unsettled. The landscape of identities has become much more complex, fluid, and fragmented. As new categories have proliferated and old categories have come to seem ill fitting, we increasingly face uncertainties and ambiguities in identifying ourselves and categorizing others. Prevailing practices of counting and classifying—and the very act of categorization itself—have been challenged. As basic categories have become the objects of self-conscious debate, critical scrutiny, strategic choice, and political claimsmaking, they have lost their self-evidence, naturalness, and taken-for-grantedness.[1]

The unsettling of basic categories has been nothing short of spectacular in the domain of sex and gender. Here a profound challenge to heteronormativity has been accompanied by the massive destabilization of binary regimes of gender and even sex itself. For scholars of sex and gender, "heteronormativity" refers to the long-prevailing cultural understanding of heterosexuality as the only legitimate and normal mode of sexuality, and of the heterosexual couple as the nucleus of family life and reproduction. This understanding has been radically disrupted. Within days of the Dolezal revelations, the Supreme Court's decision in *Obergefell v. Hodges* affirmed a constitutional right to gay marriage. The decision completed the stunningly rapid collapse of the most visible symbol of heteronormativity in the United States: as recently as 2012, forty-one states had constitutional provisions or legislation barring gay marriage.[2] The remarkable success of the marriage equality movement was the culmination of a much broader shift in recent decades toward the social and cultural acceptance—or as cultural conservatives lament, the "normalization"—of homosexuality.[3] While gay marriage debates have been most visible in the United States, the collapse of heteronormativity has been even more striking in parts of northern Europe, notably the Netherlands, where pro-gay attitudes have been enlisted as a symbol of Dutchness by anti-immigrant politicians.[4]

Challenges to prevailing understandings of sexual difference go well beyond gay marriage. Recent decades have witnessed an ongoing, publicly visible diversification of sexual diversity. Each of the multiple "sexual cultures" or "sexual worlds," as a prominent scholar of sexuality describes them, "splinters into many linked worlds. . . . There is no unified gay culture, sex-worker culture, drag culture, heterosexual culture or sado-masochist culture: there are multiplicities of scenes."[5] A telling indicator of this fragmentation is the acronym creep in designations of the reference categories for understandings of sexual (and gender) difference. From the initial core of gay and lesbian, the portfolio of categories has expanded to include bisexual, transgender, queer, questioning, intersex, asexual, ally, pansexual, and even, in a nod to certain Native American understandings of third-gender statuses, "two spirit," yielding the unwieldy LGBTQQIAAP2S.[6]

Even more striking than the diversification of sexual diversity has been the accelerating movement of transgender from the margins to the mainstream in recent decades. The mainstreaming of transgender was consecrated by a June 2014 piece in *Time* magazine, "The Transgender Tipping Point," featuring the transgender actress Laverne Cox, celebrated for her role as a transgender prison inmate in Netflix's popular series *Orange Is the New Black*, on the cover. While the notion of a single "tipping point" is no doubt too facile, the growing mainstreaming of transgender is evident in popular culture, media, legislation, organizational accommodations, and parenting practices.[7]

The transgender moment has two analytically distinguishable aspects. The first is the increasing—though of course far from universal—acceptance of the possibility and legitimacy of moving between categories.[8] This is seen in the mainstream media embrace of celebrities' gender transitions, culminating in the Caitlyn Jenner moment; in the sympathetic depictions of transgender characters in films, television, novels, and fiction for children and youth; and in the increasing willingness of parents, schools, churches, therapists, and others to support gender transitions.

The passage from one established category to another, to be sure, does not necessarily destabilize the categories themselves or the boundaries between them. The anthropologist Fredrik Barth observed in a seminal essay that ethnic boundaries can persist despite the flow of persons across them.[9] The crossing of a boundary may even strengthen that boundary. Some feminist authors have argued, for example, that transgender boundary-crossing may reinforce rather than subvert gender categories and their boundaries.[10] Others have noted the remarkable power of the binary gender system to "adapt to and re-absorb" transgender people.[11] Jenner's transition provides a case in point; it prompted considerable commentary about the reinforcement of the gender binary and about stereotypical representations of womanhood.[12]

The second development is more radically destabilizing. This is the increasing awareness, acceptance, and even institutionalization of categories other than the binary pair. As recently as 2013, two prominent scholars of transgender concluded a fascinating article on tensions between self-identity and genitalia as criteria for the determination of gender in various contexts by observing that "gender crossing can receive some validation in the liberal moment [which prioritizes autonomy and choice], but only when [the gender] binary remains unquestioned."[13] Yet in the last few years the gender binary has indeed been questioned—not just in activist and academic circles but in mainstream settings as well. And organizations are starting to make accommodations for "nonbinary people."

In the fall of 2015, for example, applicants to the University of California who preferred alternatives to male or female could choose among four additional gender identifications listed on application forms: trans male, trans female, gender queer/gender non-conforming, or different identity.[14] And an increasing number of colleges and universities—especially small liberal arts colleges—have put in place formal procedures for accommodating students who prefer to be designated by pronouns other than "he" or "she." In some campus settings, it has become routine to ask students to indicate their "preferred gender pronoun" when they introduce themselves.[15] Various sets of alternative pronouns have been proposed, though none has been broadly institutionalized.[16]

The mainstreaming of third-gender options is not confined to college campuses. After "collaborat[ing] with . . . a group of leading LGBT advocacy organizations," Facebook decided in 2014 to offer fifty-six "custom" gender options:

"When you come to Facebook, we want you to feel comfortable being your true, authentic self. An important part of this is the expression of gender, especially when it extends beyond the definitions of just 'male' or 'female'. So today, we're proud to offer a new custom gender option to help you better express your own identity on Facebook.... Moreover, people who select a custom gender will now have the ability to choose the pronoun they'd like to be referred to publicly—male (he/his), female (she/her) or neutral (they/their)."[17] The dating site OkCupid followed suit, as did other social media sites.[18]

More consequentially, some countries have started to recognize third-gender options. In 2014 the Indian Supreme Court gave legal recognition to a third-gender status for those *hijras* or others who identify as neither male nor female, and folded them into India's system of educational and employment quotas for underrepresented groups.[19] Similar forms of legal recognition exist in Nepal, Pakistan, and Bangladesh. Australia and New Zealand allow gender to be designated on passports as X—glossed as "indeterminate/intersex/unspecified" in Australia and as "indeterminate/unspecified" in New Zealand—in addition to male or female.[20] And the High Court of Australia ruled in 2014 that the New South Wales Registry of Births, Deaths, and Marriages could record an official change of sex to "non-specific," affirming the application of a petitioner who was born male and underwent sex reassignment surgery but claimed to identify as neither male nor female.[21]

The binary regime of official sex categorization at birth, too, has been loosened. Since 2013, for example, Germany has allowed parents of intersex infants to check a third, unlabeled box rather than obliging them to decide between male and female. This is not an official recognition of a third sex category; it is a placeholder, making it possible to defer official sex categorization until the child can make the decision at a later date. By acknowledging ambiguity, however, this option represents a significant shift away from the rigid binarism that has long governed the medical and legal categorization of infants in Western settings.

The change in official categorization policy is indicative of a broader shift in ways of thinking about—and treating—persons who cannot be unambiguously assigned to a binary sex category at birth.[22] In the second half of the twentieth century, prevailing medical protocols required early surgical intervention in such cases, designed to eradicate visible evidence of genital ambiguity.[23] In the last decade or so, responding in part to challenges from intersex activists, medical protocols have shifted. New guidelines place less emphasis on cultural norms regarding the proper size and appearance of genitals and greater emphasis on functionality, fertility, sexual sensation, avoiding complications from unnecessary surgery, and evidence of long-term gender identification of persons with particular "disorders of sex development."[24] In the eyes of many intersex activists, however, the changes fall far short of what is needed. Activists aim to prevent nonconsensual "normalizing" surgeries, and some seek recognition of intersex—or of "variations of reproductive development"—not as a disorder but simply as a form of difference.[25]

Challenges to prevailing categorical frameworks have been less dramatic in the domain of race and ethnicity—if only because racial and ethnic categories, in contemporary liberal societies, are not as clearly defined, deeply institutionalized, or pervasively implicated in the structuring of social life as are sex and gender. Yet the challenges have nonetheless been profound. Dominant ways of understanding racial and ethnic diversity (and religious and linguistic diversity as well) presuppose a population neatly segmented into a small number of clearly bounded, easily identifiable, relatively stable categories. This is true notably for the paradigm of multiculturalism, which implies a plurality of relatively distinct and bounded groups. But diversifying immigration patterns, rising intermarriage rates, and increasingly fluid practices of self-identification have generated a much more complex, less stable, and less easily "legible" pattern of racial and ethnic diversity. People are distributed across a much larger number of often less sharply demarcated, less easily identifiable, and less institutionalized racial and ethnic categories—to the extent that they can be placed, or can place themselves, in available categories at all.[26] The fluidity and fragmentation of the ethnoracial landscape have prompted critical reflection on the lack of fit between the brutal simplifications of prevailing categorical frameworks and the everyday experience of increasingly complex forms of heterogeneity.

In the major European countries of immigration, for example, the pattern of diversity of forty or fifty years ago—characterized by large and relatively homogeneous groups of migrant workers from a small number of countries of origin (especially Turks in Germany, North Africans in France, and South Asians in Britain)—has given way to much more complex forms of heterogeneity, generated by "smaller, transient, more socially stratified, less organised and more legally differentiated immigrant groups." London alone includes immigrant populations of 5,000 or more from each of fifty-four countries, most of them internally differentiated—to a much greater extent than earlier migrant worker communities—by education, employment, religiosity, mode of migration, legal status, generation, and so on.[27] There is a growing gap between prevailing forms of multiculturalism and identity politics and those who "fall outside or across standard classifications."[28]

Challenges to the prevailing categorical frameworks have been particularly striking in the United States, long characterized by the rigid system of racial classification that was a legacy of the one-drop rule.[†] Diversifying immigration patterns, rising intermarriage rates, and the mixed race movement have powerfully disrupted the black-white binary around which race was historically organized.[29] These and other forces—especially the emergence of a new cohort accustomed to much more fluid identifications and bearing very different collective memories and attitudes—are engendering what Jennifer Hochschild and colleagues have called a "new racial order," characterized by weaker boundaries between groups, greater heterogeneity within groups, shifting relative positions of groups, and more fluid and contextually varying racial identifications.[30] Also evident is the cultural and psychological devaluation of whiteness in certain contexts. Many observers have commented on the attractions of emblems of black culture to white youth, who may experience whiteness in terms of deprivation and lack. A Native American identification, too, can offer an enticing alternative to a white identity experienced by some as culturally and spiritually "empty."[31]

Everywhere, practices of counting, classifying, and categorizing by race and ethnicity have become increasingly politicized.[32] Whether to count and categorize by race and ethnicity; what to count; whom to count; how to count; and how to report the results—all of these questions are

---

[†] Sexual unions across socially defined racial lines have always posed problems for systems of racial classification. In the context of slavery and legally articulated racial domination in North America, such unions threatened not just the stability of racial categories but the structure of racial domination itself. It was therefore found necessary to legally regulate racial category membership, and specifically to define the status of the offspring of interracial unions. With some exceptions, the principle of "hypodescent"—assigning children of unions socially understood as mixed to the subordinate group—prevailed even in the colonial and early postcolonial era, though it was consolidated only in the early twentieth century (Davis 1991).

increasingly contested. The first of these issues—whether to count and categorize by race and ethnicity at all—has been controversial both where such counting and categorizing is deeply entrenched and where it is absent or minimal. In the United States and the Netherlands, for example, critics have argued that prevailing practices of racial and ethnic classification may harden racial and ethnic divisions and divert attention from class divisions. In France and Latin America, by contrast, critics have argued that the *absence* of racial and ethnic statistics has hindered the development of policies designed to assess and address entrenched racial and ethnic inequalities and discrimination.[33]

Debates over the second question—what to count— reflect competing understandings of fundamental social divisions. In the United States, for example, should one count race and ethnicity separately, as is done at present; fold race and ethnicity into a single question, as has been proposed as a more consistent alternative; or ask about ancestry, language, or religion rather than about race or ethnicity?[34] The issue of whom to count—which specific racial or ethnic groups—regularly generates demands for recognition of new categories and for their inclusion on census forms. The most recent example, in the United States, is the demand for a separate Middle East/North Africa category.[35] The question of how to count those of mixed ancestry, and specifically whether to introduce a new "multiracial" category or whether to permit multiple responses without introducing a new category, was heatedly debated in the United States in the 1990s.[36] The decision to allow respondents to choose more than one race beginning with the 2000 census raised the final issue mentioned above, how to report the results. Specifically, should those who choose more than one race be fractionally allocated to the different races chosen? Alternatively, should they be allocated to the minority race or races, at least for purposes of civil rights monitoring and enforcement? The Census Bureau opted for the latter.[37]

The Empire of Choice

The unsettling of basic categories has dramatically enlarged the space for choice and self-transformation. The enlargement of choice, to be sure, does not simply respond to this unsettling; it also contributes to it. Since the micropolitics of sex/gender and ethnoracial identity pivots on the tension between chosenness and givenness—between what can legitimately be chosen and what must be accepted as objectively given—it is worth considering separately the expanding empire of choice, both as cause and as consequence of the unsettling of identity categories.

Rhetorics and practices of choice and self-transformation have been central to Western modernity. They have structural roots in the erosion of older forms of social organization based on ascribed identities and inherited statuses. They have cultural roots in powerful ideals of individualism, dignity, autonomy, and self-realization (and, especially in the United States, in the myth of the "self-made man" and the tradition of self-reinvention). And they have political roots in liberalism and feminism: classical liberalism was built on the ideal of individual autonomy, while feminism has asserted women's "right to choose" how to live their lives, especially in the domains of sex and reproduction.[38]

If choice and self-fashioning have long been central to Western modernity, their importance has only increased in the late modern or postmodern era. Charles Jencks characterized postmodernity as a "time of incessant choosing," in which it is "not only the rich who become collectors, eclectic travellers in time with a superabundance of choice, but almost every urban dweller."[39] And as Peter Miller and Nicholas Rose have argued, contemporary neoliberal forms of "government at a distance" work "through the regulated choices of individual citizens, now construed as subjects of choices and aspirations to self-actualization and self-fulfillment. Individuals are to be governed through their freedom."[40]

Across a wide variety of domains, "contemporary norms of selfhood . . . stress autonomy, self-actualization, prudence, responsibility and choice."[41] What was formerly given must now be chosen: what line of work to pursue; whether, when, whom, and how to marry; whether, when, with whom, and how to have children; whether and how to practice religion; what to wear; what to eat; what cultural competencies to develop; and what cultural products to consume.[42] Central to the expanding field of choice are questions of how to form, transform, and manage our bodies. As the body itself—our "somatic, corporeal, neurochemical individuality"—gets drawn into "the field of choice, and [is] laden with all the demands that choice imposes,"[43] sex/gender and race and ethnicity become key sites of choice and self-transformation.

"Choice" is a fraught term in the field of sexual and gender politics. A woman's "right to choose" has been central to the defense of abortion rights and to third-wave feminism more generally. But the language of choice has also been used to demand conformity to sex and gender norms, while the contrary assertion that one has no choice has been used to dignify and legitimize sexual and gender difference. I return to this issue below. The point to underscore here is that one can believe sexual orientation or gender identity to be involuntary or even innate—a matter about which there is inconclusive research and ongoing disagreement—and still acknowledge the massive expansion in the space for choice of sexual conduct and gender expression or presentation.[44]

The ideal of sexual autonomy—built around the freedom to choose whether, when, how, and with whom to have sex—has been central both to the women's movement and to movements to legitimize alternative sexualities.[45] Though it remains contested by religious and other cultural conservatives, this notion of sexual autonomy has been spectacularly successful; it informs law, policy, education, and popular culture.[46] The regulation of sex in criminal law, for example, has shifted throughout most of the world from a corporatist mode, protecting corporate entities like family, race, or nation from "unnatural" forms of sexual activity, to an individualist mode. The contemporary legal regulation of sex protects vulnerable individuals (notably by criminalizing marital rape and child sexual abuse) yet at the same time allows greater latitude for a wide range of sexual activity between consenting adults (notably by decriminalizing sodomy and adultery).[47] A greatly expanded range of sexual conduct is not only legal but more or less publicly legitimate and socially acceptable. Regardless of one's orientation, one can—and indeed must—choose from a wide range of options and styles. And online dating has of course dramatically expanded the range of choice of prospective partners.

The space for choice in the domain of gender expression has expanded as well, as a much wider range of modes of behavior, dress, adornment, grooming, and bodily transformation has come to be seen as legitimate and claimed as a right.[48] As noted above, the option of choosing among a wide range of gender identification terms has been institutionalized on college campuses and social media platforms. The cultural mainstreaming of transgender options has led many families and schools to offer non-gender-conforming children more leeway in choosing their gender self-presentation, though this shift has been uneven across region, class, and milieu.[49] Choice has even been institutionalized in law: in 2013, California became the first state to grant every public school student from kindergarten through twelfth grade the right to "participate in sex-segregated school programs and activities, including athletic teams and competitions, and use facilities consistent with his or her gender identity, irrespective of the gender listed on the pupil's records."[50]

Sex/gender designations on official documents like birth certificates and passports are also increasingly chosen rather than given. More significant still is that the exercise of this choice, in a small but rapidly growing number of jurisdictions, no longer presupposes genital surgery or hormone treatments. In most of these jurisdictions, official change of sex or gender is still subject to some form of medical supervision. To change the sex designation on a birth certificate in New York State, for example, a medical professional must affirm that the applicant "has undergone appropriate clinical treatment," though no surgery or other specific treatment is required. In New York City (which has its own vital records department, independent of that of the rest of New York State), the medical supervision is still more attenuated: a physician or psychologist must declare that the chosen sex designation "more accurately reflects the applicant's sex or gender identity" according to "contemporary expert standards regarding gender identity."[51] Denmark went a step further in 2014 by dropping the requirement of any medical statement or clinical diagnosis: legal gender identity depends solely on self-identification.[52]

Notions of autonomy have informed the expansion of choice in the domain of race and ethnicity as well. Constructivist theories of ethnicity have long emphasized the variability and manipulability of ethnic identities and the fact that, in many contexts, individuals can choose among a variety of "ethnic options."[53] By contrast, race is often characterized as involuntary.[54] Camille Gear Rich, however, describes an emerging era of "elective race," in which individuals increasingly claim the right to racial self-identification and seek to "control the terms on which their bodies are assigned racial meaning."[55] Another legal scholar, Randall Kennedy, has expressly defended "free entry into and exit from racial categories, even if the choices [people] make clash with traditional understandings of who is 'black' and who is 'white.'"[56]

Understandings of autonomy that mandate and legitimate individual choice in matters of identity have been enshrined in certain institutional routines and practices. In a global shift in the way censuses are carried out, for example, questions about racial and ethnic identity that used to be answered by census personnel are now answered by respondents themselves.[57] Following this same logic, the Equal Employment Opportunity Commission in 2007 changed the way it collected data on the racial composition of the workforce: employers had previously been asked to base reports on their own perceptions, but now they are required to ask employees to self-identify.[58] The options for self-identification have expanded as well. Following the Office of Management and Budget's unsung yet massively influential Directive 15 of 1997, revising the federal standards for racial and ethnic classification and data collection, the U.S. Census Bureau and other federal government agencies that collect racial and ethnic data have allowed individuals to choose multiple racial identifications; educational institutions and most large corporations have followed suit.[59]

Outside the domain of data collection, of course, options for meaningful and effective choice of racial and ethnic identity are unequally distributed.[60] A dark-skinned person in the United States does not have a socially meaningful option to identify as white. But the growing complexity of the ethnoracial landscape, the increase in ethnoracial intermarriage, the emergence of the mixed-race movement, and the decay of the one-drop rule have expanded the scope for choice.[61] People with mixed Asian and white parentage may have a wider range of options for identification than those with mixed black and white parentage, but choice has expanded dramatically for the latter as well.[62] While the one-drop rule would have defined them as black, studies report a range of alternative identifications, including biracial, black, white, non-racial, or contextually shifting, with identification as biracial being the most common, at least for young people.[63] Given a forced choice between white and black, most of those with biracial black and white identities still choose black, reflecting the lingering influence of the one-drop rule.[64] But in an increasing range of contexts, both formal and informal, that forced choice no longer obtains: the set of socially available and legitimate racial identity categories has expanded to include options like mixed, biracial, and multiracial.

Even genetics, counterintuitively, has enlarged the scope for choice of racial and ethnic identification in certain respects. The boom in genetic ancestry testing makes increasing use of autosomal DNA, inherited from both parents. Unlike tests based on mitochondrial and Y-chromosome DNA, which yield information about a single maternal or paternal lineage, autosomal tests take account of the full, multistranded range of one's genetic ancestry. Test results, which often reveal complex mixtures of biogeographic ancestry, are enlisted—along with other, nongenetic resources—in a process of "affiliative self-fashioning" that leaves considerable room for interpretation and choice.[65]

Two further forms of racially inflected self-transformation deserve brief comment, though neither necessarily involves choice of racial or ethnic identity per se. The first is the transformation of racially or ethnically marked bodily features through cosmetic procedures, ranging "from hair-straightening treatments, to rhinoplasty, to eyelid surgery, to skin-lightening creams." These procedures are legitimized by an "ideology of . . . individual self-expression rather than (as with sex change) [by an ideology] of psychological identity," and they are marketed in ways that are expressly designed to alleviate any anxieties clients might have about "betraying" their racial or ethnic identity. But insofar as certain bodily features are perceived or "coded" in racial or ethnic terms, cosmetic procedures offer clients the opportunity to "inflect their race through changes to their bodies" by altering the racialized ways in which they are perceived.[66]

A second form of racially inflected self-transformation involves cross-racial identification. Identification with black culture—most often with rap music and hip-hop culture—has been extremely common among white youth in recent decades.[67] Usually this identification is superficial and transitory, but sometimes it takes deeper and longer-lasting forms. Even transformative and durable identification *with* another race, to be sure, does not entail identification *as* a member of that race. But the line between identifying with and identifying as may be blurred. It became blurred, of course, for Rachel Dolezal, and it may be blurred for others as well—a theme explored in Adam Mansbach's 2005 satirical novel *Angry Black White Boy*.[68]

The Policing of Identity Claims

The enlarged scope for choice and self-transformation, in the context of the unsettling of longstanding assumptions about basic identity categories, has provoked anxieties about unregulated choice and concerns about opportunistic or fraudulent identity claims. These concerns, in turn, have prompted efforts to police questionable claims in the name of authentic and unchosen identities.[†] So while theorists of reflexive modernity posit a shift from given to chosen identities, we in fact see not the disappearance but—in some contexts—the resurgence of essentialist, objectivist, and naturalist reasoning.

Transgender identity claims have been subjected to policing in the name of nature, in the name of medicine, and in the name of history. Policing in the name of nature is illustrated by the claim of Paul McHugh—the former psychiatrist in chief of the Johns Hopkins Hospital, who identifies as a conservative Catholic—that sex change is "biologically impossible" and that people who have sex reassignment surgery "do not change from men to women or vice versa [but] become feminized men or masculinized women."[69] A similar stance has been taken by some feminists, who object to the "erasing [of] female biology" implied in trans arguments that menstruation, pregnancy, and abortion are not "women's issues" (because they are not shared by trans women yet are shared by some trans men); that associating words like "vagina" with women is "trans-exclusionary"; and that "female genital mutilation" is a misnomer because clitoral cutting is not restricted to females.[70]

Policing in the name of nature is not merely discursive. It operates in practice through what the philosopher Talia Mae Bettcher has called "reality enforcement," premised on the contrast between reality and appearance and operationalized

---

† The policing that occurs when identity claims are expressly challenged is a reminder that identity is a social relation, not an individual property, and that it depends on recognition and validation from others and is therefore vulnerable to challenge and disruption. All social identities involve the interplay of self-identification and categorization by others; the explicit policing of identity claims is just one—conspicuous and conflictual—form taken by that interplay. On the processual and negotiated nature of social identity, see Jenkins 2014.

through "genital verification."[71] Such policing culminates, shockingly often, in extreme violence, as shown in a study of the press reports of murders of transgender people, which found a pattern of cisgender men killing transgender women after sexual encounters leading to the "discovery" that the victim was "really a man."[72]

Unlike policing in the name of nature, policing in the name of medicine admits—and indeed validates—the legitimacy of certain transgender claims. But it does so by subjecting them to medical and psychiatric scrutiny. Those seeking access to or insurance coverage for hormonal or surgical treatments (and, in many jurisdictions, those seeking a change in sex or gender on official documents) have been required to obtain a formal diagnosis of Gender Identity Disorder, renamed Gender Dysphoria in 2013.[73] This "highly medicalized gateway model" has denied both treatment and social validation to those who do not satisfy the criteria specified in the *Diagnostic and Statistical Manual of Mental Disorders* (DSM).[74]

Policing in the name of medicine also regulates access to sex-segregated sports.[75] In 2003 the International Olympic Committee's Medical Commission spelled out the criteria for transgender eligibility, including "external genitalia changes and gonadectomy," official legal recognition of one's sex, and hormonal therapy "sufficient . . . to minimize gender-related advantages in sport competitions." Later, the commission specified maximum permissible testosterone levels for those competing as women, again in the name of fairness, unless the high testosterone level "does not confer a competitive advantage because it is nonfunctional." As the sociologists Laurel Westbrook and Kristen Schilt note, such medical policing accommodates the liberal emphasis on autonomy and choice while strictly preserving the system of binary categories.

Policing in the name of history is illustrated by Janice Raymond's argument that while a male-to-female transsexual "can have the history of *wishing* to be a woman and *acting* like a woman, . . . this gender experience is that of a transsexual, not of a woman." Surgery may alter one's bodily constitution, but "it cannot confer the history of being born a woman in this society."[76] And it is this history—the history of having "traveled through the world as women and been shaped by all that this entails," as Elinor Burkett put it in the controversial *New York Times* op-ed discussed in the preceding chapter—that makes one a woman: "People who haven't lived their whole lives as women . . . haven't suffered through business meetings with men talking to their breasts or woken up after sex terrified they'd forgotten to take their birth control pills the day before. They haven't had to cope with the onset of their periods in the middle of a crowded subway, the humiliation of discovering that their male work partners' checks were far larger than theirs, or the fear of being too weak to ward off rapists."[77]

The policing of access to blackness—like the policing of access to womanhood—is a relatively new development. There is of course a long and ugly history of the policing of the boundaries of whiteness. Formal social closure along racial lines—culminating in the Jim Crow system of comprehensive legally mandated segregation—required the formal definition and policing of racial category membership. Southern states adopted legal definitions of blackness, using variations of the one-drop rule.[78] The 1924 Virginia "Act to Preserve Racial Integrity" made a "false" racial self-designation punishable by a year in prison.[79] And courts were drawn into adjudicating whiteness in cases involving naturalization, marriage annulment, and petitions to change racial designations on birth certificates.[80]

In the era of affirmative action, however, claims to blackness began to be more closely policed than claims to whiteness. Concerns about misrepresentations of racial identity crystallized in the case of the Malone twins. The twins had originally applied unsuccessfully for positions with the Boston Fire Department in a 1975 civil service competition, identifying themselves as white. They applied again, successfully, two years later, this time identifying themselves as black, and served for ten years until their racial classification came to the attention of the fire commissioner in connection with an internal review for promotion to lieutenant. This led to their firing, following a hearing that found their applications to have been falsified. The hearing officer ruled that the Malones were not "objectively" black by any of three criteria: phenotype, documentary evidence, or evidence of self-presentation and perception of others in their community.[81]

A second case often cited by advocates of policing claims to blackness is that of Mark Stebbins, who won a city council seat in Stockton, California, in 1983, defeating a long-serving black incumbent. Stebbins had light skin and blue eyes but also, according to a news story of the time, "a broad nose and curly brown hair that he wore in a modest Afro style." The election had not turned centrally on race, but when Stebbins had appeared at the local chapter of the Black American Political Association of California, he was asked about his race and, when pressed, said he was black. The defeated incumbent, Ralph White, launched a recall campaign, alleging that Stebbins had falsely claimed to be black in order to gain votes in the minority-dominated district (which was 46 percent Latino and 37 percent black). White produced the birth certificates of Stebbins's parents and grandparents, which listed their races as white, and remarked,

"If the momma is an elephant and the daddy is an elephant, they durn sure can't have no lion. They got to have a baby elephant." Stebbins, whose second and third marriages were to black women and who belonged to a black Baptist church and to the NAACP, admitted that he had considered himself white as a young person. But he claimed that he had gradually realized he was actually black after being involved in civil rights campaigns and community organizing, and that he considered himself "culturally, socially, and genetically" black.[82]

These and other cases prompted proposals by some legal scholars to "verify" claimed racial identifications and to penalize "racial fraud."[83] Writing in the *Vanderbilt Law Review* in 1995, Luther Wright advocated using birth certificates for racial verification. Individuals should be assigned at birth the race of their parents. In the case of parents of different races, the child should be "classified as biracial with the race of the parents clearly identified." In the case of one biracial parent, the child should be assigned "the race that predominates." This system would ensure that "an individual can never legally claim to be a member of a race that is not represented in his parents' generation." Those making false statements about their race "should be charged with fraud and subject to criminal penalties," which could include "fines, public service, or a permanent notation of racial fraud on a person's employment record."[84]

Angela Onwuachi-Willig, writing in the same law review a dozen years later, focused on the potential for manipulation and misrepresentation in the college admission process. She proposed two measures to police such "racial and ethnic fraud." Applicants would be required to "write an essay that details their racial background and ancestral heritage . . . , how such background has helped to shape their identity, . . . and how they can add to the diversity of the college environment"; and guidance counselors or teachers "who worked with the student at each grade level" would write a letter addressing, among other things, "the contributions that the applicant could make to the mission of diversity for the school based, at least in part, on the student's racial and ancestral heritages."[85]

These proposals for policing racial fraud differed in interesting ways. Wright's call for a strict regime of racial documentation on birth certificates was entirely objectivist, focused solely on ancestry. Onwuachi-Willig's proposal, too, had an objectivist strand: the school letter would serve as a check on fraudulent claims about ancestral heritage (including those based on ancestry shopping by way of DNA tests). Yet this check was not enough; her proposal targeted not only those who invented an ancestry but also those who, despite having the requisite ancestry, "do not personally identify as part of that racial group . . . and thus would not be a part of the critical mass that helps to lessen feelings of alienation for minorities on campus." The school letter, in conjunction with the applicant essay, was intended to police subjective identification as well as objective ancestry. Onwuachi-Willig expressly signaled as problematic the subjective identification of many first-generation black immigrants and mixed-race students, while presumably that of Rachel Dolezal would have been unimpeachable.[86]

Analogous concerns have arisen about "box-checkers" opportunistically identifying as Native American, especially in the context of faculty appointments at universities.[87] In 2003 the Association of American Indian and Alaska Native Professors called on universities to take steps to police "ethnic fraud"—specifically, to require evidence of enrollment in a recognized tribe; establish a case-by-case review process for those lacking such evidence; include Native American faculty in the selection process; and require from applicants "a statement that demonstrates past and future commitment to American Indian/Alaska Native concerns."[88] The tension between objectivist modes of policing, based on documentary evidence, and subjectivist modes, based on indications of "past and future commitment" to the Native cause, is evident in these proposals as well.

In the aftermath of the Dolezal affair, bloggers, journalists, and Native American activists have sparked new controversies and reignited old ones by challenging questionable claims to identification as Native American.[89] In response to this grassroots policing, the Native American and Indigenous Studies Association (NAISA) issued a "Statement on Indigenous Identity Fraud" in September 2015. NAISA is defined by its field of study, not by the ethnoracial identity of its members; the statement took pains to emphasize that one need not be indigenous to study indigenous peoples. But in a thinly veiled reference to Dolezal, the statement went on to observe that "belonging does not arise simply from individual feelings—it is not simply who you claim to be, but also who claims you. . . . The measure of truth cannot simply be a person's belief but must come from relationships with Indigenous people." The statement acknowledged, however, possible "disagreements among Indigenous people over the legitimacy of a particular person's or group's claims."[90]

These proposals for the institutional verification of racial and ethnic identities have failed to gain significant traction. In liberal contexts, the *formal* policing of racial and ethnic identities is widely seen as legally problematic and politically repugnant. Acknowledging the concerns about ethnoracial fraud and cultural appropriation, a University of Houston official articulated the mainstream institutional response: "It would be a big step backward for institutions to begin verifying or certifying employees' self-identified race or ethnicity.... If someone self-identifies their gender, we do not make them prove it—we take them at their word.... In today's diverse workplace, we understand that every employee deserves to be treated equally, with respect, and included regardless of what anyone perceives their race, ethnicity, gender or any other protected classification to be."[91] As this response suggests, the legal, cultural, and political logic of self-identification is increasingly difficult to challenge in formal institutional settings.[92] Informal policing, however, continues—indeed with renewed momentum from the Dolezal affair.[93]

The New Objectivism

The language of givenness, essence, objectivity, and nature is deployed not only by those who *contest* the legitimacy of certain identity claims but also by those who *advance* those claims. This is notably the case for many transgender people. In this mode of trans discourse, one's basic identity is not chosen but given. One must choose whether to live in conformity with, or in tension with, that basic identity, but one does not choose who one fundamentally is. Identity is cast as an objective fact, not a subjective choice.[94]

This objectivist language has been adopted in part for strategic reasons. Those seeking access to surgical or hormonal treatments have had to present themselves in ways that conform to prevailing medical understandings of Gender Identity Disorder or Gender Dysphoria, since the medical and psychiatric professionals who control access to hormonal and surgical intervention require such a diagnosis.[95] The selective pressures exerted by this medicalized gatekeeper model are responsible for the prevalence of "born in the wrong body" narratives. This has resulted in a skewed public representation of the transgender experience, since the objectivist "wrong body" narrative fails to capture the experience of many transgender or gender-variant individuals.[96]

More broadly, in a context of actual or anticipated policing of unconventional or controversial identity claims, objectivist accounts of identity serve as a response to, and as a preemptive defense against, such policing. To the claim that "you can't just choose to be a woman," the response, in effect, is that "we don't *choose* to be women; we simply *are* women." A similar strategic essentialism has been widely adopted as a response to, and a preemptive defense against, the policing of sexuality. Assertions of the immutable, inborn nature of sexual orientation have enabled gay people to reject portrayals of homosexuality as a choice that could be altered and to argue that discrimination against gays, like discrimination against blacks and women, should be considered a form of discrimination based on an unchosen and unalterable characteristic.[97]

Yet recourse to objectivist language is not simply strategic; it also reflects the deep appeal of essentialist understandings of identity outside the academy.[98] Objectivism is further nourished by the cultural authority of biomedical science. Research on a possible biological basis of transgender identity—like decades-long research on a possible biological basis of sexual orientation—remains inconclusive.[99] But periodic reports of suggestive findings are widely discussed in transgender forums and often cited uncritically as evidence of a biological basis for transgender identity.

In the domain of race and ethnicity, too, objectivist language can be used not only to challenge identity claims but to formulate (or at least to justify) the very claims that are challenged. Some college applicants, for example, seek DNA ancestry testing in order to justify identifying as black or Native American on admission or financial aid applications.[100] In a cultural context in which any discernible African ancestry has been sufficient for self- and other-identification as black, discovery of such ancestry, ironically, can ground an objectivist claim to *be* black even if one has never subjectively *identified* as black.

Such ancestry shopping is of course transparently strategic. And there are many other examples of strategically enlisting genetic findings to support individual and collective claims. In an environment that confers enormous cultural authority on genomics, however, appeals to biology in discussions of race and ethnicity are not merely strategic. Since the turn of the millennium, genetics has become a newly respectable language for talking about race and ethnicity.[101]

Objectivist language, then, is deployed both to challenge and to formulate identity claims. Alongside older arguments that appeal to God, nature, or history, newer arguments appeal to genetics or to an innate and unchosen identity. We see not only a tension between languages of chosenness and givenness, subjectivity and objectivity, but also a tension between competing objectivist languages—competing ways of grounding identity claims in something beyond individual choice and subjectivity.

The latter tension arises from the multiplicity of objectivist criteria for socially defining both race and ethnicity and sex and gender. For race and ethnicity, these include different aspects of phenotype (skin color, facial structure, hair texture, and so on); genealogical and genetic ancestry; a shared history of living and being treated as a member of an ethnic or racial category; and a range of cultural practices and competencies. For sex and gender, they include different aspects of biological sex (chromosomes, genitalia, gonads, and secondary sex characteristics); a shared history of living and being treated as a member of a sex or gender category; and a putatively innate and unchosen gender identity.

The scope for choice and self-transformation, I have argued, has expanded dramatically in the domain of sex, gender, and sexuality in recent decades as longstanding assumptions about the stability of basic categories have been profoundly shaken. Similar if less dramatic changes have occurred in the domain of race and ethnicity. The unsettling of identities and the expanding empire of choice, in turn, have provoked anxieties about the crumbling foundations of social, moral, and cognitive order. Old and new essentialisms have flourished in response, claiming that basic identities are given, not chosen; objective, not subjective.

Contrary to some influential narratives of modernity, the language of choice, autonomy, and self-fashioning has not simply displaced the language of givenness, essence, and nature in accounting for basic categorical identities. Rather, subjectivist and objectivist accounts of identity coexist, sometimes in surprising ways. They are of course in tension with one another, but they do not stand in a zero-sum relationship. While the use of essentialist language to question and police controversial identity claims is unsurprising, the use of this language to *formulate* such claims is more intriguing. Objectivist language is used not only to check unbridled subjectivity and choice but also to *ground and legitimize* new forms of subjectivity and choice. Thus while transgender subjectivities are celebrated by some for their emancipation from the merely given, they are legitimized by others as given rather than chosen. They are reinscribed in the domain of nature in a way that underscores the objectivity and givenness—and therefore the legitimacy—of unorthodox identities. The choice of ethnoracial identification, too, is legitimized by appeals to objectively mixed ethnoracial or genetic ancestry.

The contemporary politics of identity is structured by a deep—though often unacknowledged—tension between chosenness and givenness, between subjectivity and objectivity, between the possibilities of self-transformation and the constraints of nature. At the present moment, when basic categories are profoundly unsettled and intensely contested, trans is not just a social phenomenon to think *about*; it is also a conceptual tool to think *with*. It is to the development of this argument that I turn in Part Two.

Part Two

———

Thinking with Trans

Chapter 3

The Trans
of Migration

The Dolezal affair, as I have noted, marked a new kind of "trans moment": participants were no longer just thinking *about* trans, they were thinking *with* trans. Yet they were doing so in a narrow way; their thinking was limited by their interest in validating or invalidating the identities claimed by Jenner and Dolezal. By moving beyond this "logic of the trial," I suggested, we can think with trans in a broader way about the politics of sex/gender and ethnoracial identities.

I start from the premise, then, that trans is good to think with: that we can use the transgender experience—in its various forms—as a lens through which to think in new and fruitful ways about the fluidity of ethnoracial identifications.[1] In so doing I follow the lead of Susan Stryker, who, reflecting on the initial round of commentary on Jenner and Dolezal, urged scholars to "keep the conversation going" rather than shutting it down prematurely through the rejection of any analogy between changing race and changing

sex or gender. Stryker acknowledged the limits of analogical reasoning, yet she argued that an overhasty rejection of
analogy "risks foreclosing an opportunity to explore *how*
claims of race-change and claims of sex-change might be
alike, as well as how they differ."[2]

Thinking about race through the prism of sex and gender reverses a longstanding tradition of thinking about sex
and gender through the prism of race. The irony in the reversal is that in this trans moment it is the increasingly sophisticated understandings of the *fluidity and artificiality of
gender* that can be leveraged to highlight aspects of the fluidity and artificiality of race, whereas previously—especially
in the context of antidiscrimination law and politics—it was
the alleged *immutability and givenness of race* that justified the
analogy with what was understood to be the equally immutable and naturally given phenomenon of sex.[3]

But what does it mean to "think with trans"? The sheer
variety of transgender experience—a variety that has dramatically increased in the last two decades—precludes a univocal answer. To make clear what it might mean to think about
race and ethnicity through the prism of transgender, I begin
by distinguishing three very different forms of transgender
experience. I call these the trans of migration, the trans of
between, and the trans of beyond.[4]

The *trans of migration* (exemplified most clearly by those
who surgically and hormonally transform their bodies and
formally change their legal identities) involves unidirectional movement from one established sex/gender category
to another. The *trans of between* (exemplified by androgyny)
involves a positioning of oneself with reference to the two
established categories, without belonging entirely or unambiguously to either one and without moving definitively
from one to the other. The *trans of beyond* (exemplified by
a self-definition as simply trans rather than cis) involves

positioning oneself in a space that is *not* defined with reference to established categories. It involves the claim to transcend existing categories or to transcend categorization altogether. The three forms are not sharply distinct in practice, but it is useful to distinguish them analytically.

Each form of transgender, I will argue, can help us think about race and ethnicity in fruitful ways. Racial passing (including "reverse passing" like Dolezal's) exemplifies the trans of migration, a movement from one clearly defined racial or ethnic category to another. The multiracial movement, demanding recognition for those who identify with two or more racial categories—or who identify themselves simply as "multiracial"—illustrates the trans of between.[5] And indifference or opposition to racial or ethnic categorization in any form exemplifies the trans of beyond.[†]

There are major tensions, not just differences, among the trans discourses and projects. The trans of migration disturbs existing categorical frameworks least, and may even be said to reinforce them. This explains the ambivalence in trans

---

† The three forms of transgender have rough and partial analogues in other domains as well. In the domain of religion, conversion might be seen as analogous to the trans of migration. Syncretism, the mixing of elements from different religious traditions, illustrates the trans of between, as do those who identify with or participate in more than one religious community or tradition without constructing a new, syncretistic form of religious practice. Opposition to religious categorization in any form exemplifies the trans of beyond, as does atheism. In the domain of language, the shift from one language to another—for individuals or groups—illustrates the trans of migration, while creolization and bilingualism are two distinct forms of the trans of between. The development of new languages that did not emerge from transformations of established languages—sign language, for example—might exemplify the trans of beyond, though there are no projects for going beyond language that are analogous to the project of going beyond gender or beyond race. In the domain of sexuality, finally, coming out or shifting from one established sexual orientation to another exemplifies the trans of migration. Bisexuality illustrates the trans of between. And various alternative sexualities that are not defined in relation to the established categories—such as pansexual, asexual, or skoliosexual (sexual attraction to nonbinary people)—illustrate the trans of beyond.

circles about the Caitlyn Jenner moment. Even as it marked a new stage in the public acceptance of transgender identities, it seemed to reinforce and even renaturalize gender binaries: the person who had once been perceived as the most masculine of men had come out as the most feminine of women. The Dolezal story, too, did more to reinforce than to disturb racial categories. It is the trans of between and, even more so, the trans of beyond that more profoundly destabilize categorical frameworks. But for just this reason they may be inhospitable, even disturbing, to those who are invested in moving from one clearly defined gender to another.[6] This chapter addresses the trans of migration; the next two take up the trans of between and the trans of beyond.

Unidirectional Transgender Trajectories

The most familiar form of transgender experience involves the permanent movement from one sex or gender category to another, especially when accompanied by the surgical and hormonal transformation of the body. Such one-way trajectories have often been described by those undertaking them in language drawn from the realm of travel and migration. As the gender theorist Jack (also known as Judith) Halberstam has observed, the migration metaphor is at once inevitable and problematic, for it transposes "an already loaded conceptual frame—place, travel, location, home, borders— onto another contested site."[7] Still, the metaphor usefully brings into focus several key aspects of unidirectional transgender trajectories. Migration can of course take temporary, circular, serial, or pendular forms. But here I draw selectively on certain structural aspects of permanent, one-way migration trajectories in order to characterize transgender trajectories that are projected to be unidirectional and irreversible.[8]

The transgender migrant imagines the sex or gender category of destination as a permanent home.[9] Of course, things do not always work out as intended, and some gender transitions are followed by transitions back to the original gender, just as some migrants eventually return to the country of origin.[10] As the pathos that often surrounds the term "transition" suggests, however, gender migration is conceived and undertaken as a fateful, life-altering course of action. This distinguishes gender migration from the gender "travel" or "tourism" exemplified by periodic cross-dressing or other forms of exploratory or playful gender-bending or gender-crossing.[11]

Just as a complex "migration industry" provides logistical and infrastructural support for international migration, so a gender migration industry provides medical, legal, cultural, and emotional support for gender migration. Key elements of this sociotechnical ensemble include official diagnostic categories;[12] standardized treatment protocols; a network of gender identity clinics; a set of institutionalized procedures for formally changing one's sex or gender designation in a widening range of settings; a network of support and advocacy organizations; and an extensive print and web-based advice and support literature.

Like the frontier between countries, the frontiers between sex and gender categories are not open; they are policed and administered by medical, psychiatric, and legal gatekeepers. Accessing surgery or hormonal treatment requires convincing medical personnel of one's eligibility. And just as applicants for visas and for political asylum are knowledgeable and resourceful agents who may craft narratives that are more likely to be successful, so applicants for sex reassignment surgery have learned to craft the kinds of narratives that define them as "good" candidates.[13]

Debates about access to treatment have come to focus increasingly on children and adolescents. Early intervention—beginning with drugs that block puberty and the associated development of secondary sex characteristics—is widely seen as favoring more successful trans outcomes, and there is a growing demand for it as transgender narratives become more widely available. But critics worry about setting children whose identity they see as still in flux on a path leading to irreversible medical interventions that require lifelong hormone treatment, may involve complex surgical procedures, and may render them infertile.[14] Underlying the debate about the timing of intervention, then, is a debate about the fixedness or fluidity of gender identity in children. Proponents of early intervention tend to see gender identity as inborn and fixed even in early childhood; critics see greater fluidity, at least until adolescence, and argue that the desire to transition may be a passing phase, shaped by available cultural models and stories. Both of these debates, in turn, are linked to controversies over "reparative" or "conversion" therapy for gender-nonconforming children, much like the longstanding controversies about therapy aimed at altering sexual orientation.[15]

Until recently, movement between sex or gender categories in official documents required genital surgery or—in some cases—medically supervised hormonal treatment. As I noted in chapter 2, some jurisdictions have attenuated or even removed provisions for medical control over civil status. But most of these jurisdictions maintain some formal control over change in sex or gender status. In the United Kingdom, for example, gender migrants can apply to the "Gender Recognition Panel" for a "Gender Recognition Certificate" provided they are eighteen or over, have been diagnosed with gender dysphoria (though no specific medical treatment is required), have lived in their acquired gender in the United Kingdom for at least two years, and "intend to live in [their] acquired gender for the rest of [their] life."[16]

Some permanent gender migration, to be sure, takes place outside—and in opposition to—the medicalized and highly regulated and policed forms made available by the gender migration industry. Even before the terms "transsexual" and "transgender" existed, there were some "lifelong cross-dressers whose 'true' gender identities were disclosed only after their death."[17] And once changing sex became an institutionalized medical, psychiatric, and legal procedure, there emerged—from inside as well as outside the transgender community—a critique of the focus on surgically transforming the genitals. An early and influential exponent of the insider critique was Virginia Prince, who, beginning in the late 1960s, situated "transgenderals" or "transgenderists"—including herself—between transvestites and transsexuals: unlike the former, they "permanently changed social gender through the public presentation of self"; unlike the latter, they rejected genital surgery.[18]

Membership in the destination categories is policed not only formally, by medical and legal authorities, but also informally, in everyday encounters. Just as legal status as an immigrant—or even a naturalized citizen—does not guarantee social acceptance in the destination country, so legal change of sex or gender does not guarantee social recognition and acceptance of one's new sex or gender. While the legal identities of immigrants are regulated by the state, their social identities are regulated, negotiated, and recognized—or not—in everyday social interaction. The same holds for gender migrants.

Immigrants may seek to be perceived as similar, to blend in and pass for native. In the same way, gender migrants can seek to pass as unmarked, cis men or women. Assimilation was indeed long the normative path for immigrants, as passing was for gender migrants. In the last few decades, however, as part of a broad cultural shift towards the recognition of difference, alternatives to assimilation and passing have become more widely available, and more socially legitimate, for both immigrants and transgender people.[19] Just as immigrants increasingly seek to be recognized and acknowledged as legitimately different, so gender migrants increasingly seek recognition as trans men or women, rather than concealing and erasing their past in an effort to pass. Some gender migrants, however, reject the explicit or implicit claim that coming out as trans is politically or morally superior to passing. And some self-identified transsexuals distance themselves from the label "transgender" and its implications of gender non-normativity.[20]

Since the destination category in this case is not simply "man" or "woman" but the novel category "trans man" or "trans woman" (or simply "trans"), the trans of migration from one established sex/gender category to another shades into the trans of beyond, which I address in chapter 5. Yet even when gender migrants seek recognition as trans, they often also seek recognition—and equal rights—as men and women. In this sense they remain migrants from one established sex/gender category to another.

Just as immigration can provoke a nativist reaction, especially when immigrants are perceived as too different or as unwilling to assimilate (or incapable of assimilating), so migration between sex or gender categories can generate a reactive sexual or gender nativism and a restrictive politics of sex/gender citizenship, especially when gender migrants are rendered visible by their claims to rights and recognition as trans men and women. Radical feminists' efforts to restrict access to certain women's spaces to "women-born women"— efforts that led to their being dubbed TERFs, or trans-exclusionary radical feminists—illustrate such sex/gender nativism.[†] In the claim, quoted above, that "people who haven't lived their whole lives as women ... shouldn't get to define us,"[21] Elinor Burkett was in effect distinguishing between first- and second-class citizens, between lifelong women, entitled to self-determination, and newcomers to the category, to whom she would not accord that right. In terestingly, there has been no comparable "nativist" reaction against female-to-male transsexuals.

Finally, just as many currents of international migration cross steep economic gradients, so do transgender migrants cross gradients of privilege. But while international migration is often driven by large wage gaps between origin and destination countries—or by other salient differences in social, political, or economic opportunities—transgender migration does not appear to be driven by the "privilege gap" between men and women.[22] If it were, female-to-male transitions would predominate; yet there is no evidence that this is the case. Indeed, until recently, male-to-female transitions appear to have been much more common, and were certainly much more visible, than the reverse; it is only in the last decade or so that this has changed.[23]

While policing of migration from poor to rich countries is more intense and elaborate than the policing of migration in the reverse direction (or of "lateral" migration that does not cross major socioeconomic or political gradients), the opposite, ironically, is the case for gender migrants: those who transition from male to female face more intensive policing than their female-to-male counterparts. At stake, along with access to the categories, is access to sex-segregated spaces and activities; and transgender access to women's spaces— women's sports, women's colleges, and women's bathrooms,

---

† The term TERF is contested; it is rejected as a slur by those at whom it is directed. See for example Goldberg 2014.

for example—has been much more controversial than access to men's spaces. Concerns that male-to-female gender migrants might have an unfair advantage in women's sports or an unwanted and perhaps dangerous presence in women's bathrooms have no counterpart in concerns about female-to-male migrants. Some anxieties about access to women's spaces concern trans women who have not had genital surgery and who therefore represent a potential sexual threat to women in what are supposed to be nonsexual spaces.[24] Others concern the claims of trans women, whether or not they have surgically transformed their bodies, to participate in defining—and perhaps substantially redefining—the mission of women's colleges, the goals of women's organizations, the nature of women's issues, and the meaning of womanhood itself.[25]

Reconsidering "Transracial"

Central to the Dolezal debates was the question of whether one could legitimately move between racial or ethnic categories as one could between sex or gender categories. The prevailing view was that one could not. Unlike transgender, it was frequently asserted, transracial was "not a thing."

That transracial is not a thing *of the same sort* as transgender is evident. There is no institutionalized, socially recognized, legally regulated, organizationally supported, and culturally intelligible procedure for changing one's race or ethnicity in liberal societies. In South Africa under apartheid, a system in which one's official racial classification determined where one could live and work and whom one could marry, there was a procedure for applying to change one's racial classification. The premise, however, was not that one could change one's race; it was that one could rectify a mistaken classification (interestingly, a position held today by some transgender people).[26] In the era of legally sanctioned racial domination in the United States, occasional lawsuits sought to change the racial identity recorded in certain official documents. But here too the premise was that one was correcting a mistake, not changing one's race. In liberal settings, where formally recorded racial identity does not exist as part of one's official legal status—or where racial identity recorded on official documents is used almost exclusively for statistical rather than allocative purposes—there would be no point to such an official procedure of reclassification. Sex—or gender, as the category is increasingly called, even in official documents—is a far more consequential *official* identity than is race or ethnicity in contemporary liberal societies. It is thus not surprising that the invention and institutionalization of transsexualism as a medical procedure—and more recently the social acceptance of the possibility of changing gender without genital surgery—were accompanied by the development of a legal procedure for changing one's official sex or gender.

Yet the lack of a racial analogue to the socially recognized and institutionally defined procedures for changing sex and gender should not blind us to other significant commonalities between the fluidity of race and the fluidity of gender. The blunt assertion that transracial is "not a thing" is premised on the reduction of transgender to the phenomenon of legally regulated and socially organized changes of sex and gender. If "transracial" is understood by analogy with a broader understanding of transgender—incorporating notions of migration, betweenness, and beyondness—the term may indeed bring together in an illuminating way the many distinct aspects of the instability, ambiguity, and artificiality of contemporary practices of racial and ethnic classification.

Transracial Trajectories, Past and Present

What the legal scholar Daniel Sharfstein has called "racial migration"—the movement from one racial category to another—has a long history in the United States.[27] Unlike transgender migration, racial migration has proceeded overwhelmingly—though not exclusively—in the direction of the more privileged category. It has been driven by the "wages of whiteness": by the desire to enjoy opportunities systematically denied to those socially defined as black.[28] Transgender migrations have been driven by *identity*, but racial migrations have historically been driven by *interest*: not by a subjective sense of *who is what*, but by the brutal realities of *who gets what*. While a sense of identity has propelled transgender migration, it has (until recently) restrained racial migration, preventing many who might have benefited from such migration—in terms of legal rights, social status, and economic opportunities—from actually undertaking it.

Transracial trajectories have been studied chiefly under the rubric of passing.[29] Not all passing, to be sure, is captured by the metaphor of migration. "Nine-to-five passing" for purposes of employment—premised on the strict separation of the worlds of work and family—was more like commuting than migrating; and inadvertent, playful, or deliberately subversive forms of passing—which provided access to small privileges, pleasures, and courtesies otherwise denied to those socially defined as black—were even more transient, structurally akin, in certain respects, to playful or deliberately subversive forms of gender-bending or gender-crossing.[30] Other forms of passing, however, did involve unidirectional and permanent migration between racial categories. Such one-way trajectories were often accompanied, and enabled, by a physical migration between places;

and they often entailed a radical severing of ties with family and community, at great psychological and emotional cost.[31]

I noted above that some transgender migrations, although originally conceived as permanent, eventuate in a return to the category of origin. Historians have shown, similarly, that some instances of racial passing led to disappointment, disillusionment, or unmasking, and issued in a return—voluntary or involuntary—to the category and community of origin. This has been a prominent theme in fictional treatments of black-white passing and also in certain memoirs. Stories of passing are often cast as "cautionary tales" that "do not end well" for those who seek to pass.[32]

Yet stories of failure may be overrepresented in prevailing accounts of passing.[33] Since permanent movement between racial categories—at a time when such movement was ideologically and legally policed—required concealment, or at least considerable discretion, it left relatively few narrative traces; detailed accounts of passing are therefore rare. Yet historical evidence suggests that permanent movement between racial categories was in fact quite common.[34]

Paradoxically, as Sharfstein has argued, intensified ideological policing of the color line during the nineteenth and early twentieth centuries "pushed many mixed-race people into whiteness."[35] For some, this involved the concealments, physical relocations, and social dislocations associated with passing. Others, however, crossed the color line with the knowledge and tacit acceptance of their neighbors. As Sharfstein and others have shown, the actual social policing of the boundaries of whiteness in local communities—and even in legal proceedings—was much less intensive, and much less effective, than the ideological pronouncements about racial purity and the legislative codification of the one-drop rule would suggest. The color line, sharp and rigidly policed in theory, was blurred and porous in practice.

The courts, Sharfstein emphasizes, did not make it easy to police the color line. The zealous policing of whiteness—by encouraging accusations of hidden blackness—would have had "broad potential to destabilize a white society that had long included numerous people of African descent."[36] Even at the height of Jim Crow, when some state bureaucracies, most notoriously in Virginia, did undertake zealous bureaucratic policing of racial purity, few of those who had previously been tacitly accepted as white were at risk of being reclassified as black.

The opportunity for racial migration was available only to those who could be taken for white (or for not black: some redefined their racial status by claiming American Indian or Portuguese identities).[37] This of course depended in large part on phenotype, especially on skin color. But it did not depend on phenotype alone: a "person's associations, actions, and loyalties" mattered as well.[38] Migration was an option not only for those of partly African ancestry who were outwardly indistinguishable from others socially defined as white. It was also an option for many outwardly "racially ambiguous" people, the legacy of a long history of sex across racial boundaries. Depending on their social standing and comportment, many people of "mixed" appearance were tacitly accepted by local communities—and sometimes expressly recognized by courts—as white.

The decline of legally institutionalized racial domination removed the most powerful incentives for passing. Yet movement between racial categories has not ceased or even slowed in the "post-passing era"; it has proliferated and taken new forms. Movement today goes in both directions along the black-white axis (though it is by no means confined to that axis); it is more identity-driven than interest-driven (and thus more like gender migration); and it is for the most part much less fateful and consequential than classical forms of passing.

One striking current of movement between racial categories in recent decades is from white—and to a lesser extent other racial categories—to Native American.[39] From half a million in 1960, the number of those identifying as Native American (and Alaskan Native) soared to nearly 2.9 million in 2010.[40] Demographers estimate that nearly half of the growth between 1960 and 1990 reflected racial reidentification as Native American, rather than factors such as fertility, mortality, and migration.[41] Extrapolating this forward would suggest a net increase in the Native American population through racial reidentification of over a million people in the half century between 1960 and 2010.[42]

Another form of contemporary movement between racial categories is associated with the emergence in the last few decades of "mixed" and "multiracial" as widely available, legitimate, and institutionalized categories. The more differentiated palette of socially recognized categories has created new opportunities for movement between them.[43] Most significantly, it has enabled many people whom prevailing rules of classification had previously defined as black to identify themselves—and to be recognized by others—as multiracial.[44]

Most contemporary moves from one ethnoracial category to another differ substantially from permanent racial passing in an era of formalized racial subordination, and from unidirectional and permanent transgender trajectories. Both racial passing in its classic form and transgender migration involve moves not just between *categories* but between deeply consequential *statuses* that powerfully organize social life and personal experience. Some people who move between ethnoracial categories today—from black to multiracial, for example, or from white to Native American—may also move into a new social environment. But for most, a shift in ethnoracial self-identification is unlikely to be so deeply consequential, in large part because ethnoracial categories are so much less constraining than they once were. Even where ethnoracial categories remain culturally meaningful and psychologically resonant, they are often organizationally inconsequential.[45] And those for whom ethnoracial categories are the most fateful—those trapped by the triple stigmatizations of space, class, and race in American "hyperghettos"— are the least likely to have a socially effective option of moving from one categorical identity to another.[46]

The final form of migration between racial categories that I want to consider is illustrated by Rachel Dolezal's "reverse passing," which was not as unprecedented as has been widely assumed. Like passing in general, permanent reverse passing often leaves no documentary trace. But historians have found evidence of white women claiming to be black in order to circumvent legal or social prohibitions on interracial unions.[47] And thanks to the one-drop rule, reverse passing was easily accomplished: the extraordinarily wide range of phenotypes among people socially defined as black meant that it was easy to be taken for black if one lived and worked in a black environment. A famous late nineteenth-century instance involved Clarence King, a publicly renowned geologist and explorer who lived a double existence for the last thirteen years of his life, passing as the black porter James Todd in order to secretly marry and father five children with Ada Copeland, who had been born a slave; he revealed his double life to Copeland only as he was dying of tuberculosis.[48]

While reverse passing does not necessarily require bodily transformations, some people have literally changed the color of their skin. The most celebrated—though strictly temporary—example of reverse passing was that of the journalist John Howard Griffin in 1959. With guidance from a dermatologist, Griffin darkened his skin through drugs and an ultraviolet lamp and traveled through the Deep South, recounting his experiences in the book *Black Like Me*, later made into a film. Griffin's example inspired Grace Halsell to undertake a similar experiment a decade later from a woman's point of view, which she reported in the best-selling book *Soul Sister*. (Halsell went on to write another book about her experience passing as a Navajo.)[49]

Physical self-transformation in order to pass as black has also been undertaken for personal benefit. Though he did not alter his skin color, Vijay Chokal-Ingam, an Indian American son of immigrant parents (and brother of the actress Mindy Kaling), shaved his head, trimmed his "long Indian eyelashes," and applied to medical school as an African American applicant in the late 1990s, lying about nothing but his race. He was admitted and attended for two years before dropping out; later, having applied as an Indian American this time, he attended business school.[50] The theme of reverse passing to reap affirmative action benefits was also treated in the 1986 film *Soul Man*, whose protagonist darkens his skin in order to apply for a Harvard Law School scholarship that is reserved for African Americans.

Sharply opposed to such purely instrumental forms of deceptive self-presentation are cases of deep and enduring transformation of personal identity. Music has long been a privileged terrain and medium of such racially inflected self-transformation. An exemplary case is that of the jazz clarinetist Mezz Mezzrow, born Milton Mesirow into a Russian Jewish immigrant family. Mezzrow's immersion in the African American jazz worlds of Chicago and New York led him to identify not only *with* blacks—as his closest friends, collaborators, and lovers—but *as* black. He characterized himself as a "voluntary Negro" and believed that socially, psychologically, and even physically he had gradually become black. He did not conceal his origins; indeed he publicly recounted his trajectory in a 1946 memoir, *Really the Blues*. A subsequent *Ebony* profile described him as an "ex-white" man who was "in psychological makeup . . . completely a black man."[51] Mezzrow was proud of being taken for black in social encounters. And when he was imprisoned at Rikers Island in 1940 for marijuana dealing, he identi-fied as black so as to be housed with the black prisoners in the racially segregated jail.[52]

The story of the legendary rhythm and blues musician and promoter Johnny Otis, born John Veliotes into a Greek immigrant family, is in many ways similar. On his own ac-count, Otis, who grew up in a largely black neighborhood and married his black high school sweetheart, became black by choice in childhood and maintained that identity for the rest of his life:

> As a kid I decided that if our society dictated that one had to be black or white, I would be black. . . . No number of objections such as, "You were born white. . . . You can never be black," on the part of the whites, or, "you sure are a fool to be Colored when you could be white," from Negroes, can alter the fact that I cannot think of myself as white. I do not expect everybody to understand it, but it is a fact. I am black environmen-tally, psychologically, culturally, emotionally, and intel-lectually. To attempt to view my case anthropologically would be nonsense because the world, and surely America, is full of "Negroes" who are much lighter than I, and "whites" who are much darker.[53]

In addition to becoming the "godfather of R&B," Otis was noted for his civil rights activism, and he served as the founding pastor of a nondenominational, largely black community church.[54] Like Mezzrow, he did not hide his ancestry. But his identification as black was so central to his sense of self that he often used the first-person plural pronoun "we" when writing about African Americans.[55]

Dolezal's story is reminiscent in some ways of those of Mezzrow and especially Otis. Her chosen family and social relationships, her studies in African and African American art, her involvement in African American institutions, and her commitment to black political causes led her to become, like Otis, "black by choice." Pressed by an interviewer to acknowledge the deception in her self-identification as black, she responded that "nothing about being white describes who I am. . . . The closest thing that I can come to is if—if you're black or white, I'm black."[56] Her comments echo Otis's assertion that "I cannot think of myself as white" and his sense that "if . . . one had to be black or white, I would be black." Like Otis, Dolezal might describe herself as "environmentally, psychologically, culturally, emotionally, and intellectually" black.

Unlike Mezzrow and Otis, though, Dolezal felt the need to darken her skin, style her hair, and conceal her ancestry so as to pass as black. She even invented a new ancestry for herself, publicly identifying a black man as her father. Her story, unlike theirs, was tainted by deception. Moreover, times have changed. The contemporary heirs to Mezzrow and Otis, as Baz Dreisinger observes, are white rappers who adopt and market a black persona. But no white rapper claims to have become black, as Mezzrow and Otis did. Given heightened concerns about cultural theft and appropriation, the only legitimate contemporary way to "claim blackness [is to] simultaneously claim whiteness." White rappers' "license to address, speak, and perform in decidedly un-white ways" is contingent on publicly—and repeatedly—acknowledging their whiteness.[57] Because Dolezal failed to do so, her claim to blackness found minimal public acceptance.

What can be said, in summary, about the trans of migration? Permanent movement between sex or gender categories is highly institutionalized; movement between racial or ethnic categories is not. Movement between sex or gender categories is supported by a sociotechnical ensemble that includes physicians, psychologists, gender identity clinics, legal rules, organizational protocols, and advocacy groups; passing between racial and ethnic categories is an individual and largely invisible undertaking that lacks any comparable social and organizational infrastructure. Movement between sex and gender categories is driven by considerations of identity rather than interest; movement between racial and ethnic categories, while historically driven by an interest in accessing privileges reserved for whites, is today increasingly—though not exclusively—identity-driven. Movement between sex and gender categories is formally administered and officially certified; movement between racial and ethnic categories, in a liberal political and social order, depends on informal social recognition and validation. And while movement between sex and gender categories has achieved broad public acceptance, movement between racial and ethnic categories is more critically appraised and more closely policed.

Despite the lack of a socially recognized and publicly validated procedure for crossing racial lines, movement between racial and ethnic categories continues, and is no doubt more common today than ever. But it seldom takes the form of permanent passing. Passing was generated by the combination of rigid classification rules—paradigmatically the one-drop rule—and systematic, legally sanctioned categorical inequality. With classification rules much looser, mixed and intermediate categories widely available and legitimate, and formal categorical inequality a thing of the past, the incentive for permanent passing disappears. Some people continue to move permanently between racial or ethnic categories for identitarian reasons. But since the rules governing category membership are so unsettled, they can often do so without the implications of deception—of pretending to be something one is not—that are central to the concept of passing. Often, but not always: as the Dolezal affair and the cautious self-presentation of white rappers illustrate, concerns about appropriation and exploitation tend to make black—in an ironic reversal of the historic pattern—a more closely policed category today than white. At the same time, temporary, partial, and recombinatory forms of race-crossing—like analogous forms of gender-bending and gender-crossing—have proliferated. But these fall under the rubric of the trans of between, to which I now turn.

Chapter 4

The Trans
of Between

Cast as journeys of self-discovery, self-transformation, and self-realization, stories of transgender migration have a satisfying narrative form. They begin with a divided self, in a condition of pain, suffering, and alienation; they pass through crises or critical turning points on the way; and they culminate in the overcoming of alienation and the affirmation of the true self.[1] Some stories of transracial migration—those of Mezzrow, Otis, or even, on her own account, Dolezal—take a similar form. The characteristic narrative arc of passing stories, to be sure, is different.[2] They are cautionary tales: stories of loss, not of triumph. But passing stories too—built around the tension between identity and interest—have a satisfying narrative form, which may explain their persistent appeal even in the contemporary post-passing era. In pursuing their interest, at the expense of their identity, passers typically come to grief, though they may be redeemed in the end by returning to their identity.

Such considerations may help explain why the trans of migration has captured so much more public attention than the trans of between or the trans of beyond, which are less readily cast in satisfying narrative form. Yet the latter are increasingly important. Migration stories like Jenner's and Dolczal's may continue to receive disproportionate media attention; but the cutting edge of the politics of identity has shifted to efforts to carve out a space between or beyond established gender and racial categories.[3]

Transgender people, as Margaret Talbot observed, "are increasingly choosing to place themselves somewhere between male and female: taking hormones for a while, then going off them; styling their appearance in gender-confounding ways but abstaining from medical procedures."[4] Similar observations have been made about race and ethnicity. The multiracial movement has challenged the either-or logic of prevailing forms of racial classification, while others reject racial classification in any form. A "race traitor" movement seeks to abolish whiteness. Representations of fluidity and ambiguity, epitomized by Michael Jackson's self-transformation, have moved from the margins to the center of popular culture.[5] And crossover identifications and practices have proliferated through the "Afro-Americanization of white youth."[6]

For those who migrate permanently from one gender or racial category to another, betweenness is a temporary phase, a stage of the journey to be passed through and left behind.[7] For others, however, betweenness is defined not in temporal terms, as a transitory intermediate phase of a unidirectional trajectory, but in topographic terms, as a position in a space of possibilities. The space is defined with reference to established categories, but the position in that space—or what might better be called the *positioning* in that space, since the trans of between is often an active and self-conscious stance—is defined in opposition to the either-or logic of prevailing classification practices. While the trans of migration embraces the logic of exclusive identification with a single sex/gender or ethnoracial category, the trans of between refuses that exclusivity. The trans of between, in short, involves a positioning of oneself with reference to two (or sometimes more) established categories, without belonging entirely or unambiguously to either one and without moving definitively from one to the other.

Transgender Betweenness: Oscillation, Recombination, and Gradation

Transgender betweenness may take an oscillating form, involving movement back and forth between male and female identities or personae; a recombinatory form, defined by the selective mixing of elements from conventionally understood masculine and feminine repertoires; or a gradational form, defined by an intermediate position on a spectrum anchored and defined by the categories male and female. These distinctions, of course, may be blurred in practice.

Transgender oscillation generally involves cross-dressing, which may be more or less elaborate, more or less frequent, and more or less public.[8] "Cross-dressing" is not, however, a fully adequate term, especially for public and prolonged excursions across the gender line. Those who seek to be taken in public for the opposite gender may avail themselves of wigs, makeup, and props that imply or conceal features of female or male anatomy. They may practice gender-coded ways of walking, talking, sitting, gesturing, and carrying themselves. They may seek to remove facial or other body hair, take hormones temporarily, and even undergo certain forms of cosmetic surgery.[9]

Like gender migration, gender oscillation is supported by what the sociologists Richard Ekins and Dave King call a "transgender tourism" industry. This is a network of dressing and grooming services; advice-purveying guidebooks, newsletters, websites, and workshops; suppliers of clothing and accessories; and bars, clubs, restaurants, and hotels known to be friendly to, or to provide special services for, a cross-dressing clientele.[10]

The gender oscillation of drag queens and kings stands at the opposite pole from that of transvestites who cross-dress in private or seek to be taken for the other gender in public. As Judith Lorber has argued, "Drag's core elements are *performance* and *parody*." The drag performance—unlike the routine and chronic performance of gender in everyday life—is segregated in time and space. It requires a dedicated audience that—unlike the audience for everyday gender performances, including those of cross-dressers seeking to pass—is "in on the joke from the beginning." Parody, moreover, requires an exaggeration of gender-coded dress and mannerisms. By exaggerating, the drag performer calls attention to the artifice and artificiality of the performance, to its nature as "pure performance"; the passer seeks to do the opposite.[11]

While oscillating forms of transgender depend on a clear separation of male and female codes, styles, and repertoires, recombinatory forms involve their mixing. Male and female identities and personae are enacted successively, to distinct audiences, in oscillating forms, but simultaneously, or at least near-simultaneously, to one and the same audience, in re-combinatory forms. Transgender oscillators—cross-dressers who seek to pass in public as well as drag artists—have a stake in the clear legibility of their gender performances and therefore often conform (or overconform) to stereotypical gender norms. Transgender recombiners are more likely to cause "gender trouble" by disrupting expectations about consistent "packages" of gendered behavior.[12]

Recombination arises most simply through delinking gender presentation from sex category. Even if one limits gender presentation to the binary alternatives masculine and feminine, this already generates the recombinatory "masculine female" and "feminine male" along with the normative "masculine male" and "feminine female."[13] These recombinatory categories may cause gender trouble even without a self-conscious effort to subvert gender norms or disrupt the gender binary. The "gender blending" women described by the sociologist Holly (now Aaron) Devor were often mistaken for men in public encounters with strangers as a result of their masculine or ambiguous gender presentation. The same holds for some forms of "female masculinity" analyzed by Judith (Jack) Halberstam, who noted that "having one's gender challenged in the women's rest room is a frequent occurrence in the lives of many androgynous or masculine women."[14]

A recent northern European study found that transvestites who cross-dressed at least occasionally at work and in other public places did not seek to alter their voices, gestures, or bodily comportment. For them, cross-dressing "was not about being, becoming or pretending to be a woman"; it was about "expressing [their] full identity and personality."[15] Their dissonant gender presentations caused some difficulties with colleagues. A few terminated previously cordial relationships; others sought in various ways to reimpose the gender binary.[16] Yet by expressing "*trans*gender forms of embodiment and identity," by combining "masculine, feminine, and ungendered practices and attributes," these transvestites managed to "undo" gender in subtle yet consequential ways even without any activist commitment to doing so.[17]

As assimilationist practices of passing on the part of permanent gender migrants have begun to yield, in the last two decades, to differentialist demands for recognition as *trans* men and women, the lines between the trans of migration, the trans of between, and the trans of beyond have begun to blur. Several trans men and women in one study reported "consciously [holding] on to gendered characteristics that did not match their chosen gender presentations." Some of them—unlike the masculine women studied by Devor two decades earlier—attached political meaning to gender-blending; others were simply unwilling to alter what they understood as authentic aspects of themselves. As one trans man put it, "I have a lot of female socialization things that I'm not really willing to compromise because they're part of who I am."[18] The line between the trans of migration and the trans of between also blurs when gender migrants conceptualize their trajectories as movement along a continuum, rather than movement from one clear-cut category to its binary opposite.

The desire to continue to express aspects of one's pretransition self has found support from intellectuals and activists who have sought to emancipate the transsexual experience from prevailing forms of medical control and from the need to pass as a "natural" member of the gender of choice, both of which encouraged or even required rigidly stereotypical gendered presentations of self. A key text was Sandy Stone's 1991 "posttranssexual manifesto," which critically analyzed the insistence on "purity and denial of mixture" that was central to transsexuals' autobiographical narratives and intrinsic to their attempts to pass as cis: "Passing means the denial of mixture ... [and the] effacement of the prior gender role." While transsexuals seeking to pass were compelled to "eras[e] a considerable portion of their personal experience" and by extension to repress a considerable part of their identity, Stone called on transsexuals—or what she envisioned as "posttranssexuals"—to "take responsibility for *all* of their history." Here the trans of between shades over into the trans of beyond, since "the *intertextual* possibilities of the transgender body" celebrated by Stone go beyond the possibilities suggested by a bipolar continuum.[19]

The line between the trans of between and the trans of beyond also blurs in the deliberate and self-conscious approach of some transgender people to the recombination of heterogeneous and at times (from the point of view of prevailing gender norms) strikingly dissonant elements in their self-presentation. This is especially the case for those who deliberately seek to disrupt the conventions on which the "legibility" of gender depends by confounding others' attempts to "read" them as male or female.[†]

The recombinatory possibilities of transgender extend to the form of the body itself. In the highly medicalized transsexual era, "complete" transitions were generally understood as entailing genital surgery as well as other surgical and hormonal interventions. Since the early 1990s, however, the weakening of the binary model and of medical control has created space for new forms of transgender embodiment that do not involve genital surgery, or any surgery at all. This holds even for those who see themselves as transitioning

---

† A blurring of between and beyond is also evident in the expanding set of gender identification terms. "Both-and" identifiers such as "androgynous" or "ambigender" suggest a location between established categories, while "neither-nor" identifiers such as "genderqueer" or "agender" suggest an attempt to move beyond those categories, but the line is not a sharp one. (The both-and meaning of "androgynous" and "ambigender" is built into the words, the former derived from the Greek terms for male and female, the latter beginning with the Latin prefix meaning both. "Agender," by analogy to "asexual," designates someone without a gender or a gender identity. "Genderqueer" is more politically charged than the other terms; it designates a critical stance toward the gender binary as well as a gender presentation that lies outside the categories male and female.) A similar distinction can be drawn between alternative pronouns that suggest betweenness, such as "hir" (built from "his" and "her"), and those that signal beyondness, such as "per" (from "person") or "ze" (marking distance from both "he" and "she").

from male to female or female to male; indeed it holds even for self-identified transsexuals, who may choose not to have genital surgery.[20] The various bodily transformations that used to form a complete package have been unbundled; one can now mix and match elements or experiment with different forms of embodiment at different times. Trans women and men who choose to forgo genital surgery—making up, on some accounts, the large majority of those who identify as trans—often have breasts readable as female along with male genitalia or chests readable as male along with female genitalia. The ultimate recombinatory possibility is exemplified by the pregnancy of trans men, as in the case of Thomas Beatie, whose very public pregnancy became a media sensation in 2008.[21]

While oscillation and recombination are ways of *enacting* transgender betweenness, the notion of gradation points to ways of *understanding* and *representing* betweenness. If we envision gender identity and gender expression as spectra of possibilities rather than binary alternatives, as anchored but not exhausted by the category pairs man/woman and masculine/feminine, then transgender betweenness can be understood as an intermediate position on such a spectrum.

The imagery of continuous gradation rather than categorical difference is not new. As the historian Joanne Meyerowitz has shown, it informed the theory of universal bisexuality that emerged in Germany and Austria at the end of the nineteenth century and remained influential in certain scientific and medical circles in Europe and North America until the middle of the twentieth. "Bisexuality" did not refer only or primarily to sexuality; it referred to an amalgam of sex, gender, and sexuality, all understood as grounded in the continuous spectrum of biological sex itself. Proponents of this view argued that all people were "to greater and lesser degrees physically bisexual," with a "corresponding mixture of feminine and masculine traits."[22]

The theory of universal bisexuality was used to explain and justify early instances of sex reassignment surgery, including the celebrated case of Christine Jorgensen, whose transformation became front-page news in 1952 under the headline "Ex-GI Becomes Blonde Beauty."[23] Harry Benjamin, who became Jorgensen's endocrinologist in 1953 and would later play a key role in institutionalizing transsexualism as a medical and social reality, initially speculated about the "possible presence of ovarian tissue" in Jorgensen; his published writings of the 1950s subsumed transsexuals (along with transvestites and homosexuals) under the broad category of "'intersexes' of varying character, degree, and intensity." Sex reassignment surgery was initially legitimized by assimilating it to the well-established practice of surgical treatment of intersex conditions. At a time when it was not possible to live openly in a space between genders, the hypothesized mixed sex of people like Jorgensen—not evident to medical inspection, but posited to have some organic cause—was used to justify surgery that could relieve the distress of being "lost between the sexes," as Jorgensen herself put it.[24]

The early twentieth-century theory of universal bisexuality conflated sex, gender, and sexuality. From midcentury on, however, these concepts came to be increasingly sharply distinguished from one another.[25] Today, all three may be understood in gradational terms, but one's position on one continuum is generally understood to be independent of one's position on the others. The widely circulated "Genderbread Person" graphic, for example, represents gender identity, gender expression, biological sex, and sexual orientation as four independent spectra, each allowing for a range of intermediate positions. Some transgender people find the imagery of the spectrum congenial; others, however, criticize it for failing to transcend the binary categories that continue to anchor and define each spectrum.[26]

Racial and Gender Betweenness

Racial betweenness differs in certain fundamental ways from gender betweenness. Most obviously, the most familiar forms of racial betweenness are socially understood as constituted by one's ancestry, while gender betweenness is an entirely individual phenomenon to which one's ancestry is utterly irrelevant, a theme I will develop in the concluding chapter.

Every act of human procreation generates "betweenness" through genetic recombination. This genetic betweenness may or may not be expressed in phenotypic form in such a way that a child is perceived and construed as phenotypically "between" his or her parents, with the mother's eyes and the father's nose, for example.

Sexual unions across socially defined racial or ethnic lines generate the additional possibility that such genetic and (sometimes) phenotypic betweenness vis-à-vis one's parents—a universal consequence of human sexual reproduction—may be interpreted and acknowledged as a form of racial or ethnic betweenness. Then again, it may *not* be so interpreted: betweenness may be socially denied through classification rules that assign the child to the category of only one of the parents. This was notoriously the case, of course, for the one-drop rule that defined a person with any identifiable African ancestry as black.

The historical and cross-cultural variation in racial classification rules and practices might lead us to think of racial betweenness as a natural fact that may be socially acknowledged or denied. But it is problematic to naturalize racial betweenness or mixedness in this way. Betweenness and mixedness are not innocent notions. As has often been observed, the notion of mixing—like the notions of hybridity, creolization, or syncretism—implicitly posits some prior unmixed elements that the mixture comprises.[27] The notion of "natural" racial betweenness or mixedness implies, problematically, that some are mixed while others are not. Racial betweenness—like gender betweenness—is always a matter of interpretation, a way of construing something as mixed; it is a social convention, not a natural fact.[28]

Racial betweenness is conceived and practiced primarily in a recombinatory form, but there are oscillating and gradational forms of betweenness as well. Oscillation was exemplified historically by the process of "professional passing" or "nine-to-five passing" that enabled some light-skinned African Americans to work in jobs reserved for whites without the radical social break with family and community that was often required by permanent, unidirectional passing.[29] It is exemplified today by the contextual shifts in racial identification experienced by some people with multiracial backgrounds.[30] For example, some who generally identify as multiracial may seek to "pass as black" in certain contexts by deploying dress, speech style, hairstyle, and cultural preferences and by selectively concealing or revealing information. They may do so in order to fit in socially with black peers, to avoid the stigma that may attach to being seen as white in certain milieus, or to gain a perceived advantage in certain organizational contexts.[31]

Gradational betweenness has long been exemplified by intermediate positions on the continuum of skin color.[32] A much-discussed technologically mediated representation of gradational racial betweenness was the "New Face of America" image that was generated by the software program Morph 2.0 "from a mix of several races" for the cover of a special issue of *Time* magazine in 1993.[33] Gradational betweenness is also illustrated by the ways certain genetic ancestry tests shape people's understandings of their racial and ethnic heritage. Autosomal tests, as noted in chapter 2, typically report results in percentage terms as a mixture of a certain number of reference populations, and such tests almost always reveal genetic ancestry from a variety of ancestral populations. While Y-chromosome and mitochondrial DNA tests—which follow a single strand of paternal or maternal ancestry—may contribute to reifying conventional racial and ethnic categories, autosomal tests locate *everyone* in a conceptual space of betweenness.[34]

In principle, the understanding of universal genetic mixedness that is supported by the increasingly popular autosomal ancestry tests might loosen the grip of typological and categorical forms of racial thinking. In principle, it might enable us to think of race—like genetic variation itself—as a space of continuous and gradational variation. In practice, however, the notion of universal genetic betweenness is not easily transposed into commonsense ways of thinking about racial difference. While *remote* genetic ancestry is easily understood as continuous rather than categorical, *proximate* genealogical ancestry—especially the most recent and socially meaningful ancestry represented by one's parents and grandparents—continues to be defined in categorical terms. The irony, given the long and ugly history of appealing to biology to fortify racial domination, is that the putative biological substrate of race, namely genetics, is readily understood in continuous and gradational terms, while race itself remains prevailingly understood in categorical terms—and understandably so, since race operates in and through practices of social classification and categorization.

This suggests another way in which we understand racial betweenness differently from gender betweenness. We are growing accustomed to thinking of gender identity—and not simply gender presentation—as a continuum or spectrum. Yet while color and genes are similarly understood as a continuum or spectrum, we do not imagine racial identity in this way. As a result, racial betweenness is prevailingly understood in recombinatory—that is, categorical—rather than gradational terms.

Recombinatory Racial Betweenness: Classification and Identification

Recombinatory racial or ethnic betweenness is expressed in practices of social classification, modes of subjective identification, and cultural and behavioral repertoires. Historically, some systems of racial classification—notably those prevalent in the Spanish and Portuguese colonies of Latin America— elaborated a finely graded set of intermediate categories to make sense of various forms and degrees of betweenness, while others provided limited or no intermediate categories.[35] Systems of racial classification in the United States never reached the degree of elaboration found in Latin America. But intermediate categories along the black-white axis have been socially recognized and even legally defined at various times and places. The intermediate category "mulatto"— and in 1890 "quadroon" and "octoroon" as well—was an official census category between 1850 and 1920 (except in 1900). But in 1930 intermediate racial categories disappeared from the census, never to return. Their disappearance reflected the consolidation of a regime of racial classification, epitomized in the one-drop rule, that drew a sharp distinction between white and black and redefined intermediate categories as black.[36]

In the increasingly complex and fluid ethnoracial environment of the 1990s, the multiracial movement challenged this regime of classification by seeking formal and informal recognition of multiracial identities. Its campaign to include "multiracial" as an officially designated option in the census did not succeed, in part because of concerns that the black community would shrink statistically through a selective shift in identification from black to multiracial. The Census Bureau did, however, agree to recognize multiracial identities indirectly, by allowing people to identify as belonging to more than one race. While this practice does not recognize the "neither-nor" form of racial betweenness that an official "multiracial" category would have validated, it does recognize "both-and" forms of racial betweenness.

Racial and ethnic betweenness is also expressed in modes of subjective identification. Even during periods in which intermediate categories have not been officially recognized in institutions like the census, racial and ethnic betweenness has been an important trope through which self-understandings and subjective identifications have been articulated and expressed. There is rich literary, historical, and sociological evidence of the resonance of this trope.[37]

While multiracial activists lost their campaign to get the category "multiracial" officially recognized in the census, the category *has* been institutionalized in everyday life, and people can and do identify as multiracial. The weakening hold of the one-drop rule over practices of racial classification and identification has opened up a much wider range of identification options for children of racially mixed marriages, particularly black-white marriages, and for others of racially mixed background.[38] This is most clearly the case for the younger generations. An analysis of the 2000 U.S. census—when for the first time respondents could choose more than one racial identity—showed that in households with one white- and one black-identifying parent, 53 percent of the children were designated as both black and white, and another 10 percent as "other" (or as black, white, and other); only 36 percent chose single racial identities (25 percent black, 11 percent white).[39] Another study found that only 13 percent of college students with one white- and one black-identifying parent identified themselves as black, while nearly two-thirds identified themselves as biracial, including 6 percent of the sample who identified themselves as shifting between black, white, and biracial. (Of the remainder, 15 percent declined to identify with any racial category, 3 percent identified as white, and 5 percent chose another category.)[40]

Self-identification as biracial or multiracial, to be sure, does not necessarily mean that one will be identified as biracial or multiracial by others. The study just cited found that of those identifying as biracial, 60 percent chose "I consider myself biracial, but I experience the world as a black person," while only 40 percent chose "I consider myself exclusively as biracial (neither black nor white)."[41] The numbers point to the enduring influence of the one-drop rule on the way others perceive those who identify as multiracial. Moreover, the belief that one is perceived by others as black may influence one's own self-understanding and self-identification.[42] In a large-scale representative survey of young people, 75 percent who identified their race as both white and black chose black when asked to select the "one category [that] best describes your racial background," while only about half of those who identified their race as both white and Asian chose Asian as the best single racial category.[43]

Recombinatory racial or ethnic identifications may expressly preserve the parental categories. "Parental" here has both the figurative and abstract sense of the categories from which the recombinatory identity is derived—as an androgynous gender identification is derived from man and woman—and the literal sense of the categorical identifications of one's parents or grandparents. Thus one may identify, for example, as half Irish, half Italian; as half black, half white; or as three-quarters Mexican and one-quarter Filipina.

The recombinatory preservation of parental categories in the identifications of subsequent generations can rapidly become cumbersome and self-subverting if repeated over multiple generations. If one parent identifies with two categories, for example, and the second parent with a different set of two categories, the child can preserve the parental categories only by identifying with four categories. The fractional logic of recombinatory identification becomes less socially meaningful as it proceeds from halves to quarters to eighths and so on. In practice, recombinatory identification becomes selective, retaining some socially meaningful identifications but discarding others. Or it shifts from identifying with selected parental categories to identifying simply as "multiracial" or "mixed," without a core identification with any *particular* ethnoracial categories.

This latter possibility illustrates another way in which the trans of between can shade over into the trans of beyond. The category "multiracial" or "mixed" (which may be preferred to a "both-and" identification even by "first-generation" multiracials) is not located "between" anything in particular.[44] It is positioned outside—and in this sense beyond—rather than between existing categories; it thereby threatens to destabilize official practices of ethnoracial counting and categorizing. This is why proponents of using an official "multiracial" category for the census and other federal data collection efforts were ultimately unsuccessful. The "choose one or more" format that was adopted for the race question in the 2000 census preserved the basic system of racial counting and accounting, which since the 1960s has been geared to the production of data suitable for the monitoring of the enforcement of civil rights legislation. The introduction of a "multiracial" category would have disrupted that system.[45]

Performing Betweenness

Recombinatory racial or ethnic betweenness is not only a mode of classification and a style of self-understanding; it is also—like gender betweenness—something that is enacted or performed. And just as recombinatory gender betweenness draws selectively on elements from conventionally understood male and female repertoires, so recombinatory racial or ethnic betweenness draws selectively on elements from racially or ethnically coded cultural and behavioral repertoires.

Of course the notion of black, white, Asian, or Latino culture or behavioral style is deeply problematic. If black culture, for example, means the ensemble of cultural practices actually adopted in various times, places, and contexts by people who are socially defined as black, the concept is far too heterogeneous to be useful. But the alternative of defining black culture independently of that set of practices raises the questions of how it should be defined and of who has the authority to define it. And any such definition risks reifying and essentializing black culture in a way that reproduces entrenched stereotypes.[46]

The notion of racially or ethnically coded cultural, behavioral, and stylistic repertoires provides a way around this problem. The key to such repertoires is their semiotic legibility. It is this that enables people to perform race in a recognizable way, just as the semiotic legibility of conventional gender repertoires enables people to perform gender in a readily decodable way. The elements used in such performances—including both performances that call attention to themselves *as* performances and the unmarked performances of everyday life—are often highly conventionalized and stereotyped. This is what makes them reliable tools for performers and readily legible to audiences.

I noted above that recombinatory gender betweenness can occasion "gender trouble" by violating expectations about appropriate forms of gender presentation and, on a deeper level, by challenging assumptions about the binary organization of gender itself. In a similar way, the performance of recombinatory racial betweenness can produce what might be called "racial trouble" by violating expectations about appropriate forms of "racial presentation" and, on a deeper level, by challenging assumptions about the stability and categorical organization of race itself. Such trouble—and the efforts it may prompt to police and discipline performances that are seen as inappropriate—is especially likely when the performer cannot claim a mixed identity grounded in socially recognized mixed ancestry.

In the policing of unauthorized performances of recombinatory racial betweenness, norms of *appropriateness* are informed by concerns about *appropriation*. Those who are not entitled by ancestry to perform racial betweenness can be seen not only as acting inappropriately but as appropriating something that is not rightfully theirs.

The nexus between appropriateness, appropriation, and property is deeply contested. On one view, cultural practices, behavioral performances, and embodied styles of being are taken to *express*—legitimately or illegitimately—identities that are prior to and independent of those practices, performances, and styles; on the alternative view, practices and performances are taken to *constitute* identities that do not exist independently of their performative enactment. On the former view, who you are governs—or ought to govern—what you do; on the latter, what you do determines who you are.[47] On the former view, your practices and performances should express what is already and always yours: your identity, your culture, your heritage. On the latter, identity cannot serve as a yardstick by which to assess the legitimacy of practices and performances, since it is constituted by those practices and performances. The former view *presupposes* an essentialist understanding of identity; the latter *repudiates* that understanding.

The latter view, in short, takes seriously the "performative turn"—a current of thought in the social sciences and humanities that focuses on the practices and "performances" through which what might appear from a distance to be stable identities and structures are constructed, sustained, and transformed.[48] But while the performative turn has become something of an orthodoxy in gender studies, it remains more tentative and exploratory—and more controversial—in the study of race and ethnicity, no doubt because it challenges the essentialist understanding of racial and ethnic identity to which many self-styled political and cultural progressives remain committed. And it is this understanding of identity that underlies the charges of cultural appropriation that have been leveled at certain "crossover" practices and performances.[49]

Yet there is an alternative view of the performative enactment of racial betweenness that challenges the language of appropriation even as it acknowledges the historical and political concerns that inform its use. Consider, for example, the performative enactment of a socially recognizable black identity by a person who is socially defined as white. There is of course a long and ugly history of such cross-enactments that—as in the blackface or minstrelsy tradition—clearly serve to preserve the established racial hierarchy by enacting crude racial stereotypes.[50] But it is problematic to view all crossover forms of performance and enactment as racist or appropriative. Even the phenomenon of "wiggerism"—which involves whites (mainly youth) adopting cultural repertoires and behavioral styles (mainly in the domain of music, language, and dress) that are prevailingly coded and readable as black—is more complex than that.[51] In the context of a longstanding and deeply ambivalent white romanticization of "black culture," wiggerism undoubtedly does involve appropriation, and it undoubtedly does enact stereotypes. But as the philosopher Crispin Sartwell suggests in a sharp and self-reflexive essay, it can involve more than that. It can highlight the artificial and constructed nature of race; it can celebrate, not simply appropriate, "black culture"; and, most importantly, it can embody a self-conscious critique of white privilege and "white culture."[52] Sartwell concludes that when it is coupled (as in the case of Eminem) with self-critical self-consciousness and explicit "racial positioning," when the acknowledgment of one's white privilege goes hand in hand with the performance of a black identity, "wiggerism indeed becomes an agent of change."[53]

Performative enactments of blackness (in combination with the acknowledgment of whiteness) need not be focused on the cultural repertoire and aesthetic style represented by wiggerism. An alternative form of recombinatory racial betweenness combines a voluntary black *political* identity that is "aspirational and activist" with a white embodied identity defined by one's ancestry.[54] Like Rachel Dolezal, people who enact such forms of recombinatory racial betweenness do not simply identify *with* black culture, style, or causes; they identify in some way *as* black—culturally, aesthetically, or politically. But unlike Dolezal, they acknowledge their socially defined and constructed whiteness (and how they have benefited from it) even as they disavow that whiteness through their actions, affiliations, performances, and embodied ways of being.

The oscillating, gradational, and recombinatory forms of gender and racial betweenness explored in this section call into question the stability and legibility of gender and race; the either-or logic of gender and racial classification; and, perhaps most fundamentally, the notions of categorical difference that are at the heart of the gender and racial orders. In so doing, they open up the possibility of forms of difference that would exist not only *between* genders or races but *beyond* gender and race as systems of social classification. It is to this "trans of beyond" that I now turn.

Chapter 5

———

The Trans
of Beyond

If the trans of between takes its meaning from existing gender and racial categories, the trans of beyond seeks to escape from the social and cultural force fields defined by those categories. The trans of beyond may take the form of an assertion of a new category—like genderqueer, trans, or multiracial—that is not situated within the conceptual space defined by established categories. It may entail personal or political opposition to being categorized at all, or to the categorization of others. Or it may involve a normative vision or empirical diagnosis of a social world no longer organized—or no longer organized so deeply—by gender or racial categorization. I will call these neo-categorical, anti-categorical, and post-categorical forms of the trans of beyond.[1]

Beyond Gender?

What might it mean to go "beyond gender"—or at least beyond the categorical frameworks that define the gender order and organize our experience of gender? And how does the trans of beyond differ from the trans of between? After all, some forms of enacting and embodying gender betweenness already involve—implicitly or explicitly—the claim to go beyond the either-or, binary logic of gender. What I want to highlight in this chapter are other ways of going beyond gender categories.

As I noted in my discussion of the trans of between, some novel gender categories are constructed from the existing binary pair or positioned along a continuum defined by that pair. This is true for "both-and" identifiers such as "ambigender" or "bigender," for the older combining form "androgynous," and for scalar descriptors such as "masculine-of-center."

Neo-categorical forms of the trans of beyond assert or recognize categories that are not located on this continuum. These include anti-categorical categories such as genderqueer, pangendered, and ungendered, which I discuss below. They also include the categories "trans woman," "trans man," "trans*," or simply "trans."[†]

Transgender migration was long self-concealing: transsexuals and other unidirectional gender migrants sought to pass as women or men and to erase all traces of their former lives. For some, this remains the ideal. Beginning in the early 1990s, however, increasing numbers of transsexuals and

---

† As "trans" has come to be associated, in many contexts, with trans man or trans woman, trans* has come to be used in recent years as a device for expressly including those who do not identify in binary terms as well as those who do. The irony is that this replicates the inclusive intent earlier associated with "transgender" and subsequently with "trans" (Bettcher 2014a, 385; Titman 2013).

other transgender migrants have sought recognition as *trans* women and *trans* men (even though they have also claimed recognition, inclusion, and equal rights as women and men). Unlike androgynous or masculine-of-center, these categories do not suggest betweenness. And while they do of course suggest a trajectory of migration, out transsexuals or transgender migrants—unlike their "stealth" counterparts—do not move between *established* gender categories. The out male-to-female trans person migrates not from man to woman but from man to *trans* woman; and "trans woman" is not located in the same category space as "man" and "woman."

The categories "trans woman" and "trans man" obviously make reference to the categories "woman" and "man." Yet "trans woman" is not intended or understood as simply equivalent to "woman"; nor is it located between man and woman. It names a new position that transcends not simply the either-or, once-and-forever logic of the gender binary but also the prevailing one-dimensional bipolar framework through which we construct and imagine the space of gender possibilities. That is, the categories "trans woman" and "trans man"—and, even more clearly, the category "trans" itself—transcend not just the gender *binary* but the gender *continuum*. They transform the space of gender categorization from a one-dimensional continuum into a two-dimensional space, defined by the cis-trans axis as well as the male-female axis. In this two-dimensional space, the categories male and female (or some mix thereof) no longer suffice to define a gender identity; one needs the categories cis and trans as well.[2]

This redefinition of the conceptual space of gender suggests why the trans of beyond challenges the gender order in a more fundamental way than the trans of migration or even the trans of between. Self-concealing transsexuals—by seeking to pass as women or men, deploying the most conventional gender signifiers in order to do so, and framing their stories in the essentialist language of gender identity—do not disrupt the gender order; they may even reinforce it. But self-revealing transsexuals—and others expressly claiming recognition as trans women, trans men, trans*, or simply trans—disrupt the cognitive and social foundations of the sex/gender system by positioning themselves not simply between but, in part, outside its foundational categories.[3] This disruptive potential of the trans of beyond is attractive to some feminists, a point I return to below.

Anti-categorical forms of the trans of beyond take a stand not just against binary forms of gender categorization but against gender categorization per se. For some, this is a political position; for others it is primarily a personal stance. The line between the personal and the political is of course often blurred, since the lived experience of being personally unclassifiable, of not fitting in any available category, may find expression in political claims for interactional or institutional recognition of hitherto unrecognized identities.

A leading exponent of an anti-categorical position is the longstanding transgender activist Riki Wilchins. Wilchins treats all categories—even transgender itself—as traps. Her critique of category-based identities and identity politics is consistent with her emphasis on the constitutive rather than merely expressive significance of gender performance: "Gender refers not to something we *are* but to something we *do*."[4]

A quite different and even more radical anti-categorical stance is that of Christie Elan-Cane, who has long sought both personal and public recognition for an ungendered self-identity.[5] Elan-Cane came to hate being burdened with a female body, rejected the ascribed identity of woman, and eventually had a mastectomy and a hysterectomy, but never identified as a man or considered sex reassignment surgery. Elan-Cane identified for some time as an androgyne and a third-gender person but came to prefer identifying as "ungendered." In keeping with this, Elan-Cane sought recognition through the use of ungendered pronouns and terms of address, preferring the pronoun "per," derived from person, and "Pr." as a term of address. To avoid being perceived in gendered terms, Elan-Cane favors gender-neutral clothes and a shaved head.

Elan-Cane's public campaign for recognition of those with ungendered identities is in one sense neo-categorical. In a world teeming with categories, it is impossible to avoid categories altogether. Elan-Cane therefore proposes "ungendered" as a social category, while registering ambivalence about doing so: "The non-gendered identity will become a recognised social identity or category (although I dislike using the C word) alongside the existing gendered identities of male and female."[6] But Elan-Cane's fundamental stance is anti-categorical. Sex/gender categorization may be needed in some official contexts; hence Elan-Cane has taken a leading role in the campaign for the "x" passport in Britain, following the model of Australia and New Zealand. But Elan-Cane is consistently opposed to gender categorization in other contexts. "Facebook's multiple 'gender options' is a gimmick and nothing more—they have trivialised the issue. . . . It is inappropriate to ask whether one is male or female [in] the commercial sector but there should always be a third non gender-specific option when the question is asked—even if that option says 'none of your damned business.'"[7]

In a less radical way, the assertion that one does not fit in any of the available categories may be informed by a conviction of the uniqueness of one's own lived experience of gender. In describing and endorsing a "paradigm shift" in understandings of transgender, Holly Boswell criticized the restrictive focus on transsexuals and cross-dressers, concepts that are too simple—and too dependent on the existing binary categories—to capture the actual "experience of transgender" for many people. Referring to her own experience, Boswell wrote that "I seem to be neither [man nor woman], or maybe both, yet ultimately only myself." Transgender "has to do with reinventing and realizing oneself outside of the current systems of gender. . . . There are probably as many genders as there are people. Gender may be nothing more than a personal matrix of personality traits."[8] Boswell's claim to a unique gender identity—in effect, a claim to constitute a category of one—resonates with the cultural valorization of individualism in the American context. It is reminiscent of the distinctive personal faith called Sheilaism (after her own name) by an informant in the sociologist Robert Bellah's *Habits of the Heart*, which "suggests the logical possibility of over 220 million American religions, one for each of us."[9]

The personal anti-categorical stance may also be informed by a celebration of gender multiplicity and fluidity, as epitomized by Kate Bornstein's 1994 book *Gender Outlaw*, with its emphasis on play, performance, and transgression, or by Boswell's claim that "my transition will never be over."[10] This liberationist, explore-all-gender-possibilities stance has strong affinities with a genderqueer stance. And while genderqueer is itself a category—and thus might be subsumed under the notion of a neo-categorical stance—it is expressly understood (like ungendered) as what might be called an *anti-categorical category*: a category to end all categories, as it were. This family of stances differs sharply from Elan-Cane's ascetic efforts to escape the force-field of gender altogether: from the perspective of Elan-Cane, gender multiplicity, play, performance , and even transgression can be seen as "hyper-gendered" rather than ungendered.[11]

Post-categorical forms of the trans of beyond are more difficult to characterize. Here, expressly transgender stances and visions shade over into feminist stances and visions that are not ordinarily considered part of the same universe of phenomena. Indeed, normative visions of a post-gender society—and empirical diagnoses of incipient and partial moves toward such a society—have been much more fully articulated in the feminist than in the transgender literature. For my purposes, however, feminist visions of a society "beyond gender" are not simply compatible with and supportive of certain transgender projects and discourses; they are *part of* the transgender phenomenon, broadly understood, even if they are not presented in this way.[12] If "new paradigm" understandings of transgender refer, as Boswell suggests, to "the transgressing of gender norms, or being freely gendered, or transcending gender altogether in order to become more fully human," then this ought to include feminist visions of forms of social life "beyond gender."[13]

Normative accounts of what it might mean to live "beyond gender" are varied and contested, even among feminists. (Accounts of what it might mean to move "beyond race" are much clearer and—on a conceptual level—less controversial.) Feminists are divided, for example, on the question of whether overcoming gender oppression or gender inequality requires transcending gender per se. Accounts of a post-gender society envision a world in which gender categories are no longer central in organizing some combination of the following: (1) the allocation of legal and political rights, social and economic rewards, and respect; (2) the division of labor, including household labor and caring work as well as paid labor; (3) social expectations about appropriate forms of expression and behavior; (4) the perception and interpretation of the social world; and (5) the cognitive and emotional organization of the self.

The first three are straightforward. It is clear enough what it would mean to go "beyond gender" in the allocation of rights and rewards, the division of labor, and the structuring of expectations, though there are important disagreements among feminists about the desirability as well as the possibility of full "gender symmetry" in the division of labor.[14] What it might mean to go "beyond gender" in perceiving and interpreting the world and in organizing the self is less clear. The central role of gender in these last two domains comes from the fact that gender is not only a *social* structure but a *symbolic* structure, a cognitive lens through which we perceive and interpret the social world as well as our own embodied selves, assigning gendered meanings to identities, attributes, styles, tasks, and even sights, sounds, colors, and material objects.[15] Though the scope and content of the assigned meanings vary across time and place, gender appears to be a universal or nearly universal symbolic structure and cognitive lens for interpreting self and world.

The complexity of the question of what it might mean to go "beyond gender" results from the various ways in which combinations of changes in these five domains can be envisioned and evaluated. Exploring this complexity is beyond the scope of this chapter. But it may be helpful to distinguish *liberationist*, *egalitarian*, and *assimilationist* visions of going beyond gender, aimed at overcoming domination and constraint, distributional inequality, and difference, respectively.

The various feminist projects for going "beyond gender," as I observed above, are not articulated as expressly transgender projects. And I have repeatedly noted the longstanding feminist critique of certain transgender claims and practices. Feminists have been particularly critical of the trans of migration, especially in its medicalized forms, arguing that it reinforces rather than subverts the gender binary. The paradigm shift in understandings of transgender in the last two decades, however, has focused more attention on the trans of between and the trans of beyond and has highlighted their transformative potential. In so doing, that paradigm shift has opened up new possibilities for alliance between feminist and transgender projects and movements, though it has at the same time created new complexities and tensions.[16]

The possibilities for alliance are most visible in connection with what I call the liberationist strand of feminist visions of a world "beyond gender." These visions emphasize not only the liberation of women from male domination, but also, at least in some versions, the liberation of men *and* women from the constraints of gendered norms and expectations. Some feminist analyses view transgender practices and identifications as a key source of movement toward a world beyond gender.[17] Since such practices and identifications are more common among youth, they see cohort succession—the emergence of new cohorts who no longer share assumptions about the gender order that are taken for granted by earlier cohorts—as a key vector of social change.

Relations between the egalitarian strand of feminist thinking about a world "beyond gender" and expressly transgender projects and stances are much more complex and contested.[†] Feminist accounts of distributional inequality and movements to overcome it focus squarely on inequalities between men and women in power, authority, income, wealth, and so on. Transgender projects and stances disturb the conceptual and political clarity of such accounts by introducing new categories—such as trans woman and trans man—into the calculus of gender inequality and by challenging the foundational, taken-for-granted status of the category "woman" in

† All feminist thinking is of course egalitarian in some respects. The strand I am calling egalitarian focuses on distributional inequalities between men and women, while the liberationist strand focuses on the constraints exercised by the gender system on both women and men.

feminist thought.[18] For many feminists, this is at best a distraction from the core question of inequality between men and women, at worst a frontal assault on feminism.[19] But for trans activists and scholars, the focus on men and women obscures crucial forms of gender inequality and oppression that feminists have largely ignored and that radical feminists have aggravated by refusing to recognize trans women as women. That refusal has led to bitter struggles between trans activists and radical feminists about ownership and control over the category "woman," access to women's spaces, and the "trans-exclusionary" stance of radical feminists.[20]

The assimilationist strand of feminist thinking about a world "beyond gender" stands in equally sharp tension with the differentialist ethos of many transgender projects and stances. Assimilationist feminism envisions men and women ultimately becoming fundamentally similar, not least in their similar investments in domestic caregiving and paid work.[21] This envisioned diminution of difference is antithetical to the preservation or indeed proliferation of difference envisioned by most transgender projects. Far from seeking to abolish gender difference (as Elan-Cane may have done), the trans of migration presupposes and reproduces gender difference, while transgender projects that seek to carve out a space between or beyond binary gender categories celebrate the liberation and proliferation of previously unimaginable forms of gender difference; they are not assimilationist but hyper-differentialist.

Beyond Race?

The notion of racial and ethnic mixing, I noted in the preceding chapter, is not necessarily an innocent one, since it often problematically implies a mixing of elements that are themselves understood as unmixed or pure. But mixedness need not be understood in this way. The phenomenon of increasing—and increasingly salient—mixing, blending, or hybridity can be interpreted not only through the prism of racial or ethnic betweenness but, alternatively, through the prism of "beyondness." The interpretation of mixedness according to an additive or fractional "both-and" logic locates "mixed" identities *between* racial or ethnic categories. But mixedness can also be construed according to a "neither-nor" logic that locates mixed identities *outside* the prevailing category space.

The category "multiracial" expresses this neither-nor logic. "Multiracial" is not just an additional racial category alongside others; as a category with no content apart from the notion of multiplicity itself, it is located outside rather than within the prevailing system of racial categories. The conceptual space within which it is located is defined not by the categories black, white, Asian, Latino, and Native American but by the opposition between multiracial and monoracial (just as the conceptual space within which the category trans is located is defined by the opposition between transgender and cisgender). The proposal to include a "multiracial" option in the U.S. census met with strong resistance for just this reason: it threatened to disturb the logic of the system of ethnoracial counting and categorizing.[†]

Like "genderqueer" or (in some cases) "trans," "multiracial" illustrates a form of beyondness that is at once *neocategorical* and *anti-categorical*: it functions as a kind of anti-categorical category, offering a locus of identification—a categorical refuge—for those who identify with none of the established categories.

---

† More concretely, of course, a "multiracial" option threatened to reduce the official size and diminish the political strength of the black population.

Those who refuse to identify themselves in racial or ethnic terms, either because they claim to be personally unclassifiable or because they are politically opposed to such categorization, express the anti-categorical stance more clearly.[22] (As in the case of gender, no sharp distinction can be drawn between personal and political stances, since political claims-making often emerges from lived experience.)

One can distinguish liberal, radical, and performative forms of political opposition to racial categorization. In liberal perspective, ethnoracial classification is intrinsically objectionable, often invidious, and potentially harmful. Some might characterize this stance as conservative, but it is informed by classically liberal concerns. Ethnoracial classification is seen as infringing on individual privacy and autonomy, entrenching racial and ethnic divisions, and—in certain contexts—facilitating oppression and violence.[23] Strong versions of the liberal anti-categorical stance see no legitimate grounds for classifying citizens on the basis of race or ethnicity; weaker versions require cogent justification for such classification. In the language of American constitutional jurisprudence, classification by race or ethnicity should be viewed as "suspect" and should be subjected to "strict scrutiny."[24] Although counting and categorizing by race and ethnicity is pervasive in the United States and many other liberal democracies (France being the most conspicuous exception), liberal skepticism about its legitimacy has considerable standing. One indicator is that in many data collection contexts it is more legitimate to refuse to answer questions about race or ethnicity than to refuse to answer questions about sex or gender. Questions about racial or ethnic identification may be expressly flagged as optional, or a predefined option like "decline to answer" may be built into the format. The very design of the question, in these cases, reflects an awareness that collecting data on racial and ethnic identifications is considered sensitive and potentially controversial in a way that collecting data on sex or gender is not.

The "race traitor" movement associated with Noel Ignatiev exemplifies the radical anti-categorical stance. Though it seeks to challenge and disrupt "the institutions that reproduce race as a social category," the proximate focus of this movement—which distinguishes it sharply from the liberal anti-categorical stance—is on abolishing whiteness. Whites are called on to "repudiate the protection of the white skin" and to renounce the privileges of membership in the "club" of the white race, since individual "defections," taken together, may have systemic consequences. "The existence of the white race depends on the willingness of those assigned to it to place their racial interests above class, gender, or any other interests they hold. The defection of enough of its members to make [whiteness] unreliable as a determinant of behavior will set off tremors that will lead to its collapse."[25] This interest in generating a cumulatively consequential wave of defection from whiteness distinguishes the "race traitor" project from the more intensely personal repudiation of femaleness undertaken by Christie Elan-Cane, who has no political interest in abolishing femaleness, maleness, or gender categories but rather seeks recognition for the ungendered.

The performative anti-categorical stance seeks to disrupt or subvert practices of racial and ethnic categorization through performances that call attention to the arbitrariness, absurdity, manipulability, or constructedness of racial categories. Michael Awkward, for example, reads Michael Jackson's racially coded self-transmutation as a potentially transgressive instance of "transraciality"—an "astute anti-essentialist comment"—rather than as evidence of racial self-hatred.

Transraciality involves "the radical revision of one's natural markings and the adoption of aspects of the human surface (especially skin, hair, and facial features) generally associated with the racial other."[26] Like passing, it affords experience of "an altered racial designation." Yet it "potentially offers an even more effective means of uncovering the constructedness of the rules of racial being. For while the ability to pass demonstrates that one's ancestors had already moved sexually—voluntarily or not—across racial lines, transraciality represents an individually determined, surgically-and/or cosmetically-assisted traversal of boundaries that putatively separate radically distinct social groups."[27]

Some such performances may be akin to gender drag in calling attention to the artificiality of the performance itself and in relying on parody and exaggeration.[28] Eddie Murphy's 1984 "White Like Me" skit for *Saturday Night Live*, for example, shows Murphy prepping for his role as "Mr. White" by watching *Dynasty* ("See how they walk? Their butts are real tight when they walk") and reading Hallmark cards. Made over as a white man, Murphy ventures out to buy a newspaper, but the clerk insists that he take it without paying. He boards a bus, and finds that when the sole black passenger gets off, the driver and passengers break into song and dance. Applying for a loan at a bank without collateral, credit, or ID, he is initially dismissed by a black loan officer, but a white loan officer takes over, saying, "We don't have to bother with these formalities . . . just take what you want, Mr. White. Pay us back anytime. Or don't. We don't care." The skit ends with Murphy commenting, "I've got a lot of friends, and we've got a lot of makeup. So, the next time you're huggin' up with some really super, groovy white guy, or you met a really great, super keen white chick, don't be too sure. They might be black."[29]

In enacting stereotypes in order to display and comment on them, such performances tread on politically sensitive ground. While gender drag may be understood as subversive, what some commentators have called "racial drag" is much riskier. Performatively enacting stereotyped versions of race—at least when an outsider enacts stereotypes associated with a subordinate category—is vulnerable to charges of appropriation or outright racism and risks being denounced as a continuation of the blackface or minstrelsy tradition.[30]

Post-categorical visions of a social order that is "beyond race" are more conceptually straightforward and normatively uncontroversial than accounts of a social order that is "beyond gender." In a post-racial—or, more broadly, post-ethnic—social order, the allocation of rights, resources, and respect would not depend on racial or ethnic category membership. In the words of the historian David Hollinger, such a social order would "reject the idea that descent is destiny": the "ethnoracial categories central to identity politics would be more matters of choice than ascription; . . . mobilization by ethnoracial groups would be more a strategic option than a presumed destiny attendant upon mere membership in a group; and . . . economic inequalities would be confronted head-on, instead of through the medium of ethnorace."[31]

As an analytical perspective—as distinguished from a normative vision—the post-racial or post-ethnic stance "acknowledges the reality of an ethnoracially intensive past" and seeks to "assess and understand the diminution of that intensity in a variety of contexts."[32] Critics of this perspective point to the persistence of racism and categorical racial inequality; defenders counter that "post-racial" and "post-ethnic" denote a direction of change, not an end state, and point to significant weakening in the grip of ethnoracial categories.[33]

Hollinger and others emphasize the ongoing blurring of ethnoracial lines through high rates of intermarriage and cohabitation. Of black men marrying in 2013, a quarter married someone of a different race—a tenfold increase from the early 1970s, and a fivefold increase from the mid-1980s.[34] The percentage of Americans approving of marriage between blacks and whites has increased over the last half century from a mere 4 percent in 1959 to 87 percent in 2013, representing "one of the largest shifts of public opinion in Gallup history."[35]

Jennifer Hochschild and her coauthors emphasize the emergence of younger cohorts with strikingly different collective memories of and attitudes toward race. In 1987, for example, only 23 percent of young adults (under age thirty) "completely disagreed" with the statement that they "don't have much in common with people of other races," but 57 percent of young adults completely disagreed with the statement in 2009.[36]

William Julius Wilson has been arguing for decades that class background and education have become more important than race in shaping job prospects and life chances of African Americans, though he has acknowledged the importance of public-sector employment and affirmative action programs for black occupational gains.[37] Mary Waters and Phil Kasinitz have argued, more recently, that social and political exclusion in the American context are increasingly organized along legal rather than racial lines.[38] And since 9/11—especially since the December 2015 San Bernardino attack and Donald Trump's proposal to bar Muslims from entering the United States—religion has become a salient axis of exclusion as well.

All of these authors share a sensitivity to the widening divergences in education, occupation, and lifestyle within racial and ethnic categories and to the increasingly blurred and porous boundaries of those categories. The heterogeneity and boundary-blurring diminish the practical force and mobilizing power of racial and ethnic categories—the extent to which their members feel themselves to be united in a solidary, bounded community.[39] They also diminish the analytical utility of those categories, since other crucial axes of division, inequality, and exclusion—especially class, legal status, and religion—cut across racial and ethnic lines.[40] Analyzing inequalities in health or economic well-being through the statistical prism of ethnoracial categories, for example, may conceal more than it reveals about the patterns, causes, and dynamics of inequality. And public policies that are targeted by race or ethnicity may be less effective than policies that are targeted by class. The more heterogeneous the categories and the more blurred their boundaries, the less resonant and meaningful they will be in organizing the lives of their members, the less pertinent and informative they will be as categories of analysis, and the less effective they will be in guiding public policy.

None of these developments, of course, means that we live in a post-racial or post-ethnic society, just as the dramatic shifts in the boundaries, meanings, and workings of gender categories in recent decades do not mean that we live in a post-gender society. We see rather a *reconfiguration* of the racial and ethnic order, as of the gender order. As part of that reconfiguration, we can observe a relative weakening of racial and ethnic categories as principles of social organization and sources of subjectivity. That weakening is partial and selective: for those trapped in the quadruple vise of conjoined racial, spatial, class-based, and legal exclusion, ethnoracial—and what might be called ethnospatial and ethnolegal—boundaries may be hardening, not attenuating. Nonetheless, the categories "post-racial" or "post-ethnic"—like "post-gender"—can usefully clarify the terms of normative debate, articulate certain utopian possibilities, and help refine our accounts of what has changed and what has not.

Conclusion

Gender and race were long understood as distinctively stable, rigorously categorical, legibly embodied, and reliably decodable social identities. It was these features that were seen as setting gender and race apart from other social identities, such as those founded on language, religion, education, and occupation. In sociological terms, gender and race were understood as "ascribed," education and occupation as "achieved" statuses: the former as unchosen and unchanging, the latter as both choosable (albeit under structural constraints) and changeable. Language and religion were understood as somewhere in the middle: initially ascribed, yet in the modern world increasingly open to choice and change.

In recent decades, public understandings of gender have shifted dramatically. One convenient benchmark for assessing just how far-reaching this change has been is the set of five rules of gender set forth by the transgender activist and writer Riki Wilchins two decades ago: "(1) there are only two cages; (2) everyone must be in a cage; (3) there is no mid-ground; (4) no one can change; and (5) no one chooses their cage."[1] If one substitutes the more neutral "category" for the politically charged "cage," these rules formulated commonsense notions about what was right, normal, and appropriate in the domain of sex and gender. Until the last few decades, these understandings were very widely shared in Western societies. This is not to say that the rules were seldom broken: historians have traced a long and varied history of the practices through which they were bent, evaded, and transgressed. By now, however, the challenges, subversions, and violations have become so pervasive, so open, and so accepted by growing segments of the public that their status as rules is increasingly in doubt.

New categories have proliferated. The middle ground is no longer off-limits. Choice and change have become routine. And some have sought to escape from gender "cages" or categories altogether. Not long ago, sympathetic understanding of such developments was limited to small circles of activists, academics, transgender people, and the professionals and paraprofessionals catering to them. Today, a much broader public—though one still limited by age, class, and region—has come to understand gender in pluralistic, nonbinary terms, as open to the forces of change and choice, and as constituted through ongoing performances rather than simply ascribed at birth once and for all.

Yet even as gender identities have come to be reimagined in far-reaching and unprecedented ways, racial identities continue to be widely understood as unchanging and unchosen. As the reaction to the Dolezal case suggests, prevailing public understandings cast gender and race as radically different forms of embodied identities.

I have argued in this book that the differences are not as sharp as is generally assumed. The Dolezal affair was in some ways misleading. By focusing attention on idiosyncratic aspects of her story—and especially on issues of deception and fraud—the discussions of Dolezal obscured the deeper issues at stake in contemporary transformations of gender and race as embodied identities. It is productive, I have suggested, to think about race and ethnicity in relation to sex and gender as systems of social classification that have been massively destabilized in recent decades. And it is fruitful, in this trans moment, to think not just *about* trans but *with* trans, by using the multiple forms of transgender experience as an analytical lens through which to consider how racial as well as gender identities are increasingly open to choice, change, and performative enactment.

Thinking with trans brings into focus a number of similarities between gender and race as systems of social classification that have been losing the stability, self-evidence, and clarity they once possessed. The similarities include the possibility of moving—in consequential and sometimes fateful ways—from one clearly defined gender or racial category to another; the development and recognition of new forms of gender and racial betweenness; and the various attempts to establish new categories outside existing categorical frameworks, or to transcend gender or racial categorization altogether. Conceptualizing these as forms of trans—the trans of migration, the trans of between, and the trans of beyond— highlights parallel challenges to the stability and legibility of gender and race and, more fundamentally, to the basic understandings of categorical difference that are at the heart of the gender and racial orders.

Despite these formal similarities, however, gender and race remain substantively different embodied identities, open to the forces of change and choice in differing ways and to differing degrees. If the Dolezal affair concealed important similarities between gender and race, it revealed at the same time important differences. The much-tweeted claim that transracial is "not a thing" was a superficial slogan, driven more by political positioning than by intellectual analysis. Yet it pointed to an undeniable truth. Transracial is indeed not a thing in the same sense as transgender; it is not a socially recognized and validated identity. Transgender, by contrast, has been socially defined as real; it is therefore—in the words of the now-classic Thomas theorem—"real in [its] consequences."[2] Transgender has been recognized, validated, and institutionalized in cultural idioms, public narratives, ways of thinking and feeling, social practices, legal and organizational categories, political claims-making, social science research, and popular culture. For a nontrivial segment of the population, transgender is no longer a contested novelty; it is a taken-for-granted reality. Nothing comparable can be said about transracial.

The fact that transracial is not a socially recognized phenomenon like transgender is partly a matter of linguistic convention. Gender passing falls under the term "transgender," but racial passing is not designated by "transracial." Gender blending and blurring—in special performances and in everyday life—are grouped under the heading "transgender," but mixed racial identities and other forms of racial blending and blurring have not been grouped under "transracial." Efforts to subvert or transcend the gender order fall under the rubric of transgender, but efforts to subvert or transcend the racial order do not fall under any socially recognized rubric of transracial. By bringing together phenomena ordinarily treated separately, thinking with trans suggests that transracial is not the absurdity it was alleged to be in the Dolezal debates.

The contrast between the densely institutionalized, socially recognized "thingness" of transgender and the lack of social recognition for transracial, however, does not result simply from linguistic convention. The possibilities for choice and change are indeed more circumscribed in the domain of race and ethnicity than in the domain of sex and gender.

But this presents us with a paradox. Morphological, physiological, and hormonal differences between the sexes—if not as marked in humans as in many other species—are biologically real and socially consequential. Nothing remotely analogous can be said about racial divisions. Genetically governed differences between socially defined racial categories are superficial and inconsequential; genetically programmed differences between the sexes are neither. Like race, sex is a system of social classification. Unlike race, however, sex is also a well-established biological category.[†] But despite the evident biological basis of sex differences—a biological basis that is utterly lacking for racial differences—it is more socially legitimate to choose and change one's sex (and gender) than to choose and change one's race.

To account for this paradox, we need to consider the different conceptual and linguistic resources that are culturally available for thinking and talking about sex/gender and race/ethnicity. One key resource for making sense of the former, which has no counterpart in the latter domain, is the distinction between sex and gender.[3] This distinction, which became common in the 1970s, can be mapped onto a series of generative and resonant oppositions: between nature

---

† The existence of biologically based sex categories does not, of course, mean that all individuals fall cleanly and clearly into one or the other. A small fraction of infants are born with a variety of conditions that make their sex ambiguous or indeterminate. Treatment protocols that force such intersex individuals into one sex category or the other, often through surgery aiming at constructing "normal-looking" genitals, have rightly come in for sustained criticism. And theorists of sex and gender have correctly observed that such treatment is driven by the cultural imperatives of a binary classification system, not by medical necessity. But the fact that certain individuals can be assigned to the categories male or female only arbitrarily does not make the categories themselves arbitrary; and the fact that sex is culturally co-constructed does not mean it is biologically unfounded. (On changing understandings of and treatment protocols for intersex conditions, see p. 46.)

and culture, body and mind, and material and spiritual. When combined with understandings of authenticity as a touchstone of value and with understandings of identity as a deep, stable, generative inner essence, the sex-gender distinction makes it possible to understand individual gender identity as a subjective inner state that is independent of the sexed body. A corollary of this understanding—central to the epistemology of gender—is that gender identity, located within the sealed, opaque container of the self, is knowable only by the individual concerned. The sex-gender distinction, together with prevailing idioms of authenticity and identity, thus allows gender identity to be conceived as an inner essence of which each individual is the sole legitimate interpreter.

Yet while the sex-gender distinction allows gender to be understood as radically *disembodied*, it also allows gender to be *re-embodied* in two ways. First, while gender identity is understood as independent of the visible morphological features of the sexed body, it is at the same time widely understood as grounded in other—as yet unknown—properties of the body. Gender identity is thus understood *both* as a subjective inner essence, accessible to and knowable by the individual, *and* as an objective constitutional fact over which the individual has no control. The subjectivity of gender identity is seen as grounded in the objectivity of the body. This move fortifies and legitimizes the demand for public validation of subjective gender identity, since validation is claimed not simply for a subjective conviction but also for what is put forward as an objective fact.[4]

The putative objectivity of the subjective allows choice to be defended in the name of the unchosen and change to be legitimized in the name of the unchanging. What is chosen, on this understanding, is not one's gender identity but the steps one takes to express and realize that identity.

Changing one's gender does not mean changing one's gender identity; it means changing the way one is recognized and classified by others in private or public contexts. This usually involves changing one's gendered self-presentation and may also involve transforming one's body to bring it into alignment with one's gender identity.

Such projects of bodily transformation are the second way gender gets re-embodied. While gender identity is understood as analytically distinct from the sexed body, it is at the same time widely understood as an inner essence that ideally corresponds to and is expressed in the sexed body. This view is not, of course, universally shared: there are many ways to enact a transgender identity without transforming the sexed body. But congruence between inner gender identity and the visibly sexed body remains a powerful cultural ideal. The transgender twist on this ideal reverses its conventional causal and normative ordering: instead of imagining the sexed body as an unchosen and unchanging substrate and gender identity as its expression, one can now imagine gender identity as an unchosen, unchanging inner essence and the sexed body as its choosable and changeable expression.

The sex-gender distinction thus allows gender identity to be both disembodied and re-embodied, the latter through a posited (though presently unknown) bodily ground for subjective gender identity and through the reconstruction of the outwardly sexed body to match one's inner gender identity. Our conceptual and linguistic resources for thinking about race make it nearly impossible to imagine racial identity in a similar way. That is, we have no established vocabulary, no cultural tools, for thinking about racial identity in subjectivist and individualist terms as an inner essence that is independent of the body and knowable only by the individual.

A second key conceptual idiom that configures our understanding of sex/gender and race/ethnicity in very different ways is that of inheritance. We understand biological sex to be governed by the mechanisms of genetic inheritance, but in a manner that does not involve history, lineage, or intergenerational continuity. The sex of the offspring does not depend on any properties of the parents; it depends solely on whether the sperm cell that fertilizes the egg contains an X or a Y chromosome. This stochastic moment of fertilization is entirely cut off from any transgenerational history or lineage; sex determination begins anew with each generation. The sense in which race is culturally understood to be inherited, as the philosopher Cressida Heyes has observed, is radically different.[5] The processes of genetic, genealogical, and cultural inheritance that are understood to be involved in the determination of race are all conceived as multigenerational; they bring the cumulative weight of the past to bear on the present. Ancestry is thus understood as *centrally relevant* to—and indeed at least partly constitutive of—race and ethnicity, yet as *entirely irrelevant* to sex and gender.

These sharply differing understandings of inheritance establish the authority of ancestry over racial and ethnic but not sex and gender identification and classification. The history of sex/gender identity is coterminous with the history of a single embodied individual. It is conceptually entirely independent of the history of the sex/gender identity of one's parents, even if empirically one's manner of embodying and expressing a gender identity may be influenced by models furnished by one's parents. The history of racial or ethnic identity, by contrast, is intrinsically a transgenerational history. It is conceptually impossible—at least in North America, given the weight of ancestry in prevailing understandings of race—to define one's racial or ethnic identity without regard to ancestry. This means that the scope for culturally legitimate change or choice of racial or ethnic identification is bounded by the range of one's socially ratified ancestry.

The conceptual and linguistic resources I have highlighted make it easier and more legitimate to choose and change one's sex or gender than one's race or ethnicity. The stuff of which sex/gender identity is made is entirely contained within the self. The sex-gender distinction allows one to think of this stuff in dualistic terms as comprising the sexed body on the one hand and a disembodied (though putatively organically grounded) gender identity on the other. Cultural idioms of deep, stable, and authentic identity enable one to conceive gender identity as a touchstone of authenticity and value, and the sexed body as more superficial and arbitrary. Gender identity is understood as given, but the sexed body can and should be reshaped to match and express that identity. This is legitimated by the broader cultural program—central to late modernity—of reflexively shaping and transforming the body, which is understood as a plastic substance and surface on which to inscribe and express one's inner identity.

The lack of an established language for thinking about race in subjectivist and individualist terms and the authority of ancestry over racial and ethnic classifications make it more difficult for those without the requisite ancestry to choose or change their racial and ethnic identifications. The stuff of which racial and ethnic identities are made is not fully contained within the self, and the epistemology of race does not empower the individual as the sole legitimate interpreter of racial identity. Phenotypical markers of race and ethnicity—including hair, eyes, facial structure, and skin color—can of course be modified, and are indeed frequently modified, in ways that can inflect or even change the way

one is identified by others. But such racially or ethnically inflected bodily modifications are policed in ways that bodily
modifications in the domain of sex and gender are not.
Bodily transformations that signal membership in a racial
or ethnic category to which one is not entitled by ancestry
are vulnerable to being seen as deceptive or as a form of ethnoracial "betrayal." Transformations of the sexed body that
signal membership in a sex/gender category that does not
match one's chromosomes are seen as deceptive by cultural
conservatives and radical feminists, but they are accepted by
an increasingly broad public as *affirming* one's authentic
identity. The cultural logic of authenticity thus works in
radically differing ways for sex/gender and ethnoracial identities: it *authorizes* transformations of the sexed body but
stigmatizes certain transformations of the socially classified
racial body.

There are socially validated and medically regulated
procedures for altering certain racially or ethnically inter-
pretable bodily features, including eyelids, noses, and other
aspects of facial structure, just as there are for changing
genitalia, hormones, and secondary sex characteristics. But
the legitimacy of the former depends on denying that they
have anything to do with changing one's race, while the legitimacy of the latter does not require denying or hiding an
interest in changing one's sex or gender.[6] The difference is
not a technical one: the transformations of the body involved
in genital surgery are in fact much more complex and medically problematic than those involved in racially or ethnically inflected cosmetic surgery. The key difference lies rather
in the authority of ancestry over racial and ethnic classification. The individual may be understood, in the prevailing
language of liberal individualism, as owning her body, but
she does not own her ancestry.

The putative objectivity of gender identity—the claim that one's subjective gender identity is grounded in and caused by some unknown constitutional factor and is thus unchosen and unchanging—*empowers* the individual not only to choose and change her gender self-presentation but also to make choices about, and to demand changes in, the ways she is identified and classified by others. Classifications that are not congruent with the individual's self-identification can be characterized as mistakes, thanks to the individual's monopolistic access to the inner sense of self that is understood to be constitutive of gender identity.

The putative objectivity of racial identity is grounded in social relations, not just in the body. For this reason, it *constrains* the scope of individual choice and change. A key part of what constitutes racial identity—notably one's ancestry, as well as the classification practices of others—is understood to be located outside the self and open to inspection by others. For this reason, classifications that accord with an individual's phenotype and ancestry but not with her self-identification cannot be characterized as mistakes that require correction. And an individual who identifies with an ethnic or racial category to which she is not entitled by ancestry cannot intelligibly make use of the "born in the wrong body" narrative.[7]

Opportunities for choice and change, then, are indeed much more circumscribed in the domain of race and ethnicity than in the domain of sex and gender. But the space for choice and change in the domain of race and ethnicity has expanded substantially in recent decades. And it continues to expand, driven by two processes. The first is the increasing cultural salience of racial and ethnic mixing. Sexual unions across socially defined racial lines have existed whenever and wherever these lines have been drawn. In some contexts, the mixedness of the offspring of such unions has been socially denied. The American one-drop rule, which defined all offspring of black-white unions as black, was notorious for doing just that. But mixedness has been increasingly acknowledged and even celebrated. This has resulted from the multiracial movement, the prevalence of interracial marriage, the declining authority of the one-drop rule, and a diffuse sensitivity to and appreciation of hybridity. Even genetics has contributed to the visibility of mixedness: the most popular type of genetic ancestry test—the autosomal test that analyzes both paternal and maternal ancestry—reports its results in the language of "admixture" and helps popularize the notion that *everyone* is mixed.

As ancestry comes to be understood through the language of mixedness, its authority over racial and ethnic classification declines. For an ever-widening circle of people, ancestry no longer provides unambiguous answers to questions of classification and identification. Paradoxically, the more we know about our ancestry, the less unambiguously that ancestry determines our identity. Mixed ancestry not only permits but even requires choice: it invites a process of "affiliative self-fashioning," through which race and ethnicity are "constituted at the nexus of genetic science, kinship aspirations, and strategic self-making."[8] The complexity and ambiguity of ancestry also facilitate change, authorizing individuals to identify with different ancestral strands in different social and cultural contexts.

The second process that has eroded the authority of ancestry and expanded the space for choice and change is the performative turn in ways of thinking and talking about race. The shift from essentialist understandings of identity as deep, stable, and generative to post-essentialist understandings of identity as continually reconstituted through performative enactment has long been influential in the study of gender. More recently, as I observed in chapter 4, a parallel shift has begun to inform the study of race and ethnicity, though this has been more common in the humanities and cultural studies than in the social sciences.[9] Like gender, race and ethnicity are increasingly understood as something we *do*, not something we *have*—as a matter of reiterated doing rather than stable being. Through this reiterated doing, race and ethnicity are at once reproduced and, in subtle and often imperceptible yet cumulatively consequential ways, transformed.[10]

The performative turn in the study of race has focused attention on the dual nature of racial identity as both achieved and ascribed. A person who is ordinarily socially defined as black on the basis of phenotype or ancestry, for example, may be seen as "acting white."[11] This double coding—arising from a dissonance between doing and (apparent) being—can be interpreted in two ways.[12] On one interpretation, being trumps doing. The person in question may be considered to be "really black" but to be "acting white"; she may be seen as acting inauthentically and as betraying her real identity. On a second interpretation, doing trumps being. The same person may be understood to have forfeited her claim to be "really" black by virtue of acting white. The deeper and more consequential identity, on this interpretation, is the achieved identity: what one does determines who one (really) is.[13] By "acting white," one can thus cease to be effectively black, regardless of one's ancestry or phenotype. And one can also become effectively white, in a limited but socially real sense: not by passing, or by being perceived as *phenotypically* white, but by being effectively treated as *socially* white in a certain range of contexts.[14] A similar point can be made about the (apparently) white person who "acts black."[15] Attention to this "achieved" dimension of race highlights another aspect of the fragility and instability of categorical identities: their chronic need for ratification and their chronic vulnerability to policing.[16]

The performative turn is not just an academic trend; it is also a shift in popular culture. Representations of race and gender in fiction, film, and television increasingly highlight their artificiality, constructedness, and instability. They call attention to the *means of producing* legible identities. They look behind the scenes at the layers of artifice, levers of self-presentation, and manipulations of signifiers, stances, and styles through which gender and race are "achieved" in interaction rather than stably ascribed. In so doing, they tap into anxieties about what Gayle Wald called the "radical unreliability of embodied appearances," or what Marjorie Garber, in her pioneering study of cross-dressing, called a "category crisis"—"not just a category crisis of male and female, but the crisis of category itself."[17]

Attention to the means of production of legible identities is evident in the contemporary fascination with various forms of passing.[18] The renewed interest in passing is especially striking in the domain of race, since many commentators have described the "passing of passing" and see the present as a "post-passing" era.[19] Part of the appeal of passing as a topic lies in the revelation of the artifices that underlie and enable it. While passing itself is intrinsically self-concealing—it must cover its traces in order to succeed—representations of passing in fiction, memoir, and film reveal the mechanisms that make it possible. Since these depend above all on the manipulation of visual signifiers, the exploration of passing—and of related matters such as impersonation, radical makeovers, trading places, and the like—is particularly well suited for the visual media of film and television.[20]

Both popular culture and scholarship display a shift from what might be called a deep identitarian understanding of passing to a performative one. On the deep identitarian understanding, best exhibited in the domain of race, passing intrinsically involves deception and inauthenticity. To pass is to pretend to be something you are not, and to get others to misperceive you in this way. This is why classical stories of racial passing were often told in a tragic mode. The performative understanding repudiates this ontology of identity and authenticity. Passing shades into performance: everybody is passing as somebody; all identity is performative. There is no deep identity, no being apart from doing; identity is performance all the way down.[21] Contemporary accounts of passing—in scholarship as well as popular culture—are therefore imbued with less pathos and more ironic distance than earlier accounts. The mood is often comic rather than tragic; stories are more likely to highlight the incongruities and absurdities of categorical identities than their depth and pathos.

With the memory still fresh of the Charleston church massacre and the deaths that inspired the wave of Black Lives Matter protests, one needs no reminder of the analytical and political limits of a focus on passing and performance. Of course essentialist understandings of race as a deep, authentic, and unalterable identity continue to be articulated in popular culture and scholarly work. They continue to inform the everyday understandings and practices of ordinary people as well as the ideologies of people like Dylann Roof. And needless to say, opportunities for choice, change, and unconventional performative enactment remain unequally distributed in ways that reflect not only the continuing significance of ancestry but also—as highlighted in Ta-Nehisi Coates's much-discussed *Between the World and Me*—the distinctive vulnerability of the black male body.

Still, the declining authority of ancestry over racial and ethnic classification—a result of the increased salience of mixing and the greater awareness of the constructedness, artificiality, and elasticity of racial and ethnic categories—has substantially enlarged the space for choice, affiliation, and self-transformation. This holds even for a substantial and growing share of those whose ancestry, a few decades ago, would have unambiguously led them to classify themselves, and to be classified by others, as black.

The declining authority of ancestry and the expanding space for choice, change, and performative enactment do not entail the absence of constraint or power. Identities are always constituted through the interplay of self-identification and categorization by others.[22] For much of the last several centuries, the power of state categorizations and prevailing social definitions strictly limited—though of course never eliminated—the possibilities for self-identification and performative self-presentation for those externally defined as black. In recent decades, the balance has shifted, and the space of possibilities has expanded substantially. But the balance has not tilted as far toward the pole of self-identification in the domain of race as it has in the domain of gender, which is increasingly understood as an identity solely owned and controlled by its individual bearer.

The philosopher Ian Hacking has shown how categories that designate new kinds of people do not simply recognize previously unrecognized kinds of people; they contribute, rather, to "making up people" by creating "new ways for people to be." The new categories—and the new stories told about the kinds of people they designate—shape the self-understanding and conduct of people who come to recognize themselves in those categories and stories; the new categories and stories thus change "the space of possibilities for personhood." Over time, people may "come to fit their categories." But the categorized may also seek to gain control over the content and administration of the categories by challenging the authority of medical and other experts.[23]

The institutionalization of and contestation over the category "transgender" offer a powerful illustration of Hacking's argument about "making up people." Cross-dressing, gender-blending, and passing as a member of the opposite sex have long histories. But it is only in recent decades that it has become possible to be a transgender person—as a new, socially recognized kind of person, constituted by the intersection of categories, stories, self-understandings, and practices.

It is not possible to be a transracial person in this way. As I have argued, the possibilities for choosing and changing one's race have been substantially enlarged. But these possibilities remain distributed across a variety of different practices and stories—stories of passing, of multiracial identities, of affiliative self-fashioning, of cross-racial identification, and of post-racial stances. They have not been knit together into a coherent social phenomenon with a single name. The importance of names was brilliantly captured by Nietzsche's aphorism in *The Gay Science*: "What things *are called* is incomparably more important than what they are. . . . It is enough to create new names and estimations and probabilities in order to create in the long run new 'things.'"[24] In this respect, the conventional wisdom in the Dolezal affair—that transracial is "not a thing"—was right on the mark: the various manifestations of the instability of racial categories have not come together as "a thing" in part because they have not been bound together by a name.

The solidity and durability of transgender as an institutionalized and socially recognized "thing" should not be exaggerated. The shift toward public acceptance of transgender has been astonishingly rapid, but it has been uneven across regions, generations, institutions, and milieux. This unevenness sets the stage for intensified public controversy as transgender claims move from insulated settings like liberal arts colleges to mainstream settings like public school systems, and as legislatures, civil rights agencies, and courts take action to establish broad transgender rights.†

These rights are proving controversial. In November 2015, Houston voters repealed—by a wide margin—an antidiscrimination ordinance that included gender orientation among other protected classes. The church-led campaign against the ordinance focused on the slogan "No Men in Women's Bathrooms." The campaign mobilized fear of sexual predators through a video advertisement depicting a man entering a women's restroom, hiding in a stall, and then entering a stall occupied by a girl, while a voiceover warned that "any man at any time could enter a women's bathroom simply by claiming to be a woman that day."[25] The Houston ordinance in fact said nothing about bathrooms, but this did

---

† In 2013, as I noted in chapter 2, a pioneering California law granted public school students in grades K–12 the right to participate in sex-segregated activities and use sex-segregated facilities according to their self-identified gender. Efforts to challenge the law through California's initiative process failed to gather sufficient signatures in 2013 and again in 2015, but opponents have vowed to keep fighting it (Nelson 2015). Federal civil rights agencies have also been involved in expanding transgender rights. In November 2015, for example, the U.S. Department of Education's Office for Civil Rights found a suburban Chicago high school in violation of Title IX of the Education Amendments of 1972, which prohibits sex discrimination, for denying a transgender student access to the girls' locker room (U.S. Department of Education 2015). In April 2016, a federal appeals court, deferring to the Department of Education's interpretation of the statute, held that Title IX "requires schools to provide transgender students access to restrooms congruent with their gender identity." The decision—in a suit filed by the ACLU on behalf of a Virginia high school student—was narrowly drawn: the court recognized that a subsequent administration might choose to interpret Title IX in a different way, and that Congress might clarify the implications of Title IX for transgender people in a way that might or might not align with the current stance of the Obama administration. See U.S. Court of Appeals 2016, pp. 5, 15, 16, and 29.

not stop opponents from dubbing it the "bathroom bill"; they were able to make this characterization stick in part because earlier versions of the proposed measure had included specific provisions on bathroom access. And a growing number of municipal ordinances do expressly give transgender people the right to use bathrooms, locker rooms, and other sex-segregated facilities corresponding to their subjective gender identity. This provides a convenient target for opponents. In March 2016, responding to one such ordinance, North Carolina became the first state to expressly prohibit people from using bathrooms, in schools and other public buildings, that do not match the sex on their birth certificate.

The North Carolina bill provoked a storm of political and legal contention. Activists called on companies to boycott the state; the ACLU and allied groups filed suit challenging the law; and the Justice Department, asserting that the bill violated federal civil rights law, threatened to cut off federal education funding to the state. North Carolina filed suit in response, claiming that the federal government's position amounted to a "radical reinterpretation" of civil rights legislation, and the federal government in turn sued the state. In mid-May the federal Departments of Education and Justice broadened the scope of the controversy by issuing an advisory letter to schools nationwide on civil rights protections for transgender students; the letter asserted unequivocally that Title IX's prohibition of discrimination on the basis of sex "encompasses discrimination based on a student's gender identity, including discrimination based on a student's transgender status." This provoked eleven states to sue in response, claiming that the Obama administration's interpretation of Title IX rewrites the law by "administrative fiat," notably by arbitrarily "redefining the statutory term 'sex' . . . to include 'gender identity.'"[26]

As in the controversy over gay marriage, conservative churches are taking the lead in challenging transgender agendas. Opposition to strong versions of transgender rights, however, may be deeper than opposition to gay marriage. Some parents who support gay marriage, for example, may object to transgender students having the right to use locker rooms or bathrooms of their choice; they may portray this as a danger to their own children or as a violation of their right to privacy. The controversies that have erupted so far fit the pattern of what Kristen Schilt and Lauren Westbrook have called "penis panics," in that they focus on the dangers posed by the presence of men, implicitly defined as people with penises, in girls' and women's spaces.[27] Such controversies are likely to multiply in response to the widespread diffusion of transgender rights and the Obama administration's expansive interpretation of Title IX.

Rachel Dolezal's claim to identify as black provoked fiercer opposition in the summer of 2015 than Caitlyn Jenner's claim to identify as a woman. But practices associated with choosing or changing gender are likely to be more controversial in the coming years than practices associated with choosing or changing race. Sex and gender, unlike race and ethnicity, remain legally formalized identities, and access to formally sex-segregated spaces—especially women's colleges, women's sports teams, and women's bathrooms—remains a live political issue in a way that access to formally race-segregated spaces is not.[28] Cultural conservatives, moreover—especially religious conservatives—are more deeply committed to preserving sex and gender boundaries than racial and ethnic boundaries. For religious conservatives, sex and gender are central to the created order in a way that race and ethnicity are not. The blurring or crossing of sexual and gender boundaries is therefore a much graver threat than the blurring or crossing of racial or ethnic boundaries. Race will no doubt continue to be a central focus of political controversy in all kinds of ways. But apart from occasional controversies over questionable identity claims, continued debate about cultural appropriation, and disagreement about how to delimit the circle of persons concerned by antidiscrimination law or affirmative action programs, such controversy is unlikely to focus on the blurring of categorical distinctions.

Considering race in relation to gender—and reading race through the lens of the multiple forms of transgender experience—brings into sharp focus the deep contingency and arbitrariness of racial categories. This is of course not a new insight; a generation of scholarship has underscored that contingency and arbitrariness. But it is an insight that has remained largely trapped in the academy, filtering only feebly and intermittently into broader public discussions.[29] And even academic discussions have incorporated constructivist insights incompletely and ambivalently; such insights have been much more fully embraced in the study of ethnicity than in the study of race, which continues to be treated by many scholars as a domain apart.[30] Taken as an intellectual opportunity rather than a political provocation, the pairing of transgender and transracial in public discourse has the potential to leverage the shift in public understandings of gender by prompting public reflection on the artificiality, constructedness, and instability of race. By treating trans as a tool to think *with*, not just a phenomenon to think *about*, I have sought to encourage such reflection, and to provide new analytical resources for understanding the contingency and arbitrariness of racial categories, while remaining sensitive to the ways in which gender and race operate as different systems of embodied difference.

Notes

Preface

1. Wacquant 1997.
2. Stryker 2015.
3. Klaus 1991, 4; Johnson's *Dictionary of the English Language*; *Oxford English Dictionary*.
4. For critiques of the sex-gender distinction, see Butler 1990; Hood-Williams 1996; Nilsson 1996. For a qualified defense, see Plumwood 1989.

Introduction

1. Selle and Dolan 2015; Spokesman-Review 2015; Humphrey 2015; Herbst 2015.
2. The most detailed account of Dolezal's background is found in Sunderland's (2015) nuanced profile.
3. Kuruvilla 2015; Sunderland 2015.
4. Sunderland 2015. The book, by Spencer Perkins and Chris Rice, was *More Than Equals: Racial Healing for the Sake of the Gospel*. Perkins, whom Dolezal had contacted before enrolling at Belhaven, became a close friend and mentor until his death during her junior year.
5. Swayze 2015.
6. According to her father, quoted in the *Washington Post* (Moyer 2015), Dolezal applied with a portfolio of "exclusively African American portraiture," which led her to be taken for a black applicant. She later sued the university for discriminating against her as a white woman in the allocation of financial aid. For the appeals court's judgment, upholding the trial court's summary judgment against Dolezal, see http://www.thesmokinggun.com/file/rachel-dolezal-lawsuit.

7. See the sampling of work on her art website: http://racheldolezal.blogspot .com/.

8. According to Dolezal, her husband—described by their son as an "oreo"— wanted her to look "as white as possible" and rejected her interest in black culture (Sunderland 2015).

9. According to Kara Brown (2015), Dolezal "definitely nailed the hair"; see also Jackson 2015. Dolezal recounted in interviews that her interest in black hair originally emerged from her efforts to style the hair of her adopted siblings and crystallized at Belhaven (Sunderland 2015; Samuels and Bishop 2015). On her LinkedIn page Dolezal described herself as having been an "ethnic hair stylist" since 1997 (when she was a student at Belhaven); she gave a lecture on the history of black hair at Eastern Washington University in February 2015; and she reported to *Vanity Fair* that she was continuing to do braids and weaves for clients (Samuels and Bishop 2015). On Dolezal and the politics of "black hair," see Zimeta 2015.

10. See the lengthy interviews reported six months after the story broke by Sunderland (2015) and McGreal (2015).

11. Stryker 2015.

12. Morris 2015. See also Sherry Turkle's pioneering (1995) discussion of identity exploration—including, notably, gender and sexual identity exploration—in the age of the Internet, which facilitates cycling between multiple selves.

13. For broad characterizations, see Hannerz 1987 and Kraidy 2005. It is no accident that a key moment of transgender ferment in the early 1990s, focused on efforts to stake out space between or beyond established gender categories (Stryker 2006, 4–6), coincided with an explosion of interest in hybridity, syncretism, and transnationalism in broader cultural discussions.

14. Edgerton 1984, 475; Rubin 2003, 60.

15. Meyerowitz 2002, 104–8.

16. On Obama's "journey of racial self-discovery and reinvention," see Maraniss 2012.

17. On "affiliative ethnic identity," see Jiménez 2010.

18. On the emergence of understandings of "elective race," see Rich 2014.

19. The phrase "different differences" is borrowed from Epstein 2007, who is similarly concerned, in the very different context of biomedical research, to highlight both similarities and differences between gender and race.

20. Mayeri 2001, 1048–51. The relation between race/ethnicity and sex/ gender is not just a theoretical question; it is a practical question. Analogies between race and sex, for example, were central to the development of antidiscrimination law and practice (Mayeri 2001; 2007).

21. Sontag 2015. Medicaid coverage varies by state. A few states have started to cover surgery and hormone treatments, but most do not. On inequalities in access to health care for transgender people, see Gehi and Arkles 2007.

22. For influential statements of this point from the very large literature on intersectionality, see Crenshaw 1989 and McCall 2005.

23. On the similar workings of categorical difference across domains, see Tilly 1998; for a critique of Tilly, see Brubaker 2015, chap. 1.

Chapter 1. Transgender, Transracial?

1. Raymond 1994, xv–xvi; emphasis in the original.

2. Overall 2004.

3. Heyes 2009. In her Foucauldian exploration of the "ethics of self-transformation," Heyes criticized Overall for an argument that remained largely abstract and hypothetical, and for neglecting the differing histories of race and sex as identity categories, histories that "set up different possibilities for the subject seeking to change her embodied identity" (p. 141). This is an insight that I develop in the concluding chapter.

4. Overall, Heyes, and Row all focus on changes in race through surgical or other medical or cosmetic transformations that in some ways parallel transgender surgery and hormonal interventions. On racially and ethnically inflected cosmetic surgery, see pp. 56 and 164, n. 66.

5. Valentine 2007, 33–34; Stryker 2006.

6. The quotation is from Stryker 2006, 4. The public association of transgender with surgical transformation is ironic, since before "transgender" came into widespread use as an umbrella term in the early 1990s, it had been used in contradistinction to "transsexual" (and "transvestite") to designate a person who lived publicly and permanently—but without genital surgery—in a different gender from the one assigned at birth (Valentine 2007, 32, 261–62, n. 1; Stryker 2006, 4).

7. See for example Bartholet 1991; Perry 1993; Howe 1995; Kennedy 2003, chaps. 10 and 11.

8. NABSW 1972.

9. The NABSW presidents are quoted in Simon and Roorda 2009, 8, 12.

10. Kennedy 2003, 396–400, 417; the quotation is from p. 444. Racial matching is legally required in the case of Native American adoptions and foster home placements; Kennedy analyzes and criticizes this policy at pp. 480–518.

11. McKee et al. 2015.

12. Raible [n.d.].

13. Raible 2015.

14. "Voluntarism" has been primarily a term of criticism in feminist theory, notably in discussions of Judith Butler's understanding of gender as performance (Allen 1998). Here I use voluntarism in a non-pejorative way to designate a stance that highlights choice and agency and underscores the possibility and legitimacy of changing one's public, socially validated identity.

15. http://afaofpa.org/archives/blog-post-if-bruce-jenner-is-a-woman-then-rachel-dolezal-is-black/.

16. Crowder 2015; Walsh 2015.

17. Cooke 2015.

18. Fischler 2015.

19. Brown 2015.

20. *Spokesman-Review* reader comments, June 11, 2015. http://www.spokesman.com/stories/2015/jun/11/board-member-had-longstanding-doubts-about-truthfu/comments/.

21. http://forums.avemariaradio.net/viewtopic.php?f=23&t=160161 &start=20.

22. Crook 2015. Crook is the lead pastor of the Cross of Grace Church, part of a family of churches characterized as evangelical, reformed, and charismatic.

23. Holmes 2015.

24. Reader comment on a website run by the conservative Republican ex-congressman Allen B. West: http://allenbwest.com/2015/06/if-bruce-jenner-can -decide-hes-a-woman-whats-so-crazy-about-this-womans-bizarre-claim/. (The comment, accessed in July 2015, no longer appears on the site.)

25. Moore 2015. Russell Moore is the head of the Ethics and Religious Liberty Commission of the Southern Baptist Convention.

26. Greenwell 2013.

27. Burkett 2015.

28. This use of the specter of "transracial" to delegitimize transsexuals has a history in radical feminist thought, going back to Janice Raymond's pioneering critique of transsexualism, quoted at the beginning of this chapter.

29. Murphy 2015.

30. Green 2015.

31. Rich 2015.

32. http://newyork.cbslocal.com/2015/06/12/nyu-professor-naacp-rachel-dolezal/. In a subsequent *Huffington Post* contribution that addressed only race, not gender, Morning (2015) rejected the widespread charge that Dolezal had been "lying" about her race. She asked rhetorically, "How can you lie about something that doesn't have any objective truth to it in the first place?" Morning also noted that while Dolezal's identification as black did not accord with her ancestry, it did accord with the longstanding practice of identifying people's race by their behavior and social networks, and with the contemporary recognition of mixed and fluid self-identifications.

33. Harris-Perry's interview with Hobbs (June 13, 2015) can be seen at http:// www.msnbc.com/melissa-harris-perry/watch/rachel-dolezal-and-the–politics -of-passing–463796291727; emphasis in the original.

34. Sartwell 2015b.

35. Jones 2015; emphasis in the original.

36. Reed 2015.

37. Speculating that Dolezal's self-presentation would have been accepted if she had possessed some black ancestry, Nancy Leong (2015)—like Reed—finds this troubling, for it "relies on biology as a validation of identity" in a way that mirrors the one-drop rule.

38. For the argument that appeals to culture often smuggle in assumptions about race, see Michaels 1992, who provocatively concluded that the "modern concept of culture is not, in other words, a critique of racism; it is a form of racism" (684). I discuss the contested relation between appropriateness, appropriation, and property at pp. 109ff. and 158, n. 55.

39. Echoing Reed's defense of Dolezal—though without the comparison to Jenner—was the philosopher Justin E. H. Smith. Writing just after the Charleston church massacre, which marked the end of the Dolezal affair in the media, Smith argued that the questions raised by Dolezal remained relevant after the massacre,

which was premised on an essentialist understanding of race. "Rachel Dolezal grew up in a society that told her, constantly: 'You're white, you're white, you're white,' and she seems to have thought to herself, 'Really, now, can it be so simple as that?' Dylann Roof heard the same refrain, and said, 'Why yes I am!' It worked its way into his brain like a worm. I'll take Dolezal's response to the myth of whiteness over Roof's any day, as we all should, and I refuse to feel bad about the supposed frivolity of the possibilities Dolezal's life seemed, for a moment, to open up. Since when is there a moral duty to remain faithful to the accidents of your birth, and to accurately report your vital-statistical information to the whole world? I'm with Dolezal: I don't give two shits what my ancestors say about who I 'really' am. . . . We all have the right to reinvent ourselves" (Smith 2015).

40. As noted above, this comparative observation was sometimes made by the essentialists of quadrant 1.

41. On transgender civil rights jurisprudence and legislation, see Currah and Minter 2000; Currah 2002; Lloyd 2005; Vade 2005; and Currah, Juang, and Minter 2006. For a critique of the multiracial movement, see Hickman 1997.

42. Gieryn 1983.

43. Lamont and Molnár 2002.

44. Wilkinson 2015.

45. https://twitter.com/janetmock/status/610153490694950913.

46. White 2015.

47. Allen 2015.

48. See for example Blay 2015.

49. Beyer 2015.

50. Talusan 2015; emphasis in the original. The paradoxical characterization of a "decision to transition" as "involuntary" hints at the constitutive tensions in the contemporary politics of identity. These tensions will be explored more fully in chapter 2.

51. See pp. 64–65 and 166, n. 94.

52. According to Samantha Allen, Dolezal was "determined to appropriate not just blackness but the rhetoric of transgender identity as well. . . . [She] is not just trying to pass as black, she's also trying to pass as someone whose identity deserves respect on the same grounds as transgender people" (Allen 2015). Allen suggested that Dolezal was appropriating transgender language by saying "I identify as black." Given how common the "identify as" formulation is, this seems dubious. More plausible is Allen's observation that Dolezal's claim to have been "drawing self-portraits with the brown crayon instead of the peach crayon, and black curly hair" when she was five years old was modeled on transgender claims of early cross-identification. It's worth pointing out, though, that Dolezal did not describe herself as "transracial" or compare herself expressly to Jenner or other transgender people. To the best of my knowledge, her only reference to Jenner came in response to Savannah Guthrie's question in an interview for NBC. "A lot of people have made comparisons to the transgender community and how you can feel one way inside and your physical body may not match that," Guthrie observed. "Do you consider this to be something like that?" Dolezal replied, "I finally had a chance to read Caitlyn Jenner's piece . . . in the magazine. . . . And I cried . . . because I resonated with some of the themes of

isolation, of being misunderstood" (Guthrie 2015). In a later interview, Dolezal expressly rejected the notion of "transracial" and the idea that she was a black person in a white person's body: "I really feel we need to come up with better vocabulary" (McGreal 2015).

53. Kennedy 2003, chap. 7.

54. Harris 1993, 1711.

55. The notions of appropriation and cultural theft presuppose an understanding of identity, culture, and history as forms of *property*, a notion I return to in chapter 4 (see p. 109). The notion of race as property has been articulated by legal scholars, beginning with Cheryl Harris's (1993) influential analysis of "whiteness as property." In response, Chen (1997) and Lee (2015) have explored the question of whether blackness might also be analyzable as a kind of property. And Leong (2013) has analyzed "racial capitalism" as "the process of deriving social and economic value from the racial identity of another person." For a critique of the essentialism involved in understandings of culture and history as the property of a particular group, see Michaels 1992.

56. Blay 2015.

57. "Capitalized on her fake blackness": Modkins 2015. "Building a career and persona off it": Noman 2015. "Appropriated aspects of blackness": Fang 2015. "Occupied and dominated spaces": White 2015. The appropriation theme was particularly piquant since Dolezal herself had criticized the film *The Help* in 2012, noting that "a white woman makes millions off of a black woman's story" (Noman 2015).

58. The vulnerability of the black male body is a central theme in Coates 2015.

59. http://hotmessfolder.com/news/hot-mess-of-the-week-rachel-dolezal/.

60. Dolezal was herself actively involved in the Black Lives Matter movement. Just three weeks before the revelations, she traveled to Baltimore to speak at a protest against police brutality in the aftermath of the death of Freddie Gray (Shen 2015); she was also a featured speaker at an earlier Black Lives Matter teach-in at Eastern Washington University, where she was a part-time instructor in the Africana Studies program (Archer and Colburn 2015).

61. La Ganga and Pearce 2015.

62. Cobb 2015.

Chapter 2. Categories in Flux

1. The pervasive unsettling of identities across a wide range of domains has been addressed by work on transnationalism, postmodernity, hybridity, creolization, bricolage, and performativity and by developments in feminist, poststructuralist, and queer theory. To cite just a few points of entry into these very large literatures, see Kraidy 2005 and Burke 2009 on hybridity and associated themes; Alcoff 1988 on post-structuralism and the "identity crisis in feminist theory"; and Calhoun 1994 on the contours of the modern politics of identity.

2. Sanders 2012, 1423.

3. Some gay activists and writers, too, lament the "normalization" of homosexuality, though of course from a very different point of view. They criticize the "new homonormativity" for its limited, "neoliberal" embrace of gay sexuality and for domesticating homosexuality through the embrace of marriage equality. See for example Duggan 2002 and Halperin 2012, chap. 21.

4. In the Netherlands, the idea of sexual liberation—and pro-gay attitudes in particular—is "used to frame Europe as the 'avatar of both freedom and modernity' . . . while depicting Muslim citizens as backward and homophobic" (Mepschen, Duyvendak, and Tonkens 2010, 963, quoting Judith Butler 2008, 2). Mepschen et al. draw on Jasbir Puar's (2007 and 2013) influential work on "homonationalism."

5. Plummer 2012, 251; see also Halberstam 1994. On the diversity of gay and lesbian social and political movements, see Epstein 1999.

6. As an alternative to the increasingly cumbersome acronym, which invites further expansion from those who feel excluded by the existing specification of categories, the more general rubric of "gender and sexual diversity" appears to be gaining traction, notably on college campuses.

7. Stryker 2006. One recent indicator is Amazon's popular and critically acclaimed series *Transparent*, which chronicles the transition of a retired professor and its effects on her family.

8. For a lucid and sophisticated account of the history of transsexuality in the United States, see Meyerowitz 2002.

9. Barth 1969, 9–10, 21ff.

10. This argument applies both to unidirectional and permanent transsexual or transgender trajectories (Raymond 1994; Burkett 2015) and to the temporary, playful, or performative crossing of gender boundaries by transvestites and others (Lorber 1994, 21). Others disagree, emphasizing the ways in which transsexualism or transvestism can potentially disrupt the gender order (see for example Thanem and Wallenberg 2016).

11. Westbrook and Schilt 2013, 21.

12. Burkett 2015; Stark 2015.

13. Westbrook and Schilt 2013, 22.

14. Svrluga 2015.

15. Scelfo 2015; Leff 2013. Recommendations for "inclusive" pronoun practices published in the quarterly newsletter of the University of Tennessee's Office for Diversity and Inclusion in fall 2015 suggested that students and faculty "should not assume someone's gender by their appearance, nor by what is listed on a roster or in student information systems." The author, the director of the university's Pride Center, suggested that faculty ask students to "provide their name and pronouns," so as to ensure that "they are not singling out transgender or non-binary students." The same practice was recommended for student organizations. Outside of classroom or organizational settings, individuals meeting one another were encouraged to say "nice to meet you. . . . What pronouns should I use?" Once it was picked up by the media, the newsletter article provoked sufficient opposition among Republican state legislators that the university removed the article from its website and took pains to clarify that the university had no policy mandating the use of gender-neutral pronouns. The

original newsletter article is no longer available online, but its recommendations can be found in numerous news articles about the controversy (see for example Tamburin 2015).

16. Scelfo 2015; Bennett 2016. Independently of transgender concerns about pronouns, the lack of a gender-neutral singular pronoun in English has prompted complaints for at least a century and a half (Baron 2010). Many remedies have been proposed, but none has caught on. Gender-neutral honorifics have also been proposed. In the United Kingdom, "Mx" has gained acceptance in public services; it was added to OxfordDictionaries.com, published by Oxford University Press, in 2015 (Tobia 2015).

17. Facebook 2014. The proliferation of categories, here as elsewhere, is self-reinforcing. Just a year later, responding to feedback from users who found the new options constraining, Facebook announced a further change: "Now, if you do not identify with the pre-populated list of gender identities, you are able to add your own" (Facebook 2015).

18. On the varying accommodations social media sites offer to "nonbinary" people, see http://nonbinary.org/wiki/Websites_and_social_networks.

19. *Hijras* have a long history as a distinctive community, organized around a status defined by gender and sexual variance, mode of livelihood, and ritual practice. They are socially neither male nor female, though they are male or intersex at birth; and they are generally understood as impotent as a result of a congenital intersex condition or castration. Ritual performances at weddings and births, a collective myth of origin, and the widely shared understanding of their special powers to bless or curse, especially in matters of fertility, have also been central to their distinctive status. More recently, Western understandings of transgender have become available to *hijras* seeking to reconceptualize their place and secure rights and protection in a changing social and legal order (Lal 1999; Jagadish 2013). For caution about interpreting *hijras*—or the Native American *berdache* or Omani *xanith*—through the prism of contemporary Western understandings of gender (and transgender), see Murray 1994; Towle and Morgan 2002; and Valentine 2007, 153–57.

20. https://www.passports.govt.nz/Transgender-applicants; https://www.passports.gov.au/Web/SexGenderApplicants.aspx.

21. High Court of Australia 2014. As this book was going to press, an Oregon state court ruled that a petitioner's sex (previously changed legally from male to female) could be changed from female to nonbinary, marking the first court-ordered recognition of nonbinary in the context of a legal change of sex in the United States (Mele 2016).

22. The definition of "intersex"—and the term itself, as well as alternative terms such as "disorders of sex development"—is contested, but it includes, at a minimum, a variety of specific conditions that prevent unambiguous sex assignment at birth (Karkazis 2008, 22–26). On the incidence of intersex conditions, see Fausto-Sterling 2000 and (challenging Fausto-Sterling's estimates) Sax 2002.

23. These protocols for the surgical "fixing" of sex, ironically, were based on a theory of what would today be called the social construction of gender: surgery to maintain the rigidity of sexual binarism was premised on an understanding of the plasticity of gender. According to Dr. John Money, whose influential

work underlay prevailing surgical practices, a child raised as a girl from infancy would develop a female gender identity, even if the child was genetically male. This belief in the plasticity of gender was subsequently shaken, not least by the much-publicized case of David Reimer, who was raised as a girl, on the advice of Money, after his penis was destroyed in a botched circumcision. Although Money initially reported that the reassignment had been successful, Reimer himself later revealed that he had never identified as a girl, and that he had officially reassumed a male identity after learning his medical history. On the development of the traditional treatment paradigm and the subsequent challenges to it, see Karkazis 2008, chaps. 2 and 3. For a critique of the focus on genitalia as gender markers in the traditional treatment paradigm, see Kessler 1998.

24. Hughes et al. 2006.

25. The strategy of seeking recognition as a form of difference rather than a disorder echoes similar strategies adopted by some deaf and autistic rights activists (Lane, Pillard, and Hedberg 2011; Hacking 2009). The strategy is controversial among intersex activists, who differ among themselves on labels, strategies, and relations with the medical establishment (Davidson 2009). Activists' rejection of nonconsensual genital "normalizing" surgery was endorsed in 2013 by a United Nations Human Rights Council report (Méndez 2013).

26. On the challenges posed by immigration-driven "superdiversity" (Vertovec 2007) to prevailing multiculturalist frameworks for making sense of linguistic pluralism, see Blommaert and Rampton 2011.

27. Vertovec 2010, 86–87.

28. Fanshawe and Sriskandarajah 2010, 5.

29. On the continued theoretical and political significance of the "black/white paradigm," see Kim 1999.

30. Hochschild, Weaver, and Burch (2012) also point to the growing influence of genomics as contributing to the transformation of the American racial order; for the influence of genetics on understandings of race, see below, pp. 55, 65–66, and 103, and Brubaker 2015, chap. 2. On fluid and varying racial identifications, see for example Ocampo (2016), who shows that second-generation Filipino Americans shift between Asian and Latino identities in different contexts, thanks to the legacy of Spanish colonialism. Saperstein and Penner (2012) have documented a surprising degree of micro-level fluidity in racial self- and other-identification in the United States. This holds even when one excludes respondents self-identifying as Hispanic, Native American, or multiracial, for whom the fluidity of racial identification is most pronounced. The authors note, however, that "the more fluid race is at the individual level, the more entrenched racial inequality will be at the societal level" (2012, 679), since downwardly mobile individuals are more likely to identify, and be identified, as black, while the upwardly mobile are more likely to identify, and be identified, as white. Concerning the increased fluidity of self-identification, see also Liebler et al. (2014), who matched census returns from 2000 and 2010 to show that 6 percent of Americans changed their race or Hispanic origin response from one census to the next.

31. See for example hooks 1992. On whiteness as a devalued and even stigmatized identity in certain contexts, see also Storrs 1999 and TallBear 2013,

138–40. On "racial shifters" who turn to a Cherokee identity, see Sturm 2011, 54–57.

32. Kertzer and Arel 2002; Loveman 2014.

33. See Prewitt 2013 on the United States; De Zwart 2012 and Paulle and Kalir 2014 on the Netherlands; Simon 2008 on France; and Loveman 2014 on Latin America.

34. Prewitt 2013.

35. Krogstad 2014.

36. Daniel 2002.

37. Goldstein and Morning 2002; Daniel 2002, 148f.

38. The celebration of choice by some third-wave feminists, coupled with the reluctance to make judgments about the content of choices, has generated debates about "choice feminism" (Ferguson 2010; Snyder-Hall 2010; Budgeon 2015).

39. Jencks 1987, 7.

40. Miller and Rose 2008, 33f, 25. See also Elliott (2013), whose account of the "new individualism" underscores the contemporary "cultural fascination for, and institutional pressure towards, self-reinvention" (192).

41. Novas and Rose 2000, 502.

42. Giddens 1991; Beck and Beck-Gernsheim 2002. Schwartz (2004) notes the psychological costs of this vastly expanded realm of choice.

43. Rose 2007, 40, 81.

44. On the "escalating series of choices" about intimate matters in the late modern world, see Plummer 2001, 238–40; see also Plummer 2000 and Simon 1996.

45. Seidman 2001, 327.

46. On sexual autonomy and the law, see Richards 1978; Schulhofer 1998; Childs 2001; and (sharply critical of the convergence of sex law around autonomy) Rubenfeld 2013.

47. See Frank, Camp, and Boutcher 2010. New forms of sexual regulation on college campuses are also premised on protecting sexual autonomy: "yes means yes" legislation, for example, mandates that every step in a sexual encounter be expressly and mutually chosen and consented to. California's pioneering legislation, adopted in 2014, requires postsecondary educational institutions—as a condition of receiving state funds for student financial aid—to adopt a sexual assault policy that requires "affirmative, conscious, and voluntary agreement to engage in sexual activity. It is the responsibility of each person involved in the sexual activity to ensure that he or she has the affirmative consent of the other or others to engage in the sexual activity. Lack of protest or resistance does not mean consent, nor does silence mean consent. Affirmative consent must be ongoing throughout a sexual activity and can be revoked at any time. The existence of a dating relationship between the persons involved, or the fact of past sexual relations between them, should never by itself be assumed to be an indicator of consent" (State of California 2014). New York State adopted a similar policy in 2015; other states are following suit; and numerous individual colleges and universities have adopted such policies. For a critique of such policies addressed to a broad public audience, see Young 2014. For a defense of the affirmative consent standard in rape law by a legal scholar, see Little 2005.

48. The language of rights—the right to choose, and the right to self-expression—is central to Leslie Feinberg's popular 1998 book, *Trans Liberation*; for a sympathetic critique of Feinberg's focus on individual choice, see Heyes 2003, 1109–13.

49. Talbot 2013.

50. State of California 2013. For the nationwide controversy that erupted in 2016 about transgender people's access to bathrooms corresponding to their gender identity, see pp. 148–49.

51. These changes are quite recent: the surgery requirement for changing sex on birth certificates was dropped in both New York State and New York City in 2014. In 2006, a similar proposal seemed poised to pass in liberal New York City, but it was withdrawn by the Board of Health after it prompted a storm of protest in the media. For analyses of that contentious episode, see Currah and Moore 2009 and Westbrook and Schilt 2013; for a broader legal survey of the complex and varying rules governing change of sex or gender classification on official documents, see Spade 2008; and for an analysis of court cases involving gender reclassification, see Meadow 2010. The current legal requirements for changing birth certificates are collected at a website maintained by Lambda Legal, an LGBT legal services NGO: http://www.lambdalegal.org/know-your-rights/transgender/changing-birth-certificate-sex-designations.

52. Saner 2014. In New Zealand, too, changes in sex or gender on passports can be made through simple declaration, without any medical control; see https://www.passports.govt.nz/Transgender-applicants.

53. The phrase "ethnic options" was popularized by Waters 1990. For political science work that draws on constructivist understandings of ethnicity as contextually variable, see Posner 2005 and Chandra 2012.

54. For a dissenting view, criticizing the sharp contrast between race and ethnicity and exploring the role of choice in ethnic and racial minorities' negotiations of identity in the United States and Britain, see Song 2003.

55. Rich 2014, 1505; see also Rich 2013, 179.

56. Kennedy 2003, 333.

57. Loveman 2014, 171; Kertzer and Arel 2002, 34.

58. Rich 2014, 1520–21. Testifying to anxieties about unregulated self-identification, EEOC regulations allow employers to correct self-identifications that are "patently false," but they do not specify on what basis an employer might conclude that this is the case (Rich 2014, 1524–25).

59. For Directive 15, see Office of Management and Budget 1997. For the broad-based shift toward recognizing multiple racial identifications in data collection, see Hochschild, Weaver, and Burch 2012, 58–60.

60. Waters 1990.

61. Song and Aspinall 2012; Rockquemore and Arend 2002; Rockquemore and Brunsma 2008; Hochschild, Weaver, and Burch 2012.

62. Harris and Sim 2002, 621–22.

63. Rockquemore and Brunsma 2008.

64. Khanna 2010; Harris and Sim 2002, 621. Even when the choice is limited to black or white, it's significant that 17 percent of adolescents who identified their race as both white and black in one large representative sample chose white

as the single race that best describes them, while another 8 percent said they did not know or refused to answer the forced-choice question (Harris and Sim 2002, 621–22).

65. On "affiliative self-fashioning," see Nelson 2008. On the scope for interpretation and choice afforded by genetic ancestry testing, see also Hirschman and Panther-Yates 2008; Nash 2004; Hacking 2006a; and Brubaker 2015, 69–74.

66. The quotations are from Heyes 2009, 144–45. The large and growing market for racially and ethnically inflected cosmetic surgery has received increasing public attention of late. One 2014 blog post characterized it as the harbinger of "the next trans: transethnic and transracial" (Disenchanted Scholar 2014). On the widespread demand for skin lightening products in Latin America, Asia, and Africa, see Glenn 2008; Hunter 2011; Franklin 2013. See also Stokel-Walker 2013 for an account of a young Chinese immigrant to northeastern England who, tired of racist taunts, decided to alter his appearance through a series of surgical procedures; and Hoh 2014 for the story of a Brazilian man in his mid-twenties who, in a reversal of the common pattern, underwent a number of procedures to give himself single eyelids and to make his eyes appear smaller, and who changed his name to Xiahn Nishi—all after falling in love with Asian culture while an exchange student in South Korea. For the limits of a "westernization" perspective on ethnically inflected cosmetic surgery, see O'Connor 2014. For Michael Awkward's characterization of Michael Jackson's successive self-transformations as an instance of "transraciality," see pp. 125–26.

The protagonist of Jess Row's 2014 novel *Your Face in Mine* is a white man who becomes black through "race reassignment surgery." In an interview (Goldstein 2014), Row recounted describing the book to a Bangkok surgeon, who said, "That already exists, but we don't use that word for it. Racial reassignment surgery already exists." Row explained, "What he meant was, not the full-on surgical procedures I talk about in the book, most of which are made up, but the combination of actual, physical plastic surgery with hair alterations, skin-lightening creams, that are very common, especially in Asia but all around the world, that can effectively make a person able to pass from one ethnicity to the other. There are people who have, from an outsider's perspective, turned themselves very much into Caucasian-looking people through some combination of these techniques. And in Thailand especially, it's very widely accepted and embraced."

67. Rose 2008, 228–34.

68. I return to the theme of cross-racial identification in chapter 4. On the blurring between identification *with* and identification *as*, see also Dreisinger 2008.

69. McHugh 2014.

70. For a sampling of such trans claims, collected by a site that aims to document the "abuse, harassment and misogyny of transgender identity politics," see http://terfisaslur.com/erasing-female-biology/.

71. Bettcher 2014a, 392ff.; see also Bettcher 2007.

72. Schilt and Westbrook 2009. The authors interpret this strikingly gendered pattern of violence—95 percent of the murders resulting from private sexual encounters involved a cis man murdering a trans woman, and none a cis woman murdering a trans man—as evidence of the gendered significance of

violence as a means of reasserting compromised male heterosexuality. (The perpetrators often expressly claimed to have been tricked into what they experienced as a homosexual encounter.)

73. Spade 2003.

74. Green 2006, 235.

75. This paragraph is based on Westbrook and Schilt 2013. The quotations are from p. 10.

76. Raymond 1994, 114; emphasis in the original. Raymond's book was originally published in 1979, but radical feminist policing of the category "woman" was recently revived by Jeffreys (2014). Jeffreys insists on using pronouns corresponding to the (original) biological sex of transgender people, since "the use by men of feminine pronouns conceals the masculine privilege bestowed upon them by virtue of having been placed in and brought up in the male sex caste" (2014, 9).

77. Burkett 2015. An even blunter instance of policing in the name of history is furnished by Robin Morgan's categorical refusal to acknowledge transsexual folksinger Beth Elliott as a woman at the West Coast Lesbian Conference in 1973: "I will not call a male 'she'; thirty-two years of suffering in this androcentric society, and of surviving, have earned me the title 'woman'; one walk down the street by a male transvestite, five minutes of his being hassled (which he may enjoy), and then he dares, he *dares* to think he understands our pain? No, in our mothers' names and in our own, we must not call him sister" (quoted by Stryker 2008, 104, who underscores Morgan's conflation of transsexual and transvestite; emphasis in the original).

78. Davis 1991.

79. Ford 1994, 1275.

80. On naturalization, see Yang 2006, 376; on marriage annulment, Walker 2008; and on birth certificates, Domínguez 1986.

81. Ford 1994, 1232–34. The twins appealed their dismissal, but it was upheld by the Supreme Judicial Court of Massachusetts. For critiques of the reasoning in the Malone case, see Yang 2006, 390ff., and Rich 2013, 199, 205–9.

82. Stebbins's black barber, brought into the controversy, came to his defense: "I've been cutting hair for nearly 40 years. There's black hair and there's white hair. I'm a professional, and I know the difference. Now, Mark doesn't put anything on his hair. A white boy with a permanent? Nope, he's as black as I am. And coloring has nothing to do with it; my father was fair and passed as a white man. . . . The man is one of us" (Roberts 1984). The "broad nose" description is quoted in a retrospective *Los Angeles Times* story (Pearce 2015); the "baby elephant" story and Stebbins's self-characterization as "culturally, socially, and genetically" black are reported in Sweet 2005, 280. See also Wilhelm 1984.

83. For a sustained critique of proposals to police "racial fraud," see Yang 2006.

84. Wright 1995, 566–67.

85. Onwuachi-Willig 2007, 1220–21.

86. Onwuachi-Willig 2007, 1220ff.

87. Pember 2007.

88. The association is no longer active, but the statement is available at https://pantherfile.uwm.edu/michael/www/nativeprofs/fraud.htm.

89. See the series of stories published in *Inside Higher Education*: Jaschik 2015a; Jaschik 2015b; and Flaherty 2015.

90. NAISA 2015.

91. Richard A. Baker, assistant vice chancellor and vice president for equal opportunity at the University of Houston and a regional director for the American Association for Access, Equity, and Diversity, quoted in Flaherty 2015.

92. The increasing use of genetic testing to scrutinize tribal membership rolls in the United States is only apparently an exception. Tribes are legal and political entities, not (just) ethnic groups: tribal membership is a form of citizenship—codified in rules and formally regulated and administered—not (just) a form of ethnicity. The verification of tribal membership through genetic testing does not involve testing for ethnicity; it involves ascertaining whether there is a genetic basis for claimed genealogical relationships to other tribal members (TallBear 2013).

93. In August 2015, for example, conservative media outlets, citing birth certificates identifying his father as a white man, accused Shaun King, a prominent activist in the Black Lives Matter movement, of falsely claiming to be biracial in order to secure a scholarship to Morehouse College. King indicated in reply that his biological father was not the man listed on his birth certificate but rather a light-skinned black man, and various others posted accounts supporting his claim to have consistently presented himself as black since middle school. See Southall 2015, the *New York Times* story on the controversy, and, for Shaun King's own account, King 2015.

94. Casting identity as an objective fact rather than a subjective choice is not, of course, the only mode of trans discourse, any more than it is the only mode of gay discourse. The trans activist and writer Natalie Reed (2013) provides a sharp challenge to "born that way" accounts of gender identity; Ambrosino's short pieces for the *New Republic* (2014a and 2014b) make a parallel argument about sexual identity. Bettcher (2014a) analyzes the tension in the transgender field between the "wrong-body" model of an innate and unchanging gender identity at variance with the sexed body and the "beyond-the-binary" paradigm that is premised on a social constructionist account of gender. Weeks (1987) analyzes the ambiguity of the notion of sexual identity, focusing on the tension between "identity as destiny" and "identity as choice." On the noncorrespondence between sexual desire, behavior, and identity and its implications for LGBT health politics, see Epstein 2003.

95. Similarly objectivist language has been employed, in recent years, by the "transabled" movement in an effort to establish "Bodily Identity Integrity Disorder" (BIID)—a putative condition expressly modeled on Gender Identity Disorder—as an officially recognized diagnostic category that would allow those suffering from the disorder to secure access to the medical "treatment" they desire, often involving the amputation of an otherwise healthy limb. BIID was considered for inclusion in DSM-5, the fifth edition of the *Diagnostic and Statistical Manual of Mental Disorders*, but in the end it was not included. On the ethical and legal issues involved, see C. Elliott 2000 and T. Elliott 2009. On the objectivist narratives deployed by members of an online transabled community, see Davis 2012.

96. On this point see Stone 2006, 228; Green 2006, 235; Spade 2003; and Valentine 2007, 265 n. 13.

97. See for example Kimmel 1993 and Stein 2011. Both are critical of "born that way" claims, arguing that they have limited use—and may even backfire—as a political strategy.

98. For sympathetic accounts of transsexuals' essentialist understandings of identity, see Prosser 1998 and Rubin 2003.

99. Fausto-Sterling 2012.

100. See Harmon 2006. Some ancestry testing sites highlight this possibility. DNA Testing Adviser.com, which bills itself as "the independent guide to DNA testing," notes on its main web page that "proving minority status can be helpful in race-based college admissions and job applications." http://www.dna-testing-adviser.com/EthnicAncestry.html.

101. On the striking "return of biology" in public discussions of race and ethnicity in the last decade or so, see Brubaker 2015, chap. 2.

Chapter 3. The Trans of Migration

1. In suggesting that trans is "good to think with," I echo Lévi-Strauss's classic discussion of totemism, which argues that particular animals are used to represent clans not because they are "good for eating" (*bonnes à manger*) but because they are "good for thinking" (*bonnes à penser*). See Lévi-Strauss 1964, 89 (translation modified); 1962, 128.

2. Stryker 2015.

3. On the immutability concept in equal protection jurisprudence, see Braman 1998 and Marcosson 2001.

4. I draw here on Kessler and McKenna (2000), who distinguish bodily transformation to fit subjective gender identity, crossing gender boundaries, and going beyond gender; Roen (2002), who distinguishes "either/or" transsexual from "both/neither" transgender positions; and especially Ekins and King (2006), who distinguish migrating, oscillating, negating, and transcending forms of transgender. For the history of the term "transgender," see Stryker 2006, 4ff., and Valentine 2007, 32ff.

5. I argue in chapter 5, p. 123, that the multiracial movement also illustrates how the trans of between can shade over into the trans of beyond.

6. On the deep tensions structuring the transgender field, see Roen 2002; Bettcher 2014a; and Halberstam 1998b.

7. Halberstam 1998a, 165, 170; the quotation is from p. 170. See also Aizura 2012.

8. This section builds on Ekins and King's (2006) discussion of transgender "migrating stories" while taking the migration metaphor in a somewhat different direction.

9. Migration that is imagined as permanent may be reiterated, leading to a third destination (Ossman 2013). There are some examples of such "serial"

forms of transgender trajectories, but obviously the structural possibilities are different.

10. On gender "detransitions" or "retransitions," see Clark-Flory 2015.

11. See Ekins and King (2006) on playful gender excursions as a form of gender "tourism" rather than migration. The notion of gender "travel" is captured colloquially by the French slang term for transvestite: *travelo*.

12. Gender Identity Disorder was introduced into the DSM-3 in 1980; it was renamed Gender Dysphoria in 2013 in the DSM-5. Gender Identity Disorder is also institutionalized in the World Health Organization's International Classification of Diseases.

13. On the social reflexivity through which those seeking access to surgery learned to craft the right kinds of narratives, see Stone 2006, 228.

14. For a nuanced account of these debates, focusing on a trans boy who started testosterone treatments and had a double mastectomy at age sixteen, see Margaret Talbot's (2013) *New Yorker* story. For reservations about early medical intervention, see Dreger 2013 and the op-eds by Vilain and Bailey (2015) and Friedman (2015); for critical responses to Friedman, see Ford 2015 and Lopez 2015.

15. In 2015, Ontario banned therapy that seeks to change the sexual orientation or gender identity of minors after the suicide of Leelah Alcorn, an American transgender adolescent who had been subjected to such therapy; President Obama expressed his support for such a ban. Critics argue that banning any attempt to change gender identity—if gender identity is taken to be whatever even a young child says it is—would in effect push children toward gender transitions. In support of a ban, see Karasic and Ehrensaft 2015; for a critique, see Dreger 2015a. A central figure in these linked controversies has been Kenneth Zucker, chiefly because of his endorsement of conversion therapy for some gender-nonconforming children (though he has also endorsed medical interventions to enable others to make gender transitions). On the controversy surrounding Zucker and the Gender Identity Clinic he headed until late 2015 at Toronto's Center for Addiction and Mental Health, see Schwartzapfel 2013 and, for a defense of Zucker, Dreger 2015b. On the controversy over therapies that seek to alter sexual orientation—now widely seen as unethical as well as ineffective, and now banned, when they target minors, in four U.S. states including California— see Waidzunas 2013 and 2015. Waidzunas interestingly notes that while a 2009 American Psychological Association resolution on "Appropriate Affirmative Responses to Sexual Orientation Distress and Change Efforts" rejected attempts to change sexual orientation—defined as a pattern of arousal and desire that is independent of one's identity—the accompanying report gave a qualified endorsement to "sexual orientation identity exploration" for clients interested in pursuing a "heterosexual identity and lifestyle in alignment with their religious values" (Waidzunas 2013, 1; American Psychological Association Task Force 2009).

16. The UK regulations are found at https://www.gov.uk/apply-gender-recog nition-certificate/changing-your-gender.

17. Garber 1992, 67ff.

18. Ekins and King 2005a; 2005b; 2006, 13, 79–84; the quotation is from Stryker 2006, 4. Prince appears to have been the first to use the term "transgender"

or its lexical variants. The first major outsider critique of the industry—the "conglomerate of medical and other professional practitioners who coalesce to institutionalize transsexual treatment and surgery on the medical model"—was Janice Raymond's *The Transsexual Empire* (1994, xvi; the book was originally published in 1979). Important critiques of medicalization from within the transgender community include Stone 2006 (originally published in 1991) and Spade 2003.

19. For a nuanced discussion of the politics of passing, focused on the tension between the "transgender position of refusing to fit within categories of woman and man" and the "transsexual imperative to pass convincingly as either a man or a woman," see Roen 2002 (the quotation is from p. 505).

20. Roen 2002; Bettcher 2014a, 385.

21. Burkett 2015.

22. Although gender migration is generally not *driven* by the privilege gap, it may contribute to increasing *awareness* of that gap. This is suggested by Schilt's (2006, 2010) finding that transgender men who remained in the same jobs often received more rewards and respect after transitioning, and thereby developed a greater sensitivity to the gendered dynamics of workplace inequality. Connell similarly found that transgender people in the workplace develop a more robust feminist consciousness and a heightened awareness of gender inequality (2010, 47–50).

23. On the longstanding relative invisibility of trans men, see Meyerowitz 2002, 148ff., 206, 274ff. A Dutch study of the early 1990s, based on comprehensive records, showed that nearly three-quarters of those who had taken hormones to change sex were male-born; but Meyerowitz (2002, 9, 148) notes most doctors' sense that the sex ratio subsequently evened out. Studies summarized in Zucker and Lawrence 2009, pp. 14–15, reported higher rates of male-to-female than female-to-male transitions, but most of these studies were based on data collected in whole or in part at least two decades ago, and Zucker and Lawrence caution that no proper epidemiological studies of gender dysphoria have been conducted.

24. For the cultural logic behind these anxieties, see Westbrook and Schilt 2013. The presence of people with penises in sex-segregated women's spaces, they suggest, transforms what ought to be a "nonsexual space into a dangerously (hetero)sexual one. Within this heteronormative logic, all bodies with male anatomies, regardless of gender identity, desire female bodies, and [some] . . . are willing to use force to get access to those bodies" (p. 17).

25. On the difficulties trans men and women pose for women's colleges, see the *New York Times Magazine* piece by Padawer (2014).

26. For racial reclassification in South Africa, see Bowker and Starr 1999, chap. 6.

27. Sharfstein 2007.

28. On the "wages of whiteness," see Roediger 2007.

29. I focus here on *individual* migration between racial categories. Historians and sociologists have also studied the *collective* movement between racial categories. The seminal study in this tradition is Ignatiev's *How the Irish Became White* (1995); see also Loveman and Muniz (2007) on the "whitening" of Puerto Rico.

30. On "nine-to-five passing," see Hobbs 2014, 124–25, 151ff., 175–76.

31. The theme of loss is central to Hobbs's account.

32. Hubbard 2003, 840.

33. Since passing was an intergenerational phenomenon, moreover, it is important to note that while "the passer lived with anxiety, his or her children often did not" (Sharfstein 2003, 1494).

34. Rates of passing have recently been quantified by the economists Emily Nix and Nancy Qian (2015). Using new matching techniques and taking advantage of the recent digitization of historical census records and of increases in computation power, Nix and Qian examined the entire population of individuals identified as black in a given census year for the period 1880–1940 and estimated the fraction who were identified as white in a subsequent census, as well as the fraction of the latter who returned to a black identification later. They conclude that at least 19 percent of blacks passed as white, and that of these about 10 percent were again identified as black in the following census.

35. Sharfstein 2007, 597.

36. Sharfstein 2003, 1503.

37. On claims to Native American and Portuguese identity, see Sharfstein 2007, 625–26.

38. Rothman 2003, 205.

39. For qualitative studies of the shift to identifying as Native American, see Fitzgerald 2007 and Sturm 2011. On dynamics of ethnic reidentification, see also Nagel 1997, chap. 4, and Kelly and Nagel 2002.

40. This figure does not count the additional 2.3 million people who identified themselves as Native American and some other race (an option that has been available only in the last two censuses).

41. For census figures, see U.S. Census Bureau 2012; for the estimate of reidentification, Passel 1997. For a more recent demographic study, see Liebler and Ortyl 2013.

42. The pool of new identifiers may be drawn from those who claim some—often distant—Native ancestry. When the census last asked an ancestry question, in 2000, about eight million reported some Native ancestry, suggesting further potential for future growth in those identifying their racial identity, or at least one of their racial identities, as Native American (Passel 1997; for the results of the 2000 ancestry question, see https://www.census.gov/prod/2004pubs /c2kbr-35.pdf).

43. I discuss the complex, fluid, and multidirectional patterns of identification arising from the new visibility and legitimacy of "multiracial" as an identity option in chapter 4.

44. Note that this shift may occur on an aggregate level without necessarily occurring on an individual level. This can happen when individuals who would have identified (and would have been identified) as black under old rules of classification grow up identifying themselves—and being identified by others—as multiracial. These individuals do not experience a change in identification or categorization, yet a consequential shift may occur on the aggregate level if enough individuals follow this pattern.

45. On the distinction between "thin" and "thick" ethnoracial identities (a thick identity being one that "organizes a great deal of social life and both individual and collective action"), see Cornell and Hartmann 1998, 73.

46. On the "hyperghetto," see Wacquant 2008.

47. See Hodes 2003, 114–15. See also Drake and Cayton 1993, 167 (originally published in 1945): "To avoid injuring the feelings and standing of his family, the white partner often commits sociological suicide and buries himself in the black community."

48. The story is told in Sandweiss 2009.

49. The cases of Griffin and Halsell are analyzed in Baz Dreisinger's *Near Black* (2008), the most sustained account of reverse passing.

50. Chokal-Ingam 2015. Chokal-Ingam is planning a book on the subject; the project is described in detail at http://almostblack.com/the-book/.

51. The *Ebony* article is quoted in Dreisinger 2008, 105; see also Wald 2000, 57.

52. For Mezzrow's own story, see *Really the Blues*, cowritten with Bernard Wolfe (1946). See also Wald 2000; Dreisinger 2008, chap. 4; Melnick 1999.

53. Otis 1968, xl.

54. Otis describes the church in his memoir, *Upside Your Head! Rhythm and Blues on Central Avenue*.

55. As Dreisinger notes (2008, 98–99), Otis is not entirely consistent; he sometimes uses the third person when speaking of blacks. Dreisinger interprets this as conveying "moments of anxiety about . . . his adopted identity." But the shift might also simply indicate Otis's awareness of the limits as well as the importance of choice in matters of identity.

56. Guthrie 2015.

57. Dreisinger 2008, 118, 129–31; the quotations are from pp. 129 and 130.

Chapter 4. The Trans of Between

1. A classic example is Jan Morris's *Conundrum* (1974).

2. Passing stories are seldom told by their protagonists, since the telling of the story would undermine the passing. I refer here to the genre conventions of fictional and historical representations of passing.

3. I do not mean to suggest that betweenness is a new phenomenon. Androgyny has a long history in myth, philosophy, fashion, and the norms and practices of certain specific milieux (Zhou 2008). And as I discuss later in this chapter, the idea of betweenness was central to the pioneering German sexological research of the late nineteenth and early twentieth century (Meyerowitz 2002, 22–29). Sollors (1999) traces the theme of racial betweenness in literature on a vast historical canvas spanning many centuries and languages. What is new, in recent decades, are forms of the politics of identity that expressly seek to establish legitimate and recognized positions between or beyond existing categories.

4. Talbot 2013.

5. Gubar 1996, xv ff.; Wald 2000, introduction; Dreisinger 2008, especially chap. 5 and epilogue.

6. West 1994, 121. Explorations of sex/gender and ethnoracial betweenness are part of a broader cultural moment, attuned to hybridity, syncretism, creolization, and bricolage in religion, language, cuisine, music, and other domains; see for example Hannerz 1987; Kraidy 2005; and Burke 2009. In a discussion of syncretism, Stewart (1999, 41) notes the tendency to "valoriz[e] recognitions of mixture where formerly they had been stigmatized as inauthentic." Stewart takes as emblematic Salman Rushdie's characterization of his novel *The Satanic Verses* as a celebration of "hybridity, impurity, intermingling, the transformation that comes of new and unexpected combinations of human beings, cultures, ideas, politics, movies, songs. It rejoices in mongrelization and fears the absolutism of the Pure. . . . It is a love song to our mongrel selves" (Rushdie 1990, 4; emphasis omitted).

7. On the understanding of the intermediate phase as temporary, see Bolin 1994, 457. The lived experience of having a gender-ambiguous body during the stage of betweenness is described by Nordmarken 2014.

8. I rely here on Ekins and King's (2006, chap. 3) discussion of "oscillating stories." On cross-dressing more generally, see Garber 1992; Bullough and Bullough 1993; and Ekins 1997.

9. Those who cross-dress in private, of course, or in support groups or settings that specifically cater to cross-dressers, may be entirely unconcerned with being publicly "read" as the opposite gender. Even those who occasionally cross-dress in public may be unconcerned with passing (Thanem and Wallenberg 2016, 261–63).

10. Ekins and King 2006, 106. The London-based Style Me Quirky, for example, offers "transvestites, transsexuals, transgender, t-girls and anyone with a gender subversive nature a service for you to turn into the gender of your choice" (http://www.stylemequirky.com/dressing-service/transgender-dressing-service/). This can be done individually, or as a "social makeover" that combines "socialising with friends and meeting new friends while enjoying the experience of a full makeover and dressing experience." Style Me Quirky emphasizes that its services are not for those who seek to pass in any conventional sense: "We are the Lady Gaga of transgender dressing services. Our philosophy is that we want . . . clients to feel fabulous not normal." See also Halberstam 1998a, 251–52, on the "drag king workshop" run by New York performance artist Diane Torr, which teaches female participants how to present themselves and pass (temporarily) as men.

11. Lorber 2004; emphasis in the original.

12. On "gender trouble," see Butler 1990; Thanem and Wallenberg 2016.

13. On these recombinatory possibilities, see Nicholas 2014, 32; see also Bem (1995, 330), arguing for a strategy of "proliferating gender categories" as an alternative to seeking to eliminate them.

14. The quotation is from Halberstam 1998a, 20. The women studied by Devor (1987) did not consider themselves transgender. They identified unambiguously as women, and they were not seeking to disrupt the social legibility of gender.

But if "transgender" refers to the "widest imaginable range of gender-variant practices and identities" (Stryker 2008, 19), then their gender-variant presentations can be considered part of the transgender phenomenon. A decade later, by the time Halberstam published her book on female masculinity (1998a), the category transgender was much more widely available to designate gender-variant identities other than transsexual ones; Halberstam (1998b) herself elaborated the notion of "transgender butch" as a subject position different from yet not—despite the "border wars" between the two—radically opposed to that of the female-to-male transsexual. As the anthropologist David Valentine observes, the recombinatory possibilities of female masculinity and male femininity are not in fact symmetrically available: "Unlike Halberstam's valorization of 'transgender butch' [or of female masculinity more generally], there is no analogous *culturally valorized space* for male-bodied 'transgender fems,' gay men who adopt, play with, or assert femininity as a central aspect of their senses of self, beyond the figure of the performing drag queen." The result is that drag queens and feminine men are "available for absorption into the category of transgender (and into transgender studies)" without anything analogous to the struggles between butch lesbians and trans men over ownership of masculinity in those born as women (2007, 151–53; the quotation is from p. 153; emphasis in the original).

15. Thanem and Wallenberg 2016, 263.

16. Efforts to reestablish the gender binary have also been described by Connell 2010, 41–42.

17. Thanem and Wallenberg 2016, 266–68; emphasis in the original.

18. Connell 2010, 43; see also Gardiner 2012, 601.

19. Stone 2006, 226, 231–2; emphasis in the original. I return to Stone's foundational text in chapter 5.

20. As Stryker (2008, 19) points out, the line has blurred between those who identify as transsexuals (and who may or may not choose to have genital surgery) and transgender people who do not so identify, yet who do transition between one gender identity and another and do engage in some (if not all) of the body modification practices usually associated with transsexuals.

21. On Beatie and the "unexpected configurations" of transgender bodies, see Currah 2008; on transgender men, pregnancy, and parenting, see Ryan 2009.

22. Meyerowitz 2002, 22–29; the quotation is from p. 22.

23. Meyerowitz 2002, 66, 98–103; the *New York Daily News* headline is quoted on p. 62. Jorgensen's surgery was performed in 1951 in Denmark; until the mid-1960s, most Americans seeking sex reassignment surgery—overwhelmingly male-to-female cases in those years—were referred to physicians abroad (ibid., 146–48).

24. Meyrowitz 2002, 103. Benjamin is quoted at p. 102, Jorgensen at p. 66.

25. On the differentiation of sex and gender, see Meyerowitz 2002, 111–29; on the differentiation of gender and sexuality, ibid., 170–176; Valentine 2007, 15–16, 57–63.

26. The original version of the "Genderbread Person" (Killerman 2012a) represented gender identity as a single continuum, ranging from woman to

man. A revised version (Killerman 2012b) represented it as two paired but independent continua, ranging from nongendered to woman-ness and from nongendered to man-ness; a similar change was made for gender expression, sex, and sexual attraction. The revision responded to the argument that being more feminine doesn't necessarily make one less masculine.

27. See for example Gilroy 2000, 250.

28. On the differing ways of construing "multiracial," which yield widely varying estimates of the size of the multiracial population, see Morning 2000.

29. Myrdal 1962, 685; Hobbs 2014, 150–51.

30. On the "protean," contextually shifting identity of some biracials with one white- and one black-identifying parent, see Rockquemore and Brunsma 2008, 47.

31. Khanna and Johnson 2010; Rockquemore and Arend 2002, 60.

32. A growing body of research on discrimination by color—as analytically distinct from, though empirically intertwined with, discrimination by categorical race—demonstrates how position on the color continuum matters in a variety of formal and informal settings; see for example Hunter 2007.

33. *Time*'s "new Eve," representing "the future, multiethnic face of America," was described as "15% Anglo-Saxon, 17.5% Middle Eastern, 17.5% African, 7.5% Asian, 35% southern European and 7.5% Hispanic." *Time*, November 18, 1993, p. 2.

34. Brubaker 2015, 72–74.

35. Loveman 2014, 61–66; Stamatov 2014.

36. Hochschild and Powell 2008, 66–71. Enumerators for the 1890 census were instructed to "be particularly careful to distinguish between blacks, mulattoes, quadroons, and octoroons. The word 'black' should be used to describe those persons who have three-fourths or more black blood; 'mulatto,' those persons who have from three-eighths to five-eighths black blood; 'quadroon,' those persons who have one-fourth black blood; and 'octoroon,' those persons who have one-eighth or any trace of black blood." Hochschild and Powell observe drily that "no instruction explained how to determine fractions of black blood" (p. 68). The shifting racial categories used in the United States census are displayed in a convenient and informative format in "What Census Calls Us: A Historical Timeline": http://www.pewsocialtrends.org/interactives /multiracial-timeline/.

37. See especially Sollors's (1999) magisterial work of literary criticism.

38. For qualitative studies of the new identification options opened up by the weakening of the one-drop rule, see Daniel 2002; Rockquemore and Brunsma 2008.

39. Roth 2005. For a thoughtful analysis of the methodological difficulties involved in studying identification as multiracial, see Gullickson and Morning 2011.

40. Rockquemore and Brunsma 2008, 39.

41. Rockquemore and Brunsma 2008, 45. On the other hand, self-identifying as black does not necessarily mean that one will be identified as black by others. Pew Research Foundation data from 2009 indicate that only 27 percent of

Americans thought of President Obama as mostly black, while 52 percent thought of him as mostly mixed race (P. Taylor 2014).

42. Khanna 2010.

43. Harris and Sim 2002, 622.

44. Daniel (2002) distinguishes "first-generation" multiracials—children of racially mixed marriages whose parents do not themselves identify as multiracial—from "multigenerational" multiracials. The latter have parents or more distant ancestors who have been socially defined as black despite their mixed backgrounds; "these individuals, and/or their parents and ancestors, have resisted identifying solely with the African-American community" (p. 6). On the problems of limiting studies of multiracial identification to "first-generation" individuals, see Gullickson and Morning 2011.

45. Daniel 2002, chap. 7.

46. Michaels 1992; Appiah 1996, 83–104; Ford 2005, chaps. 1 and 2.

47. See Michaels 1992, 683–85, and 1997, 133–37.

48. I return to the performative turn in the concluding chapter, pp. 142–45.

49. Some radical feminists, too, are committed to an essentialist understanding of identity, as indicated by their policing of transgender identity claims in the name of nature and/or history. See pp. 26–27 and 59. Their opposition to Jenner (and to the trans of migration more generally) parallels progressives' opposition to Dolezal, and their concern about illegitimate access to women's spaces parallels progressives' concern about opportunistic or fraudulent access to positions and opportunities intended for racial and ethnic minorities. But radical feminists are not opposed to the behavioral enactment of gender betweenness, even if they might criticize the emphasis on play and pleasure that sometimes informs such enactment. They may even welcome gender-bending or gender-blending, insofar as it disrupts expectations about gender-appropriate behavior. In this they differ from progressives who oppose performative racial blending.

50. That such stereotypes may have an ambivalent valence is suggested by the title of Eric Lott's pioneering *Love and Theft: Blackface Minstrelsy and the American Working Class* (2013), originally published in 1993; see also Gubar 1997.

51. The rest of this paragraph draws on Sartwell 2005; see also Sartwell 2015a. On wiggerism, see also Roediger 2002, 221ff. On upwardly mobile, phenotypically "Mexican-looking" children of Mexican immigrants in New York who identify as black rather than Mexican during their adolescence as a way of participating in a specifically black variant of what Neckerman, Carter, and Lee (1999) call a "minority culture of mobility" (and as a way of avoiding stigmatization as undocumented), see Smith 2014. For a nuanced ethnographic account of "Puerto Rican wannabes," see Wilkins 2008, chaps. 6 and 7. On the long history of "playing Indian" in the United States, see Deloria 1998. On "affiliative" forms of cross-ethnic identification generally, see Jiménez 2010.

52. Sartwell notes the difficulties in writing about "black culture" or "white culture" and concedes that he will be "purveying stereotypes even as I examine them." The "black culture" performed by wiggers, and the "white culture" from

which they disaffiliate, are of course stereotypical social constructions. But as Sartwell observes, "We need to be able to examine the content of the social constructions themselves, and we need to be able to acknowledge their continuing centrality to our experience" (2005, 37).

53. Sartwell 2005; the quotations are from pp. 45 and 48. In a cultural landscape in which hip-hop has become the "universal language" of youth, and in which "black" has become, in the domain of popular culture, a valorized category, a pole of attraction and affiliation, while "white" has come to symbolize lack and inauthenticity, it's not surprising that crossover practices and identifications have proliferated. To quote Sartwell again: "It should surprise no one that white people not only buy hip-hop records, but romanticize hip-hop culture and seek to emigrate into it. . . . Coding black is a way to rebel against one's own culture and one's own family, not just in some general sense in which each generation rebels against the previous one, but specifically against the content of whiteness as polite good taste, deference, and self-effacement. The culture we have made is immensely dull and safe, and we've made it specifically by excluding from ourselves anything interesting and dangerous. . . . It's odd, in fact, that there are any really white kids left" (pp. 42–43). On the crossover appeal of hip-hop, see also Kitwana 2005.

54. "Unlike identity politics," write Guinier and Torres (2002, 15–16), "political race is not about being but instead is about doing"; the concept "affirms the value of the individual's choosing to affiliate with the named group." The quotation in the text is from p. 12. See also Wright 2010 on the combination of a white "visual identity" with a black "practical identity"; and Green 2009.

Chapter 5. The Trans of Beyond

1. On neo-, anti-, and post- stances in the very different context of modernization theory, see Alexander 1995.

2. The complexities go well beyond this two-dimensional space. Vade (2005), for example, argues for conceptualizing the "gender galaxy" as a "three-dimensional non-linear space in which every gender has a location that may or may not be fixed."

3. Sandy Stone's "posttranssexual manifesto," originally published in 1991, played a key role in enabling as well as conceptualizing this shift. Stone expressly sought to position herself outside the gender continuum, to "speak from outside the boundaries of gender, beyond the constructed oppositional nodes which have been predefined as the only positions from which discourse is possible" (2006, 230). Reflecting on the significance of this text a quarter century later, Susan Stryker (2008, 128–29) noted that Stone was calling on (post-) transsexuals to "speak out in a 'heteroglossic,' Babel-like profusion of tongues about all the imaginable genres of gender difference there could be, if only the medically dominated discourse of transsexuality were shattered."

4. Wilchins 2002, 24. In her emphasis on gender performance, Wilchins follows Judith Butler and post-structuralist theory.

5. My discussion of Elan-Cane follows Ekins and King 2006, 158ff.

6. Elan-Cane 2000.

7. Elan-Cane is quoted in Kyriacou 2014.

8. Boswell 1997, 54.

9. Bellah et al. 1985, 221.

10. Boswell is quoted by Ekins and King (2006, 199), Bornstein is discussed at p. 203. Multiplicity and play are also suggested by such terms as "polygendered," which echoes in the domain of gender Freud's notion of "polymorphous perversity" in the domain of sexuality.

11. Ekins and King 2006, 159–60.

12. It is important to distinguish transgender as a term of self-identification from transgender as an analytically defined field of phenomena. As a field of investigation, transgender studies regroups phenomena previously studied under other headings. Transgender studies would not be the productive field it has become if it were limited to persons and practices that expressly define themselves as transgender. None of the participants in the support group for transgender-identified people with HIV in New York studied by David Valentine, for example, referred to themselves as transgender: "They talk about themselves as girls, sometimes as fem queens, every now and then as women, but also very often as gay" (2007, 3). Yet they fell within the purview of his study because they were "identified by others as being transgender" (p. 26). Similarly, forms of gender-blending and androgyny that are not expressly framed as transgender fall within the domain of the field as instances of the trans of between. By the same logic, if the trans of beyond comprises efforts to escape from the social and cultural force fields defined by existing categorical frameworks, then feminist visions of forms of social life "beyond gender" can fruitfully be studied as instances of the trans of beyond. For sophisticated accounts of the emergence of the field of transgender studies, see Stryker 2006 and Valentine 2007, chap. 4.

13. Boswell 1997, 54.

14. For feminist debates on gender symmetry, see Orloff 2009.

15. On gender as a symbolic structure, see Ortner and Whitehead 1981; Ortner 1996; and Bourdieu 2001. Ortner underscores the "relationship of mutual metaphorization" through which gender "becomes a powerful language for talking about the great existential questions of nature and culture, while a language of nature and culture . . . can become a powerful language for talking about gender, sexuality, and reproduction" (1996, 179).

16. For overviews of feminist stances toward trans issues and explorations of the possibility of feminist-trans alliances, see Heyes 2003 and Bettcher 2014b. For efforts to elaborate a specifically trans feminism, see Bettcher 2014a and Serano 2016. For a critique of the tendency of some feminists to embrace certain forms of trans as progressive while criticizing others as reactionary, distinguishing for example "good genderqueers" from "bad transsexuals," see Schilt 2010, 173–75.

17. See especially Risman, Lorber, and Sherwood (2012), who see gender-queer and transgender youth as a key force generating "crisis tendencies in the gender order" (pp. 12–16).

18. On transgender challenges to the category "woman," see for example Wilchins 1997, 81–83, and, for a more extended discussion, drawing primarily on Judith Butler, Wilchins 2004, 133–45.

19. See, most recently, Jeffreys 2014.

20. See for example the *New Yorker* account by Michelle Goldberg (2014) and the critical response by the transgender writer and activist Julia Serano (2014).

21. For a sharp analysis and critique of this strand of feminist thought, with particular reference to the "universal caregiver" model articulated by Nancy Fraser, see Orloff 2009. For a critique of feminist theory for failing to take seriously the "pleasures of gender" experienced by trans and cis people alike, see Schilt and Meadow 2012.

22. See Rockquemore and Brunsma 2008, 48–49. For a sustained and sympathetic analysis of "race transcenders," who refuse to identify themselves in racial terms, even while acknowledging that they are racially identified by others, see Hoyt 2016.

23. In signaling the dangers of official racial or ethnic classification, commentators point to the obvious examples of Nazi Germany, Vichy France, the American South under Jim Crow, South Africa under apartheid, and colonial and postcolonial Rwanda. In considering these potential dangers it is important to distinguish the aggregate and in principle anonymous forms of classification represented by modern statewide censuses from the individualizing modes of classification in population registration systems and special-purpose censuses designed to identify specific target populations. In the implementation of the Final Solution, for example, the former played only a small role, while the latter were crucial (Seltzer 1998).

24. See Strauss 2011.

25. Ignatiev and Garvey 1996; the quotations are from pp. 3, 4, and 10. The "race traitor" theme receives a sophisticated exploration in Mansbach's *Angry Black White Boy* (2005); see also the discussion of the novel in Davis 2014, 52–65.

26. As examples of other "texts of transraciality," Awkward cites John Howard Griffin's 1961 *Black Like Me,* reporting on his experiences traveling in the Deep South disguised as a black man; George Schuyler's satirical 1931 novel *Black No More,* premised on the discovery of a medical procedure that can turn blacks white; Melvin Van Peebles's 1970 film *Watermelon Man,* the story of a casually racist suburban white man who wakes up one morning to find himself transformed into a black man; and the 1986 film *Soul Man,* a comedy about a white man who darkens his skin to qualify for a Harvard Law School scholarship reserved for African Americans. To these might be added a number of more recent examples, including the 2006 reality TV show *Black.White,* which followed two families as they exchanged race, and a 2007 French show, *Dans le peau d'un noir,* that used the same device.

27. Awkward 1995, chap. 7; the quotations are from pp. 180 and 184.

28. See p. 95.

29. The skit can be viewed at http://www.nbc.com/saturday-night-live/video/white-like-me/n9308.

30. On progressive skepticism of "racial drag," see the blog post by Rachel S (2006).

31. Hollinger 2008, 1033–34; see also Hollinger 1995 and 2011.

32. Hollinger 2011, 175.

33. For nuanced critical discussions of post-racialism, see Bobo 2011 and P. C. Taylor 2014.

34. The 2013 figures are from Wang 2015; the earlier figures are from Kalmijn 1993, 130. Black intermarriage rates continue to be skewed by gender; only 12 percent of black women marrying in 2013 married across racial lines. The intermarriage rates of Latinos and Asians are about 50 percent higher than those of blacks (Wang 2012).

35. Newport 2013.

36. Hochschild, Weaver, and Burch 2012, chap. 5; the quotation is from pp. 115–16. While Hochschild and colleagues delineate the emergence of a "new racial order," they do not characterize it as "post-racial." See also Hochschild's (2015) comment on the "Ferguson moment." A comprehensive review of General Social Survey data over several decades by Bobo et al. (2012) traces a "sweeping fundamental change" in basic "racial principles" among white Americans, though it also documents stability or much less dramatic change in other dimensions of racial attitudes, including those pertaining to social distance (apart from intermarriage) and support for government policies to reduce racial inequalities (the quotations are from pp. 74 and 39). This review, I should note, does not endorse a post-racial perspective; it thoroughly documents the continued importance of race, even as it also documents dramatic change in certain types of racial attitudes.

37. Wilson's influential and controversial book *The Declining Significance of Race* (2012) was first published in 1980; see also Wilson 2011, 59–60. Nobody, of course, would look to the deeply racialized American criminal justice system for evidence to back up Wilson's thesis. Yet while the skewed *racial* composition of the incarcerated population has—for good reason—commanded wide public attention, the skewed *class* composition of that population has been largely ignored. As Loïc Wacquant has argued, the spectacular growth in incarceration has in fact been narrowly targeted not only by race but also by class and space, amounting to the "*hyper*incarceration of (sub)proletarian African-American men from the imploding ghetto" (2010, 74; emphasis in the original). Public attention has focused on the shockingly large racial discrepancies in incarceration rates, yet class differentials within racial categories are even larger than differentials between racial categories. See Pettit and Western 2004, 162, and Wacquant 2010, 79–80.

38. Waters and Kasinitz 2015, 117–18, 244–45.

39. There is a substantial literature on the increasing divergence of life chances among the black population, driven by the growth of a substantial black middle class and—at the other end of the spectrum—by the massive joblessness and hyper-incarceration of uneducated black men, and further complicated by the substantial (and largely middle-class) black immigration of recent decades from the Caribbean and Africa (Anderson 2015). When asked in 2007 which of two statements came closest to their views—"Blacks today can

no longer be thought of as a single race because the black community is so diverse" or "Blacks can still be thought of as a single race because they have so much in common"—a bare majority of African Americans (53 percent) chose the latter, while more than a third (37 percent) chose the former (Pew Research Center 2007, 4). Growing literatures also document the increasing heterogeneity and within-group inequality among Asians, Latinos, Native Americans, and whites. On the question of the "groupness" of racial and ethnic categories, see Brubaker 2004, especially chap. 1.

40. On the changing relation between categories of difference—including race, ethnicity, and gender—and patterns of inequality, see Brubaker 2015, chap. 1.

Conclusion

1. Wilchins 1997, 156. Wilchins's rules (or laws, as she called them) echo Harold Garfinkel's formulation of a considerably more elaborate set of rules in his pioneering study of the ways in which Agnes, a male-to-female transsexual, sought to manage and validate her status as a woman. Garfinkel intended these rules to characterize commonsense understandings of the "properties of 'natural, normally sexed persons' as cultural objects" (1967, 122).

2. "If men define situations as real, they are real in their consequences" (Thomas and Thomas 1928, 572).

3. For the emergence of this distinction, see Meyerowitz 2002, chap. 3.

4. There are, of course, dissenters from this view; see p. 166, n. 94.

5. Heyes 2009, 144. I build on Heyes's insightful discussion but develop it in a somewhat different direction.

6. Heyes 2009, 144–45.

7. Heyes 2009, 144.

8. Nelson 2008, 763.

9. The performative turn in the humanities has drawn heavily on Judith Butler and poststructuralist theory; the performative turn in the social sciences draws its inspiration primarily from other sources, including Erving Goffman, Victor Turner, and ethnomethodology as well as the practice theory associated with Pierre Bourdieu and others (Giesen 2006, 325–26; Morris 1995, 571ff.).

10. For a review of the performative turn in the study of gender, see Morris 1995. For the extension of the performative turn to the study of race and ethnicity, see West and Fenstermaker 1995, arguing that "doing gender" as a situated practical accomplishment (West and Zimmerman 1987) could be generalized to "doing difference"; Mirón and Inda 2000, applying Butler (and more indirectly Austin, Derrida, and Foucault) to the understanding of race as "a kind of speech act"; Warren 2001, analyzing the performative dimension of race in the classroom; Rottenberg 2003, criticizing Mirón and Inda for simply "transposing" Butler; and, more recently, Ehlers 2012 and Clammer 2015.

11. For a review of the evidence on the hypothesis that African American students who excel in school are socially penalized for "acting white," see Wildhagen 2008, chap. 2.

12. See Michaels 1992 and 1997.

13. For example, black power activists in the 1960s distinguished on performative grounds between "Negro" and "Black." In their view, "'Negroes' did not think and act like true black people. The presumption was that 'Negroes' wanted to be white or were controlled by whites and therefore they were not truly black. They were 'white' black people. One of the goals of Black Power was to coerce 'Negroes' into being 'Black.' . . . The Black Power movement shows clearly that blackness can be conceptualized as something that one does or that one can fail to do. . . . [It shows that] race is not only socially assigned . . . but it can also be achieved or not achieved by an individual's behavior" (Austin 2006, 60).

14. For the pressures on minority employees to "act white" in employment contexts, see Carbado and Gulati 2013. For a broader discussion of pressures to "cover"—to "tone down a disfavored identity to fit into the mainstream"—in the domains of sexual orientation, race, and gender, see Yoshino 2002 and 2006 (the former is a lengthy law review article, the latter a book written for a broad audience; the definition is from the latter, p. ix).

15. "Acting black" is explored in depth in Mansbach's *Angry Black White Boy*.

16. On the policing of ethnic and national identities, see Brubaker et al. 2006, 229ff. On the dynamics of policing within minority and especially marginal populations, focusing on marginal elites' efforts to monitor and prevent the assimilation of non-elites, see Laitin 1995, 39–41. On queer theory as a resource for analyzing—and resisting—pressures to conform to racial "scripts," see Ford 2007.

17. Wald 2000, 6; Garber 1992, 17. Garber defines a "category crisis" as "a failure of definitional distinction, a borderline that becomes permeable, that permits border-crossings from one (apparently distinct) category to another" (1992, 16). Expanding on this notion in another context, she observes that "what seems like a binary opposition, a clear choice between opposites that define cultural boundaries, is revealed to be not only a construct but also—more disturbingly—a construct that no longer works to contain and limit meaning" (1996, xiv).

18. See for example Ginsberg 1996; Sánchez and Schlossberg 2001; and Pfeiffer 2003.

19. Dreisinger (2008, 121) notes the surprising "upsurge in racial passing narratives," as does Nerad (2014, 12–14).

20. Nerad 2014, 14.

21. Nerad 2014, 9.

22. See Jenkins 2008, chap. 5, and 2014.

23. The interaction between new categories and the people subsumed under them leads Hacking to describe his position as "dynamic nominalism" (Hacking 1986, 228f). The quotations in the text are from pp. 223 and 229; see also the related arguments in Hacking 1995 and 2006b.

24. Nietzsche's aphorism (from *The Gay Science*, aphorism #58, as translated by Walter Kaufmann; emphasis in the original) is quoted, in a different translation, by Hacking (2006b), who notes its pertinence to his own argument

about "making up people," though Hacking does not address the transgender phenomenon. Nietzsche's amplification of his aphorism is equally pertinent to the transgender experience: "The reputation, name, and appearance, the usual measure and weight of a thing, what it counts for—originally almost always wrong and arbitrary, thrown over things like a dress and altogether foreign to their nature and even to their skin—all this grows from generation unto generation, merely because people believe in it, until it gradually grows to be part of that thing and turns into its very body."

25. Fernandez and Blinder 2015; Dart 2015. The ad can be viewed at https://www.youtube.com/watch?v=WYpko86x6GU.

26. As this book goes to press, the matter is radically unsettled, and school districts nationwide face a great deal of uncertainty as they try to navigate between the threat of being held in violation of Title IX (and of losing federal funding) and pressures from parents, churches, and conservative groups—all under the harsh glare of publicity. See Blinder, Pérez-Peña, and Lichtblau 2016; Schuck 2016; U.S. Departments of Education and Justice 2016; U.S. District Court 2016.

27. Schilt and Westbrook 2015.

28. There are no comparably intense controversies over transgender access to men's colleges, men's sports teams, and men's bathrooms. Racially or ethnically segregated dorms are controversial, but controversy does not turn on who can access such spaces; it turns on whether separate living facilities are desirable.

29. On the persisting strength of racial essentialism, see Morning 2011, 221–48.

30. For the claim that race is a domain of its own, see Bonilla-Silva 1997 and Winant 2000. For the argument that race and ethnicity are best treated as part of a single integrated domain of phenomena, see Brubaker 2009 and Wimmer 2013.

Bibliography

Aizura, Aren Z. 2012. "The Persistence of Transgender Travel Narratives." In *Transgender Migrations: The Bodies, Borders, and Politics of Transition*, edited by Trystan T. Cotten, 139–56. New York: Routledge.

Alcoff, Linda. 1988. "Cultural Feminism versus Post-Structuralism: The Identity Crisis in Feminist Theory." *Signs* 13, no. 3: 405–36.

Alexander, Jeffrey C. 1995. "Modern, Anti, Post, Neo." *New Left Review* 210: 63–101.

Allen, Amy. 1998. "Power Trouble: Performativity as Critical Theory." *Constellations* 5, no. 4: 456–71.

Allen, Samantha. 2015. "Dolezal's Damaging 'Transracial' Game." *Daily Beast*, June 16. http://www.thedailybeast.com/articles/2015/06/16/dolezal-s-damaging-transracial-game.html.

Ambrosino, Brandon. 2014a. "I Wasn't Born This Way. I Choose to Be Gay." *New Republic*, January 28. http://www.newrepublic.com/article/116378/macklemores-same-love-sends-wrong-message-about-being-gay.

———. 2014b. "What My Angry Critics Get Wrong about My Choice to Be Gay." *New Republic*, February 6.

http://www.newrepublic.com/article/116517/what-my
-angry-critics-get-wrong-about-my-choice-be-gay.

American Psychological Association Task Force. 2009.
"Report of the American Psychological Association
Task Force on Appropriate Therapeutic Responses
to Sexual Orientation." https://www.apa.org/pi/lgbt/
resources/therapeutic-response.pdf.

Anderson, Monica. 2015. "A Rising Share of the U.S. Black
Population Is Foreign Born." Pew Research Center, April 9.
http://www.pewsocialtrends.org/2015/04/09/a-rising
-share-of-the-u-s-black-population-is-foreign-born/.

Appiah, Kwame Anthony. 1996. "Race, Culture, Identity:
Misunderstood Connections." In *Color Conscious: The
Political Morality of Race*, by Kwame Anthony Appiah
and Amy Gutmann, 30–105. Princeton, NJ: Princeton
University Press.

Archer, Jaclyn, and Zoe Colburn. 2015. "Black Lives Matter
Teach-In Sheds Light on Racial Injustice." *Easterner*,
January 26. http://easterneronline.com/34931/eagle-life
/black-lives-matter-teach-in-sheds-light-on-racial-injustice/.

Austin, Algernon. 2006. *Achieving Blackness: Race, Black
Nationalism, and Afrocentrism in the Twentieth Century*.
New York: New York University Press.

Awkward, Michael. 1995. *Negotiating Difference: Race,
Gender, and the Politics of Positionality*. Chicago: University of Chicago Press.

Baron, Dennis. 2010. "The Gender-Neutral Pronoun: After
150 Years Still an Epic Fail." *The Web of Language* (blog),
August 2. https://illinois.edu/blog/view/25/31097.

Barth, Fredrik. 1969. Introduction to *Ethnic Groups and
Boundaries: The Social Organization of Culture Difference*,
edited by Fredrik Barth, 9–38. Boston: Little, Brown.

Bartholet, Elizabeth. 1991. "Where Do Black Children
Belong? The Politics of Race Matching in Adoption."

University of Pennsylvania Law Review 139, no. 5: 1163–1256.

Beck, Ulrich, and Elisabeth Beck-Gernsheim. 2002. *Individualization: Institutionalized Individualism and Its Social and Political Consequences*. London: SAGE.

Bellah, Robert N., Ann Swidler, Richard Madsen, Steven M. Tipton, and William M. Sullivan. 1985. *Habits of the Heart: Individualism and Commitment in American Life*. Berkeley: University of California Press.

Bem, Sandra L. 1995. "Dismantling Gender Polarization and Compulsory Heterosexuality: Should We Turn the Volume Down or Up?" *Journal of Sex Research* 32, no. 4: 329–34.

Bennett, Jessica. "She? Ze? They? What's in a Gender Pronoun." *New York Times*, January 30. http://www.nytimes.com/2016/01/31/fashion/pronoun-confusion-sexual-fluidity.html.

Bettcher, Talia Mae. 2007. "Evil Deceivers and Make-Believers." *Hypatia* 22, no. 3: 43–65.

———. 2014a. "Trapped in the Wrong Theory: Rethinking Trans Oppression and Resistance." *Signs* 39, no. 2: 383–406.

———. 2014b. "Feminist Perspectives on Trans Issues." In *The Stanford Encyclopedia of Philosophy*, edited by Edward N. Zalta. http://plato.stanford.edu/archives/spr2014/entries/feminism-trans/.

Beyer, Dana. 2015. "Moving On: 'FTLOG, Caitlyn Jenner Is Not Pretending to Be a Woman.'" *Huffington Post*, June 13. http://www.huffingtonpost.com/dana-beyer/moving-on----ftlog-caitly_b_7575558.html.

Blay, Zeba. 2015. "Why Comparing Rachel Dolezal to Caitlyn Jenner Is Detrimental to Both Trans and Racial Progress." *Huffington Post*, June 12. http://www.huffingtonpost.com/2015/06/12/rachel-dolezal-caitlyn-jenner_n_7569160.html?ncid=fcbklnkushpmg00000047.

Blinder, Alan, Richard Pérez-Peña, and Eric Lichtblau.
2016. "Countersuits over North Carolina's Bias Law."
New York Times, May 9. www.nytimes.com/2016/05/10
/us/north-carolina-governor-sues-justice-department
-over-bias-law.html?_r=0.

Blommaert, Jan, and Ben Rampton. 2011. "Language and
Superdiversity." *Diversities* 13, no. 2: 1–21.

Bobo, Lawrence D. 2011. "Somewhere between Jim
Crow and Post-Racialism: Reflections on the Racial
Divide in America Today." *Daedalus* 140, no. 2: 11–36.

Bobo, Lawrence D., Camille Z. Charles, Maria Krysan, and
Alicia D. Simmons. 2012. "The *Real* Record on Racial
Attitudes." In *Social Trends in American Life: Findings from
the General Social Survey since 1972*, edited by Peter
Marsden, 38–83. Princeton, NJ: Princeton University Press.

Bolin, Anne. 1994. "Transcending and Transgendering:
Male-to-Female Transsexuals, Dichotomy, and Diversity."
In *Third Sex, Third Gender: Beyond Sexual Dimorphism in
Culture and History*, edited by Gilbert Herdt, 447–85.
New York: Zone Books.

Bonilla-Silva, Eduardo. 1997. "Rethinking Racism: Toward
a Structural Interpretation." *American Sociological Review*
62, no. 3: 465–80.

Bornstein, Kate. 1994. *Gender Outlaw: On Men, Women, and
the Rest of Us*. New York: Routledge.

Boswell, Holly. 1997. "The Transgender Paradigm Shift
towards Free Expression." In *Gender Blending*, edited by
Bonnie Bullough, Vern L. Bullough, and James Elias,
53–57. Amherst, NY: Prometheus Books.

Bowker, Geoffrey C., and Susan L. Star. 1999. *Sortings
Things Out: Classification and Its Consequences*. Cambridge, MA: MIT Press.

Bourdieu, Pierre. 2001. *Masculine Domination*. Translated
by Richard Nice. Cambridge: Polity.

Braman, Donald. 1998. "Of Race and Immutability." *University of California Los Angeles Law Review* 46: 1375.

Brown, Kara. 2015. "Rachel Dolezal Definitely Nailed the Hair, I'll Give Her That." *Jezebel*, June 12. http://jezebel .com/rachel-dolezal-definitely-nailed-the-hair-ill-give-her -1710899988.

Brown, Michael. 2015. "If You Can Be Transgender, Why Can't You Be Transracial?" *Charisma Podcast Network*, June 15. http://www.charismanews.com/opinion/in-the -line-of-fire/50078-if-you-can-be-transgender-why-can-t -you-be-transracial.

Brubaker, Rogers. 2004. *Ethnicity without Groups*. Cambridge, MA: Harvard University Press.

———. 2009. "Ethnicity, Race, and Nationalism." *Annual Review of Sociology* 35, no. 1: 21–42.

———. 2015. *Grounds for Difference*. Cambridge, MA: Harvard University Press.

Brubaker, Rogers, Margit Feischmidt, Jon Fox, and Liana Grancea. 2006. *Nationalist Politics and Everyday Ethnicity in a Transylvanian Town*. Princeton, NJ: Princeton University Press.

Budgeon, Shelley. 2015. "Individualized Femininity and Feminist Politics of Choice." *European Journal of Women's Studies* 22: 303–18.

Bullough, Vern L., and Bonnie Bullough. 1993. *Cross Dressing, Sex, and Gender*. Philadelphia: University of Pennsylvania Press.

Burke, Peter. 2009. *Cultural Hybridity*. Cambridge: Polity.

Burkett, Elinor. 2015. "What Makes a Woman?" *New York Times*, June 6. http://www.nytimes.com/2015/06/07 /opinion/sunday/what-makes-a-woman.html.

Butler, Judith. 1990. *Gender Trouble: Feminism and the Subversion of Identity*. New York: Routledge.

Calhoun, Craig J. 1994. "Social Theory and the Politics of Identity." In *Social Theory and the Politics of Identity*, edited by Craig J. Calhoun, 9–36. Oxford: Blackwell.

Carbado, Devon W., and Mitu Gulati. 2013. *Acting White? Rethinking Race in "Post-Racial" America*. Oxford: Oxford University Press.

Chandra, Kanchan, ed. 2012. *Constructivist Theories of Ethnic Politics*. New York: Oxford University Press.

Chen, Jim. 1997. "Embryonic Thoughts on Racial Identity as New Property." *University of Colorado Law Review* 68: 1123–63.

Childs, Mary. 2001. "Sexual Autonomy and Law." *Modern Law Review* 64, no. 2: 309–23.

Chokal-Ingam, Vijay. 2015. "Why I Faked Being Black for Med School." *New York Post*, April 12. http://nypost.com /2015/04/12/mindy-kalings-brother-explains-why-he -pretended-to-be-black/.

Clammer, John. 2015. "Performing Ethnicity: Performance, Gender, Body and Belief in the Construction and Signalling of Identity." *Ethnic and Racial Studies* 38, no. 13: 2159–66.

Clark-Flory, Tracy. 2015. "Detransitioning: Going from Male to Female to Male Again." *Vocativ*, June 15. http:// www.vocativ.com/culture/lgbt/detransitioning-male -female-male-again/.

Coates, Ta-Nehisi. 2015. *Between the World and Me*. New York: Spiegel & Grau.

Cobb, Jelani. 2015. "Murders in Charleston." *New Yorker*, June 18. http://www.newyorker.com/news/news-desk /church-shooting-charleston-south-carolina.

Connell, Catherine. 2010. "Doing, Undoing, or Redoing Gender? Learning from the Workplace Experiences of Transpeople." *Gender & Society* 24, no. 1: 31–55.

Cooke, Charles C. W. 2015. "Should Self-Identification Trump Objective Truth?" *National Review*, June 12. http://www.nationalreview.com/article/419698/woman-who-insists-shes-african-american-isnt-charles-c-w-cooke.

Cornell, Stephen E., and Douglas Hartmann. 1998. *Ethnicity and Race: Making Identities in a Changing World*. Thousand Oaks, CA: Pine Forge Press.

Crenshaw, Kimberle. 1989. "Demarginalizing the Intersection of Race and Sex: A Black Feminist Critique of Antidiscrimination Doctrine, Feminist Theory and Antiracist Politics." *University of Chicago Legal Forum*, no. 1, article 8, 139–67.

Crook, Scott. 2015. "The Problem with 'Self-Identifying' (A Gospel Response to Bruce Jenner and Rachel Dolezal)." *Cross of Grace*, June 17. http://crossgrace.org/christian-life/problem-self-identifying-gospel-response-bruce-jenner-rachael-dolezal/.

Crowder, Steven. 2015. "Actually, 'Trans-racial' Is Much More Reasonable Than 'Transgender' . . ." *Louder with Crowder* (blog), June 16. http://louderwithcrowder.com/actually-trans-racial-is-much-more-reasonable-than-transgender/.

Currah, Paisley. 2002. "The Transgender Rights Imaginary." *Georgetown Journal of Gender and the Law* 4: 705–20.

———. 2008. "Expecting Bodies: The Pregnant Man and Transgender Exclusion from the Employment Non-Discrimination Act." *WSQ: Women's Studies Quarterly* 36, no. 3: 330–36.

Currah, Paisley, Richard M. Juang, and Shannon Price Minter, eds. 2006. *Transgender Rights*. Minneapolis: University of Minnesota Press.

Currah, Paisley, and Shannon Minter. 2000. "Unprincipled Exclusions: The Struggle to Achieve Judicial and Legislative Equality for Transgender People." *William & Mary Journal of Women and the Law* 7, no. 1: 37–66.

Currah, Paisley, and Lisa Jean Moore. 2009. "'We Won't Know Who You Are': Contesting Sex Designations in New York City Birth Certificates." *Hypatia* 24, no. 3: 113–35.

Daniel, G. Reginald. 2002. *More Than Black? Multiracial Identity and the New Racial Order*. Philadelphia: Temple University Press.

Dart, Tom. 2015. "'Bathroom Predator' Spin on Houston Equal Rights Bill Puts Texans in Hot Seat." *The Guardian*, October 25. http://www.theguardian.com/us-news/2015/oct/25/hero-campaign-texas-equal-rights-ordinance-houston.

Davidson, Robert J. 2009. "DSD Debates: Social Movement Organizations' Framing Disputes Surrounding the Term 'Disorder of Sex Development.'" *Liminalis: Journal for Sex/Gender Emancipation and Resistance* 3: 60–80.

Davis, F. James. 1991. *Who Is Black? One Nation's Definition*. University Park: Pennsylvania State University Press.

Davis, Jenny L. 2012. "Narrative Construction of a Ruptured Self: Stories of Transability on Transabled.org." *Sociological Perspectives* 55, no. 2: 319–40.

Davis, Kimberly Chabot. 2014. *Beyond the White Negro: Empathy and Anti-Racist Reading*. Chicago: University of Illinois Press.

Deloria, Philip Joseph. 1998. *Playing Indian*. New Haven, CT: Yale University Press.

Devor, Holly. 1987. "Gender Blending Females: Women and Sometimes Men." *American Behavioral Scientist* 31, no. 1: 12–40.

De Zwart, Frank. 2012. "Pitfalls of Top-down Identity Designation: Ethno-Statistics in the Netherlands." *Comparative European Politics* 10, no. 3: 301–18.

Disenchanted Scholar. 2014. "The Next Trans: Transracial and Transethnic." *Philosophies of a Disenchanted Scholar* (blog), August 6. https://disenchantedscholar.wordpress.com/2014/08/06/the-next-trans-transracial-and-transethnic/.

Domínguez, Virginia R. 1986. *White by Definition: Social Classification in Creole Louisiana*. New Brunswick, NJ: Rutgers University Press.

Drake, St. Clair, and Horace R. Cayton. 1993. *Black Metropolis: A Study of Negro Life in a Northern City*. Rev. and enl. ed. (Orig. pub. 1945.) Chicago: University of Chicago Press.

Dreger, Alice. 2013. "Pink Boys: What's the Best Way to Raise Children Who Might Have Gender Identity Issues?" *Pacific Standard*, July 18. http://www.psmag.com/books-and-culture/pink-boys-gender-identity-disorder-62782.

———. 2015a. "The Big Problem with Outlawing Gender Conversion Therapies." *Wired*, June 4. http://www.wired.com/2015/06/big-problem-outlawing-gender-conversion-therapies/.

———. 2015b. "Gender Mad." *Alice Domurat Dreger* (blog), December 19. http://alicedreger.com/gendermad.

Dreisinger, Baz. 2008. *Near Black: White-to-Black Passing in American Culture*. Amherst: University of Massachusetts Press.

Duggan, Lisa. 2002. "The New Homonormativity: The Sexual Politics of Neoliberalism." In *Materializing Democracy: Toward a Revitalized Cultural Politics*, edited by Russ Castronovo and Dana D. Nelson, 175–94. Durham, NC: Duke University Press.

Edgerton, M. T. 1984. "The Role of Surgery in the Treatment of Transsexualism." *Annals of Plastic Surgery* 13, no. 6: 473–76.

Ehlers, Nadine. 2012. *Racial Imperatives: Discipline, Performativity, and Struggles against Subjection*. Bloomington: Indiana University Press.

Ekins, Richard. 1997. *Male Femaling: A Grounded Theory Approach to Cross-Dressing and Sex-Changing*. London: Routledge.

Ekins, Richard, and Dave King. 2005a. Introduction. *International Journal of Transgenderism* 8, no. 4: 1–4.

———. 2005b. "Virginia Prince: Transgender Pioneer." *International Journal of Transgenderism* 8, no. 4: 5–15.

———. 2006. *The Transgender Phenomenon*. London: SAGE.

Elan-Cane, Christie. 2000. "The Fallacy of the Myth of Gender." Paper presented at the Sixth International Gender Dysphoria Conference, Manchester, England. http://www.gender.org.uk/conf/2000/elancane.htm.

Elliott, Anthony. 2013. "The Theory of New Individualism." In *Subjectivity in the Twenty-First Century*, edited by Romin W. Tafarodi, 190–209. New York: Cambridge University Press.

Elliott, Carl. 2000. "A New Way to Be Mad." *The Atlantic*, December. http://www.theatlantic.com/magazine/archive/2000/12/a-new-way-to-be-mad/304671/.

Elliott, Tracey. 2009. "Body Dysmorphic Disorder, Radical Surgery and the Limits of Consent." *Medical Law Review* 17, no. 2: 149–82.

Epstein, Steven. 1999. "Gay and Lesbian Movements in the United States: Dilemmas of Identity, Diversity and Political Strategy." In *The Global Emergence of Gay and Lesbian Politics*, edited by Barry D. Adam, Jan W. Duyvendak, and André Krouwel, 30–91. Philadelphia: Temple University Press.

———. 2003. "Sexualizing Governance and Medicalizing Identities: The Emergence of 'State-Centered' LGBT

Health Politics in the United States." *Sexualities* 6, no. 3: 131–71.

———. 2007. *Inclusion: The Politics of Difference in Medical Research*. Chicago: University of Chicago Press.

Facebook. 2014. "When you come to Facebook . . ." *Facebook Diversity*, February 13. https://www.facebook.com /photo.php?fbid=567587973337709&set=a.19686571374 3272.42938.105225179573993&type=1.

———. 2015. "Last year we were proud . . ." *Facebook Diversity*, February 26. https://www.facebook.com/face bookdiversity/posts/774221582674346.

Fang, Jenn. 2015. "Race, Transracialization, and Other Thoughts on Rachel Dolezal." *Reappropriate* (blog), June 16. http://reappropriate.co/2015/06/race-trans racialization-and-other-thoughts-on-rachel-dolezal/.

Fanshawe, Simon, and Dhananjayan Sriskandarajah. 2010. " 'You Can't Put Me in a Box': Super-Diversity and the End of Identity Politics in Britain." Institute for Public Policy Research. http://www.ippr.org/assets/media /images/media/files/publication/2011/05/you_cant_put _me_in_a_box_1749.pdf.

Fausto-Sterling, Anne. 2000. *Sexing the Body: Gender Politics and the Construction of Sexuality.* New York: Basic Books.

———. 2012. *Sex/gender: Biology in a Social World*. New York: Routledge.

Feinberg, Leslie. 1998. *Trans Liberation: Beyond Pink or Blue*. Boston: Beacon Press.

Ferguson, Michaele L. 2010. "Choice Feminism and the Fear of Politics." *Perspectives on Politics* 8, no. 1: 247–53.

Fernandez, Manny, and Alan Blinder. 2015. "Opponents of Houston Rights Measure Focused on Bathrooms, and Won." *New York Times*, November 4. http://www.nytimes .com/2015/11/05/us/houston-anti-discrimination-bath room-ordinance.html.

Fischler, David. 2015. "Rachel Dolezal, Bruce Jenner, and the End of Reality." *Stand Firm*, June 16. http://www.standfirminfaith.com/?/sf/page/31877.

Fitzgerald, Kathleen J. 2007. *Beyond White Ethnicity: Developing a Sociological Understanding of Native American Identity Reclamation*. Lanham, MD: Lexington Books.

Flaherty, Colleen. 2015. "Preventing Ethnic Fraud." *Inside Higher Ed*, September 22. https://www.insidehighered.com/news/2015/09/22/how-might-colleges-and-universities-best-prevent-ethnic-fraud-faculty-hires#.VgF0TBZS5R0.facebook.

Ford, Christopher A. 1994. "Administering Identity: The Determination of 'Race' in Race-Conscious Law." *California Law Review* 82, no. 5: 1231–85.

Ford, Richard T. 2005. *Racial Culture: A Critique*. Princeton, NJ: Princeton University Press.

———. 2007. "What's Queer about Race?" *South Atlantic Quarterly* 106, no. 3: 477–84.

Ford, Zack. 2015. "New York Times Op-Ed Encourages People to Be 'Skeptical' of Trans Identities." *ThinkProgress*, August 24. http://thinkprogress.org/lgbt/2015/08/24/3694486/transgender-kids-health-myths/.

Frank, David John, Bayliss J. Camp, and Steven A. Boutcher. 2010. "Worldwide Trends in the Criminal Regulation of Sex, 1945 to 2005." *American Sociological Review* 75, no. 6: 867–93.

Franklin, Imani. 2013. "Living in a Barbie World." Senior honors thesis, Stanford University. https://fsi.fsi.stanford.edu/sites/default/files/Imani_Franklin.pdf.

Friedman, Richard A. 2015. "How Changeable Is Gender?" *New York Times*, August 22. http://www.nytimes.com/2015/08/23/opinion/sunday/richard-a-friedman-how-changeable-is-gender.html.

Garber, Marjorie B. 1992. *Vested Interests: Cross Dressing and Cultural Anxiety*. New York: Routledge.

———. 1996. Foreword to Catalina de Erauso, *Lieutenant Nun: Memoir of a Basque Transvestite in the New World*. Boston: Beacon Press.

Gardiner, Judith Kegan. 2012. "Female Masculinity and Phallic Women—Unruly Concepts." *Feminist Studies* 38, no. 3: 584–611.

Garfinkel, Harold. 1967. *Studies in Ethnomethodology*. Englewood Cliffs, NJ: Prentice-Hall.

Gehi, Pooja S., and Gabriel Arkles. 2007. "Unraveling Injustice: Race and Class Impact of Medicaid Exclusions of Transition-Related Health Care for Transgender People." *Sexuality Research and Social Policy* 4, no. 4: 7–35.

Giddens, Anthony. 1991. *Modernity and Self-Identity: Self and Society in the Late Modern Age*. Stanford, CA: Stanford University Press.

Gieryn, Thomas F. 1983. "Boundary-Work and the Demarcation of Science from Non-Science: Strains and Interests in Professional Ideologies of Scientists." *American Sociological Review* 48, no. 6: 781–95.

Giesen, Bernhard. 2006. "Performing the Sacred: A Durkheimian Perspective on the Performative Turn in the Social Sciences." In *Social Performance: Symbolic Action, Cultural Pragmatics, and Ritual*, edited by Jeffrey C. Alexander, Bernhard Giesen, and Jason L. Mast, 325–67. Cambridge: Cambridge University Press.

Gilroy, Paul. 2000. *Against Race: Imagining Political Culture beyond the Color Line*. Cambridge, MA: Belknap Press of Harvard University Press.

Ginsberg, Elaine K., ed. 1996. *Passing and the Fictions of Identity*. Durham, NC: Duke University Press.

Glenn, Evelyn Nakano. 2008. "Yearning For Lightness: Transnational Circuits in the Marketing and

Consumption of Skin Lighteners." *Gender & Society* 22, no. 3: 281–302.

Goldberg, Michelle. 2014. "What Is a Woman?" *New Yorker*, August 4.

Goldstein, Jessica. 2014. "The Facts and Fiction of Racial Reassignment Surgery." *ThinkProgress*, August 21. http://thinkprogress.org/culture/2014/08/21/3473996/facts-and-fiction-racial-reassignment-surgery-novelist/.

Goldstein, Joshua, and Morning, Ann. 2002. "Back in the Box: The Dilemma of Using Multiple-Race Data for Single-Race Laws." In *The New Race Question: How the Census Counts Multiracial Individuals*, edited by Joel Perlmann and Mary C. Waters, 119–36. New York: Russell Sage Foundation and Levy Economics Institute.

Green, Amber Robinson. 2009. "White Skins, Black Cultural Identities: Examining the Emergence of Black Cultural Identity in the White Person." PsyD dissertation, Alliant International University, San Francisco. http://gradworks.umi.com/33/58/3358399.html.

Green, Eli R. 2006. "Debating Trans Inclusion in the Feminist Movement: A Trans-Positive Analysis." *Journal of Lesbian Studies* 10, nos. 1–2: 231–48.

Green, Kai M. 2015. "'Race and Gender Are Not the Same!' Is Not a Good Response to the 'Transracial'/Transgender Question, *or* We Can and Must Do Better." *The Feminist Wire*, June 14. http://www.thefeministwire.com/2015/06/race-and-gender-are-not-the-same-is-not-a-good-response-to-the-transracial-transgender-question-or-we-can-and-must-do-better/.

Greenwell, Andrew. 2013. "Oh Gender, Thy Name is Legion: The Dangers of the Gender Identity Movement." *Catholic Online*, July 27. http://www.catholic.org/news/hf/family/story.php?id=51873.

Griffin, John Howard. 1961. *Black Like Me*. Boston: Houghton Mifflin.

Gubar, Susan. 1997. *Racechanges: White Skin, Black Face in American Culture*. New York: Oxford University Press.

Guinier, Lani, and Gerald Torres. 2002. *The Miner's Canary: Enlisting Race, Resisting Power, Transforming Democracy*. Cambridge, MA: Harvard University Press.

Gullickson, Aaron, and Ann Morning. 2011. "Choosing Race: Multiracial Ancestry and Identification." *Social Science Research* 40, no. 2: 498–512.

Guthrie, Savannah. 2015. "Rachel Dolezal: 'Nothing about Being White Describes Who I Am.'" NBC News, June 16. http://www.nbcnews.com/nightly-news/video/rachel -dolezal-nothing-about-being-white-describes-who-i-am -465644099755.

Hacking, Ian. 1986. "Making Up People." In *Reconstructing Individualism: Autonomy, Individuality, and the Self in Western Thought*, edited by Thomas C. Heller and Christine Brooke-Rose, 222–36. Stanford, CA: Stanford University Press.

———. 1995. "The Looping Effects of Human Kinds." In *Causal Cognition: A Multidisciplinary Debate*, edited by Dan Sperber, David Premack, and Ann J. Premack, 351–94. Oxford: Clarendon.

———. 2006a. "Genetics, Biosocial Groups and the Future of Identity." *Daedalus* 135: 81–95.

———. 2006b. "Making Up People." *London Review of Books*, August 17.

———. 2009. "Humans, Aliens and Autism." *Daedalus* 138, no. 3: 44–59.

Halberstam, Jack. 1994. "F2M: The Making of Female Masculinity." In *The Lesbian Postmodern*, edited by Laura Doan, 210–29. New York: Columbia University Press.

Halberstam, Judith. 1998a. *Female Masculinity*. Durham, NC: Duke University Press.

———. 1998b. "Transgender Butch." *GLQ: A Journal of Lesbian and Gay Studies* 4, no. 2: 287–310.

Halperin, David M. 2012. *How to Be Gay*. Cambridge, MA: Belknap Press of Harvard University Press.

Hannerz, Ulf. 1987. "The World in Creolization." *Africa* 57: 546–59.

Harmon, Amy. 2006. "Seeking Ancestry in DNA Ties Uncovered by Tests." *New York Times*, April 12. http://www.nytimes.com/2006/04/12/us/12genes.html.

Harris, Cheryl I. 1993. "Whiteness as Property." *Harvard Law Review* 106, no. 8: 1707–91.

Harris, David R., and Jeremiah Joseph Sim. 2002. "Who Is Multiracial? Assessing the Complexity of Lived Race." *American Sociological Review* 67, no. 4: 614–27.

Herbst, Diane. 2015. "Inside Story: How Rachel Dolezal's Cover as a Black Woman Was Blown." *People*, June 20. http://www.people.com/article/rachel-dolezal-black-woman-cover-blown-hate-crimes.

Heyes, Cressida J. 2003. "Feminist Solidarity after Queer Theory: The Case of Transgender." *Signs* 28, no. 4: 1093–1120.

———. 2009. "Changing Race, Changing Sex: The Ethics of Self-Transformation." In *"You've Changed": Sex Reassignment and Personal Identity*, edited by Laurie J. Shrage, 135–54. Oxford: Oxford University Press.

Hickman, Christine B. 1997. "The Devil and the One Drop Rule: Racial Categories, African Americans, and the U.S. Census." *Michigan Law Review* 95, no. 5: 1161–1265.

High Court of Australia. 2014. "NSW Registrar of Births, Deaths and Marriages v Norrie." http://www.hcourt.gov.au/assets/publications/judgment-summaries/2014/hca-11-2014-04-02.pdf (summary); http://eresources.hcourt.gov.au/downloadPdf/2014/HCA/11 (full judgment).

Hirschman, Elizabeth C., and Donald Panther-Yates. 2008. "Peering Inward for Ethnic Identity: Consumer Interpretation of DNA Test Results." *Identity: An International Journal of Theory and Research* 8: 47–66.

Hobbs, Allyson Vanessa. 2014. *A Chosen Exile: A History of Racial Passing in American Life*. Cambridge, MA: Harvard University Press.

Hochschild, Jennifer. 2015. "What Does Obama's Election Tell Us about 'The Ferguson Moment'?" http://furman center.org/research/iri/essay/what-does-obamas-election-tell-us-about-the-ferguson-moment.

Hochschild, Jennifer, and Brenna Powell. 2008. "Racial Reorganization and the United States Census 1850–1930: Mulattoes, Half-Breeds, Mixed Parentage, Hindoos, and the Mexican Race." *Studies in American Political Development* 22, no. 1: 59–96.

Hochschild, Jennifer L., Vesla M. Weaver, and Traci R. Burch. 2012. *Creating a New Racial Order: How Immigration, Multiracialism, Genomics, and the Young Can Remake Race in America*. Princeton, NJ: Princeton University Press.

Hodes, Martha. 2003. "The Mercurial Nature and Abiding Power of Race: A Transnational Family Story." *American Historical Review* 108, no. 1: 84–118.

Hoh, Amanda. 2014. "Brazilian Man Undergoes Surgery to Look Asian." *Sydney Morning Herald*, June 2. http://www.smh.com.au/lifestyle/brazilian-man-undergoes-surgery-to-look-asian-20140602-zrv8n.html.

Hollinger, David A. 1995. *Postethnic America: Beyond Multiculturalism*. New York: Basic Books.

———. 2008. "Obama, the Instability of Color Lines, and the Promise of a Postethnic Future." *Callaloo* 31, no. 4: 1033–37.

———. 2011. "The Concept of Post-Racial: How Its Easy Dismissal Obscures Important Questions." *Daedalus* 140, no. 1: 174–82.

Holmes, Jasmine. 2015. "We Long to Belong." *Desiring God*, June 12. http://www.desiringgod.org/articles/we-long -to-belong.

Hood-Williams, John. 1996. "Goodbye to Sex and Gender." *Sociological Review* 44, no. 1: 1–16.

hooks, bell. 1992. "Eating the Other: Desire and Resistance." In *Black Looks: Race and Representation*, by bell hooks, 21–39. Boston: South End Press.

Howe, Ruth-Arlene. 1995. "Redefining the Transracial Adoption Controversy." *Duke Journal of Gender Law & Policy* 2, no. 1: 131–64.

Hoyt, Carlos A., Jr. 2016. *The Arc of a Bad Idea*. New York: Oxford University Press.

Hubbard, Dolan. 2003. Review of *Crossing the Line: Racial Passing in Twentieth-Century US Literature and Culture*. *MFS: Modern Fiction Studies* 49, no. 4: 838–40.

Hughes, I. A., C. Houk, S. F. Ahmed, and P. A. Lee. 2006. "Consensus Statement on Management of Intersex Disorders." *Journal of Pediatric Urology* 2, no. 3: 148–62.

Humphrey, Jeff. 2015. "How the Coeur d'Alene Press Broke the Rachel Dolezal Story." *KXLY.com*, June 15. http://www.kxly.com/news/north-idaho-news/how -the-coeur-dalene-press-broke-the-dolezal-story /33598298.

Hunter, Margaret. 2007. "The Persistent Problem of Color-ism: Skin Tone, Status, and Inequality." *Sociology Compass* 1, no. 1: 237–54.

———. 2011. "Buying Racial Capital: Skin-Bleaching and Cosmetic Surgery in a Globalized World." *Journal of Pan African Studies* 4, no. 4: 142–64.

Ignatiev, Noel. 1995. *How the Irish Became White*. New York: Routledge.

Ignatiev, Noel, and John Garvey, eds. 1996. *Race Traitor*. New York: Routledge.

Jackson, Kristin Collins. 2015. "5 Hair Rules Rachel Dolezal Must Have Had to Follow to Fake a Convincing Texture." *Bustle*, June 12. http://www.bustle.com/articles /89966-5-natural-hair-rules-rachel-dolezal-must-have -had-to-follow-to-fake-a-convincing-texture.

Jagadish, Pooja S. 2013. "Mainstreaming Third-Gender Healers: The Changing Perceptions of South Asian Hijras." *Vanderbilt Undergraduate Research Journal* 9: 1–8.

Jaschik, Scott. 2015a. "Fake Cherokee?" *Inside Higher Ed*, July 6. https://www.insidehighered.com/news/2015 /07/06/scholar-who-has-made-name-cherokee-accused-not-having-native-american-roots.

———. 2015b. "Indian Enough for Dartmouth?" *Inside Higher Ed*, September 17. https://www.insidehighered .com/news/2015/09/17/indian-activists-raise-questions -about-woman-appointed-lead-native-american-pro-gram.

Jeffreys, Sheila. 2014. *Gender Hurts: A Feminist Analysis of the Politics of Transgenderism*. Abingdon, Oxon, UK: Routledge.

Jencks, Charles. 1987. *What Is Post-Modernism?* 2nd ed., rev. and enl. London: Academy Editions.

Jenkins, Richard. 2008. *Rethinking Ethnicity*. 2nd ed. (Orig. pub. 1997.) Los Angeles: SAGE.

———. 2014. *Social Identity*. 4th ed. (Orig. pub. 1996.) New York: Routledge.

Jiménez, Tomás R. 2010. "Affiliative Ethnic Identity: A More Elastic Link between Ethnic Ancestry and Culture." *Ethnic and Racial Studies* 33, no. 10: 1756–75.

Jones, Angela. 2015. "Rachel Dolezal Is Really Queer: Transracial Politics and Queer Futurity." *Social (In)Queery*, June 17. http://socialinqueery.com/2015/06/17/rachel -dolezal-is-really-queer-transracial-politics-and-queer -futurity/.

Kalmijn, Matthijs. 1993. "Trends in Black/White Inter-marriage." *Social Forces* 72, no. 1: 119–46.

Karasic, Dan, and Diane Ehrensaft. 2015. "We Must Put an End to Gender Conversion Therapy for Kids." *Wired*, July 6. http://www.wired.com/2015/07/must-put-end -gender-conversion-therapy-kids/.

Karkazis, Katrina Alicia. 2008. *Fixing Sex: Intersex, Medical Authority, and Lived Experience*. Durham, NC: Duke University Press.

Kelly, Mary E., and Joane Nagel. 2002. "Ethnic Re-identification: Lithuanian Americans and Native Americans." *Journal of Ethnic and Migration Studies* 28, no. 2: 275–89.

Kennedy, Randall. 2003. *Interracial Intimacies: Sex, Marriage, Identity, and Adoption*. New York: Pantheon.

Kertzer, David I., and Dominique Arel. 2002. "Censuses, Identity Formation, and the Struggle for Political Power." In *Census and Identity: The Politics of Race, Ethnicity, and Language in National Censuses*, edited by David I. Kertzer and Dominique Arel, 1–42. Cambridge: Cambridge University Press.

Kessler, Suzanne J. 1998. *Lessons from the Intersexed*. New Brunswick, NJ: Rutgers University Press.

Kessler, Suzanne J., and Wendy McKenna. 2000. "Who Put the 'Trans' in Transgender? Gender Theory and Everyday Life." *International Journal of Transgenderism* 4, no. 3. http://web.archive.org/web/20070720021141/http:/www.symposion.com/ijt/gilbert/kessler.htm.

Khanna, Nikki. 2010. "'If You're Half Black, You're Just Black': Reflected Appraisals and the Persistence of the One-Drop Rule." *Sociological Quarterly* 51, no. 1: 96–121.

Khanna, Nikki, and Cathryn Johnson. 2010. "Passing as Black: Racial Identity Work among Biracial Americans." *Social Psychology Quarterly* 73, no. 4: 380–97.

Killerman, Sam. 2012a. "The Genderbread Person." http://itspronouncedmetrosexual.com/2012/01/the-genderbread-person/.

———. "The Genderbread Person v2.0." http://itspronouncedmetrosexual.com/2012/03/the-genderbread-person-v2-0/.

Kim, Janine Young. 1999. "Are Asians Black? The Asian-American Civil Rights Agenda and the Contemporary Significance of the Black/White Paradigm." *Yale Law Journal* 108, no. 8: 2385–2412.

Kimmel, Michael S. 1993. "Sexual Balkanization: Gender and Sexuality as the New Ethnicities." *Social Research* 60, no. 3: 571–87.

King, Shaun. 2015. "Race, Love, Hate, and Me: A Distinctly American Story." *Daily Kos*, August 20. http://www.dailykos.com/story/2015/08/20/1413881/-Race-love-hate-and-me-A-distinctly-American-story?showAll=yes.

Kitwana, Bakari. 2005. *Why White Kids Love Hip-Hop: Wankstas, Wiggers, Wannabes, and the New Reality of Race in America*. New York: Basic Civitas.

Klaus, Carl H. 1991. "Elements of the Essay." In *Elements of Literature: Essay, Fiction, Poetry, Drama, Film*, edited by Carl H. Klaus, Robert Scholes, Nancy Comley, and Michael Silverman. 4th ed. New York: Oxford University Press.

Kraidy, Marwan. 2005. *Hybridity, Or the Cultural Logic of Globalization*. Philadelphia: Temple University Press.

Krogstad, Jens Manuel. 2014. "Census Bureau Explores New Middle East/North Africa Ethnic Category." *Pew Research Center*, March 24. http://www.pewresearch.org/fact-tank/2014/03/24/census-bureau-explores-new-middle-eastnorth-africa-ethnic-category/.

Kuruvilla, Carol. 2015. "Rachel Dolezal's Father Talks about Her Evangelical Christian Upbringing." *Huffington Post*, June 16. http://www.huffingtonpost.com/2015/06/16/rachel-dolezal-evangelical-christian_n_7598562.html.

Kyriacou, Anastasia. "Meet Someone Who Isn't Male or Female and Wants a New Type of Passport." *PinkNews*, October 24. http://www.pinknews.co.uk/2014/10/24/interview-christie-elan-cane-on-x-passports-and-the-campaign-for-non-gendered-legitimacy/.

La Ganga, Maria L., and Matt Pearce. 2015. "Rachel Dolezal's Story, a Study of Race and Identity, Gets 'Crazier and Crazier.'" *Los Angeles Times*, June 15. http://www.latimes.com/nation/la-na-spokane-naacp-rachel-dolezal-resigns-20150615-story.html#page=1.

Laitin, David D. 1995. "Marginality: A Microperspective." *Rationality and Society* 7, no. 1: 31–57.

Lal, Vinay. 1999. "Not This, Not That: The Hijras of India and the Cultural Politics of Sexuality." *Social Text* 61: 119–40.

Lamont, Michèle, and Virág Molnár. 2002. "The Study of Boundaries in the Social Sciences." *Annual Review of Sociology* 28, no. 1: 167–95.

Lane, Harlan L., Richard Pillard, and Ulf Hedberg. 2011. *The People of the Eye: Deaf Ethnicity and Ancestry*. New York: Oxford University Press.

Lee, Philip. 2015. "Identity Property: Protecting the New IP in a Race-Relevant World." *West Virginia Law Review* 117: 1183–1223.

Leff, Lisa. 2013. "'Preferred' Gender Pronouns Gain Traction at Colleges." *Huffington Post*, November 30. http://www.huffingtonpost.com/huff-wires/20131130/us-redefining-gender/?utm_hp_ref=green&ir=green&m=true.

Leong, Nancy. 2013. "Racial Capitalism." *Harvard Law Review* 126: 2153–2226.

———. 2015. "This Is Not a Post about Rachel Dolezal." *RightsBlog*, June 15. http://www.nancyleong.com/race-2/this-is-not-a-post-about-rachel-dolezal/.

Lévi-Strauss, Claude. 1962. *Le Totémisme aujourd'hui*. Paris: Presses Universitaires de France.

———. 1964. *Totemism*. Translated by Rodney Needham. London: Merlin Press.

Liebler, Carolyn, and Timothy Ortyl. 2013. "More Than a Million New American Indians in 2000: Who Are They?" Washington, DC: U.S. Census Bureau, Center for Econmic Studies.

Liebler, Carolyn A., Sonya Rastogi, Leticia E. Fernandez, James M. Noon, and Sharon R. Ennis. 2014. "America's Churning Races: Race and Ethnic Response Changes between Census 2000 and the 2010 Census." U.S. Census Bureau, Center for Administrative Records Research and Applications, Working Paper #2014-09.

Little, Nicholas J. 2005. "From No Means No to Only Yes Means Yes: The Rational Results of an Affirmative Consent Standard in Rape Law." *Vanderbilt Law Review* 58: 1321–64.

Lloyd, Abigail W. 2005. "Defining the Human: Are Transgender People Strangers to the Law." *Berkeley Journal of
Gender, Law & Justice* 20: 150–95.

Lopez, German. 2015. "The Catastrophically Bad New York
Times Op-Ed on Transgender Research, Debunked." *Vox
Identities*, August 24. http://www.vox.com/2015/8/24
/9197789/new-york-times-transgender-research.

Lorber, Judith. 1994. *Paradoxes of Gender*. New Haven, CT:
Yale University Press.

———. 2004. Preface. In *The Drag Queen Anthology: The
Absolutely Fabulous but Flawless Customary World of Female
Impersonators*, edited by Steven P. Schacht and Lisa
Underwood, xv–xvi. New York: Harrington Park Press.

Lott, Eric. 2013. *Love and Theft: Blackface Minstrelsy and the
American Working Class*. (Orig. pub. 1993.) New York:
Oxford University Press.

Loveman, Mara. 2014. *National Colors: Racial Classification
and the State in Latin America*. New York: Oxford University Press.

Loveman, Mara, and Jeronimo O. Muniz. 2007. "How
Puerto Rico Became White: Boundary Dynamics and
Intercensus Racial Reclassification." *American Sociologi-
cal Review* 72, no. 6: 915–39.

Mansbach, Adam. 2005. *Angry Black White Boy*. New York:
Three Rivers Press.

Maraniss, David. 2012. "How Obama Became Black."
Washington Post, June 14. https://www.washingtonpost
.com/opinions/how-obama-became-black/2012/06/14
/gJQA8CnKdV_story.html.

Marcosson, Samuel A. 2001. "Constructive Immutability."
Journal of Constitutional Law 3: 646–721.

Mayeri, Serena. 2001. "'A Common Fate of Discrimination': Race-Gender Analogies in Legal and Historical
Perspective." *Yale Law Journal* 110, no. 6: 1045–87.

———. 2007. "Reconstructing the Race-Sex Analogy." *William & Mary Law Review* 49: 1789–1857.

McCall, Leslie. 2005. "The Complexity of Intersectionality." *Signs* 30, no. 3: 1771–1800.

McGreal, Chris. 2015. "Rachel Dolezal: 'I Wasn't Identifying as Black to Upset People. I Was Being Me.'" *Guardian*, December 13. http://www.theguardian.com/us -news/2015/dec/13/rachel-dolezal-i-wasnt-identifying-as -black-to-upset-people-i-was-being-me.

McHugh, Paul. 2014. "Transgender Surgery Isn't the Solution." *Wall Street Journal*, June 12. http://www.wsj .com/articles/paul-mchugh-transgender-surgery-isnt-the -solution-1402615120.

McKee, Kimberly, et al. 2015. "An Open Letter: Why Co-opting 'Transracial' in the Case of Rachel Dolezal Is Problematic." *Medium*, June 16. https://medium.com /@Andy_Marra/an-open-letter-why-co-opting-transra cial-in-the-case-of-rachel-dolezal-is-problematic -249f79f6d83c#.eo89u8p3v.

Meadow, Tey. 2010. "'A Rose Is a Rose': On Producing Legal Gender Classifications." *Gender & Society* 24, no. 6: 814–37.

Mele, Christopher. 2016. "Oregon Court Allows a Person to Choose Neither Sex." *New York Times*, June 13. www .nytimes.com/2016/06/14/us/oregon-nonbinary-trans gender-sex-gender.html.

Melnick, Jeffrey Paul. 1999. *A Right to Sing the Blues: African Americans, Jews, and American Popular Song*. Cambridge, MA: Harvard University Press.

Méndez, Juan E. 2013. "Report of the Special Rapporteur on Torture and Other Cruel, Inhuman or Degrading Treatment or Punishment, Juan E. Méndez." United Nations General Assembly, Human Rights Council. http://www.ohchr.org/Documents/HRBodies/HRCouncil /RegularSession/Session22/A.HRC.22.53_English

.pdf?utm_source=AIC+mailing+list&utm_campaign
=0940e5a7fc-&utm_medium=email.

Mepschen, Paul, Jan Willem Duyvendak, and Evelien H. Tonkens. 2010. "Sexual Politics, Orientalism and Multicultural Citizenship in the Netherlands." *Sociology* 44, no. 5: 962–79.

Meyerowitz, Joanne. 2002. *How Sex Changed: A History of Transsexuality in the United States.* Cambridge, MA: Harvard University Press.

Mezzrow, Mezz, and Bernard Wolfe. 1946. *Really the Blues.* New York: Random House.

Michaels, Walter Benn. 1992. "Race into Culture: A Critical Genealogy of Cultural Identity." *Critical Inquiry* 18, no. 4: 655–85.

———. 1997. "Autobiography of an Ex-White Man: Why Race Is Not a Social Construction." *Transition*, no. 73 (January): 122–43.

Miller, Peter, and Nikolas S. Rose. 2008. *Governing the Present: Administering Economic, Social and Personal Life.* Cambridge: Polity.

Mirón, Louis F., and Jonathan Xavier Inda. 2000. "Race as a Kind of Speech Act." *Cultural Studies* 5: 85–107.

Modkins, Stephanie. 2015. "How Rachel Dolezal Capitalized on Her Fake Blackness." *Examiner*, June 15. http://www.examiner.com/article/how-rachel-dolezal-capitalized-on-her-fake-blackness.

Moore, Russell. 2015. "What Should the Church Say to Bruce Jenner?" *Russell Moore* (blog), April 24. http://www.russellmoore.com/2015/04/24/what-should-the-church-say-to-bruce-jenner/.

Morning, Ann. 2000. "Who Is Multiracial? Definitions and Decisions." *Sociological Imagination* 37, no. 4: 209–29.

———. 2011. *The Nature of Race: How Scientists Think and Teach about Human Difference*. Berkeley: University of California Press.

———. 2015. "It's Impossible to Lie about Your Race." *Huffington Post*, July 1. http://www.huffingtonpost.com /ann-morning/its-impossible to-lie-about-your-race_b _7708598.html.

Morris, Jan. 1974. *Conundrum*. New York: Harcourt Brace Jovanovich.

Morris, Rosalind C. 1995. "All Made Up: Performance Theory and the New Anthropology of Sex and Gender." *Annual Review of Anthropology* 24, no. 1: 567–92.

Morris, Wesley. 2015. "The Year We Obsessed over Identity." *New York Times*, October 6. http://www.nytimes .com/2015/10/11/magazine/the-year-we-obsessed-over -identity.html.

Moyer, Justin Wm. 2015. "'Are You an African American?' Why an NAACP Official Isn't Saying." *Washington Post*, June 12. https://www.washingtonpost.com/news /morning-mix/wp/2015/06/12/spokane-naacp-president -rachel-dolezal-may-be-white/.

Murray, Stephen O. 1994. "On Subordinating Native American Cosmologies to the Empire of Gender." *Current Anthropology* 35, no. 1: 59–61.

Myrdal, Gunnar. 1962. *An American Dilemma*. New York: Harper & Row.

Murphy, Meghan. 2015. "You Can't 'Feel' Race, but Can You 'Feel' Female? On Rachel Dolezal, Caitlyn Jenner, and Unspeakable Questions." *Feminist Current*, June 17. http:// feministcurrent.com/12254/you-cant-feel-race-but-can -you-feel-female-on-rachel-dolezal-caitlyn-jenner-and -unspeakable-questions/.

NABSW. 1972. "National Association of Black Social
    Workers Position Statement on Trans-Racial Adop-
    tions," September. http://c.ymcdn.com/sites/nabsw.org
    /resource/collection/E1582D77-E4CD-4104–996A
    -D42D08F9CA7D/NABSW_Trans-Racial_Adoption_1972
    Position(b).pdf.

Nagel, Joane. 1997. *American Indian Ethnic Renewal: Red
    Power and the Resurgence of Identity and Culture*. Oxford:
    Oxford University Press.

NAISA (Native American and Indigenous Studies Associa-
    tion). 2015. "NAISA Council Statement on Indigenous
    Identity Fraud." http://www.naisa.org/naisa-council
    -statement-on-indigenous-identity-fraud-2.html.

Nash, Catherine. 2004. "Genetic Kinship." *Cultural Studies*
    18: 1–33.

Neckerman, Kathryn M., Prudence Carter, and Jennifer
    Lee. 1999. "Segmented Assimilation and Minority
    Cultures of Mobility." *Ethnic and Racial Studies* 22, no. 6:
    945–65.

Nelson, Alondra. 2008. "Bio Science: Genetic Genealogy
    Testing and the Pursuit of African Ancestry." *Social
    Studies of Science* 38, no. 5: 759–83.

Nelson, Steven. 2015. "'Bathroom Police' Initiative Fails
    to Make California Ballot." *US News & World Report*,
    December 22. http://www.usnews.com/news/articles
    /2015-12-22/bathroom-police-initiative-fails-to-make
    -california-ballot.

Nerad, Julie. 2014. "Introduction: The (Not So) New Face
    of America." In *Passing Interest: Racial Passing in US
    Novels, Memoirs, Television, and Film, 1990–2010*, edited
    by Julie Nerad, 1–38. Albany, NY: SUNY Press.

Nestle, Joan, Clare Howell, and Riki Anne Wilchins, eds.
    2002. *GenderQueer: Voices from beyond the Sexual Binary*.
    Los Angeles: Alyson Books.

Newport, Frank. 2013. "In U.S., 87% Approve of Black-White Marriage, vs. 4% in 1958." *Gallup*. July 25. http://www.gallup.com/poll/163697/approve-marriage-blacks-whites.aspx.

Nicholas, Lucy. 2014. *Queer Post-Gender Ethics: The Shape of Selves to Come*. Basingstoke, Hampshire, UK: Palgrave Macmillan.

Nilsson, Frida. 1996. "The Breakdown of the Sex/Gender Distinction in Anthropological Discourse." *Nordic Journal of Feminist and Gender Research* 4, no. 2: 114–27.

Nix, Emily, and Nancy Qian. 2015. "The Fluidity of Race: 'Passing' in the United States, 1880–1940." National Bureau of Economic Research. http://www.nber.org/papers/w20828.

Noman, Natasha. 2015. "One Tweet Perfectly Shows Everything Wrong with What Rachel Dolezal Did." *Identities.mic*, June 12. http://mic.com/articles/120609/one-tweet-exposes-the-hypocrisy-of-rachel-dolezal-s-views-on-race#.xVAKr5vX2.

Nordmarken, Sonny. 2014. "Becoming Ever More Monstrous: Feeling Transgender In-Betweenness." *Qualitative Inquiry* 20, no. 1: 37–50.

Novas, Carlos, and Nikolas Rose. 2000. "Genetic Risk and the Birth of the Somatic Individual." *Economy and Society* 29, no. 4: 485–513.

Ocampo, Anthony. 2016. *The Latinos of Asia: How Filipino Americans Break the Rules of Race*. Stanford, CA: Stanford University Press.

O'Connor, Maureen. 2014. "Is Race Plastic? My Trip into the 'Ethnic Plastic Surgery' Minefield." *New York Magazine*, July 27. http://nymag.com/thecut/2014/07/ethnic-plastic-surgery.html#.

Office of Management and Budget. 1997. "Revisions to the Standards for the Classification of Federal Data on Race

and Ethnicity." http://www.whitehouse.gov/omb/fedreg
_1997standards.

Onwuachi-Willig, Angela. 2007. "The Admission of Legacy
Blacks." *Vanderbilt Law Review* 60: 1141–1231.

Orloff, Ann. 2009. "Should Feminists Aim for Gender
Symmetry? Why a Dual-Earner/Dual-Caregiver Society
Is Not Every Feminist's Utopia." In *Gender Equality:
Transforming Family Divisions of Labor*, edited by Janet
C. Gornick and Marcia K. Meyers, 129–60. London:
Verso.

Ortner, Sherry B. 1997. "So, *Is* Female to Male as Nature Is
to Culture?" In *Making Gender: The Politics and Erotics of
Culture*, 173–80. Boston: Beacon Press.

Ortner, Sherry B., and Harriet Whitehead. 1981. "Intro-
duction: Accounting for Sexual Meanings." In *Sexual
Meanings: The Cultural Construction of Gender and
Sexuality*, edited by Sherry B. Ortner and Harriet
Whitehead, 1–27. Cambridge: Cambridge University
Press.

Ossman, Susan. 2013. *Moving Matters: Paths of Serial Migration*. Stanford, CA: Stanford University Press.

Otis, Johnny. 1968. *Listen to the Lambs*. New York: W. W.
Norton.

Overall, Christine. 2004. "Transsexualism and 'Transracialism.'" *Social Philosophy Today* 20: 183–93.

Padawer, Ruth. 2014. "When Women Become Men at
Wellesley." *New York Times*, October 15. http://www
.nytimes.com/2014/10/19/magazine/when-women
-become-men-at-wellesley-college.html.

Passel, Jeffrey S. 1997. "The Growing American Indian
Population, 1960–1990: Beyond Demography." *Population Research and Policy Review* 16, nos. 1–2: 11–31.

Paulle, Bowen, and Barak Kalir. 2014. "The Integration
Matrix Reloaded: From Ethnic Fixations to Established

Versus Outsiders Dynamics in the Netherlands." *Journal of Ethnic and Migration Studies* 40, no. 9: 1354–74.

Pearce, Matt. 2015. "Decades before Rachel Dolezal, There Was Mark Stebbins in a Stockton Scandal." *Los Angeles Times*, June 19. http://www.latimes.com/nation/la-na -stockton-dolezal-20150619-story.html.

Pember, Mary Annette. 2007. "Ethnic Fraud?" *Diverse: Issues in Higher Education* 23, no. 25: 20–23.

Perry, Twila L. 1993. "The Transracial Adoption Controversy: An Analysis of Discourse and Subordination." *New York University Review on Law & Social Change* 21: 33.

Pettit, Becky, and Bruce Western. 2004. "Mass Imprison- ment and the Life Course: Race and Class Inequality in U.S. Incarceration." *American Sociological Review* 69, no. 2: 151–69.

Pew Research Center. 2007. "Blacks See Growing Values Gap Between Poor and Middle Class." http://www.pew socialtrends.org/files/2010/10/Race-2007.pdf.

Pfeiffer, Kathleen. 2003. *Race Passing and American Individualism*. Amherst: University of Massachusetts Press.

Plummer, Ken. 2000. "Intimate Choices." In *Understanding Contemporary Society: Theories of the Present*, edited by Gary Browning, Abigail Halcli, and Frank Webster, 432–44. London: SAGE.

———. 2001. "The Square of Intimate Citizenship: Some Preliminary Proposals." *Citizenship Studies* 5, no. 3: 237–53.

———. 2012. "Critical Sexuality Studies." In *The Wiley- Blackwell Companion to Sociology*, edited by George Ritzer, 243–68. Malden, MA: Wiley-Blackwell.

Plumwood, Val. 1989. "Do We Need a Sex/Gender Distinc- tion?" *Radical Philosophy* 51: 2–11.

Posner, Daniel N. 2005. *Institutions and Ethnic Politics in Africa*. New York: Cambridge University Press.

Prewitt, Kenneth. 2013. *What Is Your Race? The Census and Our Flawed Efforts to Classify Americans*. Princeton, NJ: Princeton University Press.

Prosser, Jay. 1998. *Second Skins: The Body Narratives of Transsexuality*. New York: Columbia University Press.

Puar, Jasbir K. 2007. *Terrorist Assemblages: Homonationalism in Queer Times*. Durham, NC: Duke University Press.

———. 2013. "Rethinking Homonationalism." *International Journal of Middle East Studies* 45, no. 2: 336–39.

Rachel S. 2006. "Trans Identity—Sex Changes, Race Changes, Drag, and Passing." *Alas* (blog), May 18. https://amptoons.com/blog/?p=2366.

Raible, John. n.d. "What Is Transracialization?" *John Raible Online* (blog). https://johnraible.wordpress.com/about -john-w-raible/what-is-transracialization/.

———. 2015. "#Transracialization: It Really Is a Thing." *John Raible Online* (blog), June 18. https://johnraible .wordpress.com/2015/06/18/transracialization-it-really -is-a-thing/.

Raymond, Janice G. 1994. *The Transsexual Empire: The Making of the She-Male*. Rev. ed. (Orig. pub. 1979.) New York: Teachers College Press.

Reed, Natalie. 2013. "Born This Way (Reprise): The New Essentialism." *Sincerely, Natalie Reed* (blog), March 9. http://freethoughtblogs.com/nataliereed/2013/03/09 /born-this-way-reprise-the-new-essentialism/.

Reed, Adolph. 2015. "From Jenner to Dolezal: One Trans Good, the Other Not So Much." *Common Dreams*, June 15. http://www.commondreams.org/views/2015/06/15 /jenner-dolezal-one-trans-good-other-not-so-much.

Rich, Camille Gear. 2013. "Affirmative Action in the Era of Elective Race: Racial Commodification and the Promise of the New Functionalism." *Georgetown Law Journal* 102: 179–218.

———. 2014. "Elective Race: Recognizing Race Discrimination in the Era of Racial Self-Identification." *Georgetown Law Journal* 102, no. 5: 1501–72.

———. 2015. "Rachel Dolczal Has a Right to Be Black." *CNN.com*, June 16. http://www.cnn.com/2015/06/15 /opinions/rich-rachel-dolezal/.

Richards, David A. J. 1978. "Sexual Autonomy and the Constitutional Right to Privacy: A Case Study in Human Rights and the Unwritten Constitution." *Hastings Law Journal* 30: 957–1018.

Risman, Barbara, Judith Lorber, and Jessica Holden Sherwood. 2012. "Toward a World Beyond Gender: A Utopian Vision." Paper prepared for American Sociological Association Annual Meeting. https://www.ssc.wisc. edu/~wright/ASA/Risman-Lorber-Sherwood%20Real%20 Utopia%20Proposal%20–%20Beyond%20Gender.pdf.

Roberts, Wade. 1984. "The 'White' Man Who Insists He's Black." *Ebony*, June, 31–34.

Rockquemore, Kerry Ann, and Patricia Arend. 2002. "Opting for White: Choice, Fluidity and Racial Identity Construction in Post Civil-Rights America." *Race and Society* 5, no. 1: 49–64.

Rockquemore, Kerry, and David L. Brunsma. 2008. *Beyond Black: Biracial Identity in America*. 2nd ed. Lanham, MD: Rowman & Littlefield.

Roediger, David R. 2002. *Colored White: Transcending the Racial Past*. Berkeley: University of California Press.

———. 2007. *The Wages of Whiteness: Race and the Making of the American Working Class*. London: Verso.

Roen, Katrina. 2002. "'Either/Or' and 'Both/Neither': Discursive Tensions in Transgender Politics." *Signs* 27, no. 2: 501–22.

Rose, Nikolas. 2007. *The Politics of Life Itself: Biomedicine, Power, and Subjectivity in the Twenty-First Century*. Princeton: Princeton University Press.

Rose, Tricia. 2008. *The Hip Hop Wars: What We Talk about When We Talk about Hip Hop—and Why It Matters*. New York: Basic Books.

Roth, Wendy D. 2005. "The End of the One-Drop Rule? Labeling of Multiracial Children in Black Intermarriages." *Sociological Forum* 20, no. 1: 35–67.

Rothman, Joshua D. 2003. *Notorious in the Neighborhood: Sex and Families across the Color Line in Virginia, 1787–1861*. Chapel Hill: University of North Carolina Press.

Rottenberg, Catherine. 2003. "Passing: Race, Identification, and Desire." *Criticism* 45, no. 4: 435–52.

Row, Jess. 2014. *Your Face in Mine*. New York: Riverhead.

Rubenfeld, Jed. 2013. "The Riddle of Rape-by-Deception and the Myth of Sexual Autonomy." *Yale Law Journal* 122, no. 6: 1372–1443.

Rubin, Henry. 2003. *Self-Made Men: Identity and Embodiment among Transsexual Men*. Nashville, TN: Vanderbilt University Press.

Rushdie, Salman. 1990. *In Good Faith*. New York: Granta.

Ryan, Maura. 2009. "Beyond Thomas Beatie: Trans Men and the New Parenthood." In *Who's Your Daddy? And Other Writings on Queer Parenting*, edited by Rachel Epstein, 55–71. Toronto: Sumach Press.

Samuels, Allison (text), and Justin Bishop (photographs). 2015. "Rachel Dolezal's True Lies." *Vanity Fair*, July 19. http://www.vanityfair.com/news/2015/07/rachel-dolezal-new-interview-pictures-exclusive.

Sánchez, María Carla, and Linda Schlossberg, eds. 2001. *Passing: Identity and Interpretation in Sexuality, Race, and Religion*. New York: New York University Press.

Sanders, Steve. 2012. "The Constitutional Right to (Keep Your) Same-Sex Marriage." *Michigan Law Review* 110: 1421–81.

Sandweiss, Martha A. 2009. *Passing Strange: A Gilded Age Tale of Love and Deception across the Color Line*. New York: Penguin.

Saner, Emine. 2014. "Europe's Terrible Trans Rights Record: Will Denmark's New Law Spark Change?" *The Guardian*, September 1. http://www.theguardian.com /society/shortcuts/2014/sep/01/europe-terrible-trans -rights-record-denmark-new-law.

Saperstein, Aliya, and Andrew M. Penner. 2012. "Racial Fluidity and Inequality in the United States." *American Journal of Sociology* 118, no. 3: 676–727.

Sartwell, Crispin. 2005. "Wigger." In *White on White/Black on Black*, edited by George Yancy, 35–48. Lanham, MD: Rowman & Littlefield.

———. 2015a. "Should Miley Cyrus Wear Dreadlocks?" *Los Angeles Times*, September 25. http://www.latimes.com /opinion/op-ed/la-oe-0927-sartwell-appropriated-culture -20150927-story.html.

———. 2015b. "Transrace." *Cheese It, the Cops!* (blog), June 15. http://eyeofthestorm.blogs.com/eye_of_the_storm /2015/06/racedrag.html.

Sax, Leonard. 2002. "How Common Is Intersex? A Response to Anne Fausto-Sterling." *Journal of Sex Research* 39, no. 3: 174–78.

Scelfo, Julie. 2015. "A University Recognizes a Third Gender: Neutral." *New York Times*, February 3. http://www .nytimes.com/2015/02/08/education/edlife/a-university -recognizes-a-third-gender-neutral.html.

Schilt, Kristen. 2006. "Just One of the Guys? How Transmen Make Gender Visible at Work." *Gender & Society* 20, no. 4: 465–90.

———. 2010. *Just One of the Guys? Transgender Men and the Persistence of Gender Inequality*. Chicago: University of Chicago Press.

Schilt, Kristen, and Tey Meadow. 2012. "The Pleasures of Gender." Paper presented at the American Sociological Association Annual Meeting.

Schilt, Kristen, and Laurel Westbrook. 2009. "Doing Gender, Doing Heteronormativity: 'Gender Normals,' Transgender People, and the Social Maintenance of Heterosexuality." *Gender & Society* 23, no. 4: 440–64.

———. 2015. "Bathroom Battlegrounds and Penis Panics." *Contexts* 14, no. 3. http://contexts.org/articles/bathroom -battlegrounds-and-penis-panics/.

Schuck, Peter H. 2016. "A Bathroom of One's Own?" *New York Times*, May 18. www.nytimes.com/2016/05/18/opinion /a-bathroom-of-ones-own.html.

Schulhofer, Stephen J. 1998. *Unwanted Sex: The Culture of Intimidation and the Failure of Law*. Cambridge, MA: Harvard University Press.

Schwartz, Barry. 2004. *The Paradox of Choice: Why More Is Less*. New York: Ecco.

Schwartzapfel, Beth. 2013. "Born This Way?" *American Prospect*, March 14. http://prospect.org/article/born-way.

Seidman, Steven. 2001. "From Identity to Queer Politics: Shifts in Normative Heterosexuality and the Meaning of Citizenship." *Citizenship Studies* 5, no. 3: 321–28.

Selle, Jeff, and Maureen Dolan. 2015. "Black Like Me?" *CDAPress*, June 11. http://www.cdapress.com/news /local_news/article_385adfeb-76f3-5050-98b4-d4bf021c423f .html.

Seltzer, William. 1998. "Population Statistics, the Holocaust, and the Nuremberg Trials." *Population and Development Review* 24, no. 3: 511–52.

Serano, Julia. 2014. "Op-Ed: An Open Letter to the New Yorker." *Advocate*, August 5. http://www.advocate.com /commentary/2014/08/05/op-ed-open-letter-new-yorker.

———. 2016. *Whipping Girl: A Transsexual Woman on Sexism and the Scapegoating of Femininity*. 2nd ed. Emeryville, CA: Seal Press.

Sharfstein, Daniel J. 2003. "The Secret History of Race in the United States." *Yale Law Journal* 112: 1473–1509.

———. 2007. "Crossing the Color Line: Racial Migration and the One-Drop Rule, 1600–1860." *Minnesota Law Review* 91: 592–656.

Shen, Fern. 2015. "Dolezal, Accused of Lying about Her Race, Spoke at Baltimore Protest." *Baltimore Brew*, June 13. https://www.baltimorebrew.com/2015/06/13/dolezal -accused-of-lying-about-her-race-spoke-at-baltimore -protest/.

Simon, Patrick. 2008. "The Choice of Ignorance: The Debate on Ethnic and Racial Statistics in France." *French Politics, Culture & Society* 26, no. 1: 7–31.

Simon, Rita J., and Rhonda M. Roorda. 2009. *In Their Siblings' Voices: White Non-Adopted Siblings Talk about Their Experiences Being Raised with Black and Biracial Brothers and Sisters*. New York: Columbia University Press.

Simon, William. 1996. *Postmodern Sexualities*. London: Routledge.

Smith, Justin E. H. 2015. "Why Rachel Dolezal Still Matters after Charleston." *Jehsmith* (blog), June 19. http://www .jehsmith.com/1/2015/06/why-rachel-dolezal-still -matters-after-charleston.html.

Smith, Robert Courtney. 2014. "Black Mexicans, Conjunctural Ethnicity, and Operating Identities: Long-Term Ethnographic Analysis." *American Sociological Review* 79, no. 3: 517–48.

Snyder-Hall, R. Claire. 2010. "Third-Wave Feminism and the Defense of 'Choice.'" *Perspectives on Politics* 8, no. 1: 255–61.

Sollors, Werner. 1999. *Neither Black nor White yet Both: Thematic Explorations of Interracial Literature*. Cambridge, MA: Harvard University Press.

Song, Miri. 2003. *Choosing Ethnic Identity*. Cambridge: Polity/Blackwell.

Song, Miri, and Peter Aspinall. 2012. "Is Racial Mismatch a Problem for Young 'Mixed Race' People in Britain? The Findings of Qualitative Research." *Ethnicities* 12, no. 6: 730–53.

Sontag, Deborah. 2015. "'A Whole New Being': How Kricket Nimmons Seized the Transgender Moment." *New York Times*, December 12. http://www.nytimes.com/2015/12/13/us/kricket-nimmons-transgender-surgery.html?_r=0.

Southall, Ashley. 2015. "Activist Shaun King Denies Claims He Lied about Race and Assault." *New York Times*, August 19. http://www.nytimes.com/2015/08/20/us/activist-shaun-king-denies-claims-he-lied-about-race-and-assault.html?_r=1.

Spade, Dean. 2003. "Resisting Medicine, Re/modeling Gender." *Berkeley Women's Law Journal* 18: 15–37.

———. 2008. "Documenting Gender." *Hastings Law Journal* 59: 731–841.

Spokesman-Review. 2015. "Credibility of Local NAACP Leader Rachel Dolezal Questioned." *Spokesman-Review*, June 11. http://www.spokesman.com/stories/2015/jun/11/board-member-had-longstanding-doubts-about-truthfu/.

Stamatov, Peter. 2014. "Imperial Sorting Grids: Institutional Logics of Diversity and the Classificatory Legacies of the First Wave of European Overseas Expansion." Paper prepared for 237 Reunion Conference, UCLA.

Stark, Jill. 2015. "Call Yourself a Woman? Feminists Take On Transgender Community in Bitter Debate." *Sydney Morning Herald*, November 22. http://www.smh.com .au/national/what-makes-a-woman-feminists-take-on -transgender-community-in-bitter-debate-20151113-gkyk6u .html#ixzz7460BmkEe6.

State of California. 2013. Assembly Bill No. 1266. http:// leginfo.legislature.ca.gov/faces/billNavClient.xhtml?bill _id=201320140AB1266.

———. 2014. Senate Bill No. 967. https://leginfo.legisla ture.ca.gov/faces/billNavClient.xhtml?bill_id=2013 20140SB967.

Stein, Edward. 2011. "Sexual Orientations, Rights, and the Body: Immutability, Essentialism, and Nativism." *Social Research* 78, no. 2: 633–58.

Stewart, Charles. 1999. "Syncretism and Its Synonyms: Reflections on Cultural Mixture." *Diacritics* 29, no. 3: 40–62.

Stokel-Walker, Chris. 2013. "When Does Plastic Surgery Become Racial Transformation?" *BuzzFeed*, May 16. http://www.buzzfeed.com/chrisstokelwalker/when-does -plastic-surgery-become-racial-transformation.

Stone, Sandy. 2006. "The 'Empire' Strikes Back: A Posttrans-sexual Manifesto." In *The Transgender Studies Reader*, edited by Susan Stryker and Stephen Whittle, 221–35. (Orig. pub. 1991.) New York: Routledge.

Storrs, Debbie. 1999. "Whiteness as Stigma: Essentialist Identity Work by Mixed-Race Women." *Symbolic Interaction* 22, no. 3: 187–212.

Strauss, Marcy. 2011. "Reevaluating Suspect Classifications." *Seattle University Law Review* 35, no. 1: 135–74.

Stryker, Susan. 2006. "(De)Subjugated Knowledges: An Introduction to Transgender Studies." In *The Transgender Studies Reader*, edited by Susan Stryker and Stephen Whittle, 1–17. New York: Routledge.

———. 2008. *Transgender History*. Berkeley, CA: Seal Press.

———. 2015. "Caitlyn Jenner and Rachel Dolezal: Identification, Embodiment, and Bodily Transformation." *AHA Today* (blog), July 13. http://blog.historians.org/2015 /07/caitlyn-jenner-and-rachel-dolezal-identification -embodiment-bodily-transformation/.

Sturm, Circe. 2011. *Becoming Indian: The Struggle over Cherokee Identity in the Twenty-First Century*. Santa Fe, NM: School for Advanced Research Press.

Sunderland, Mitchell. 2015. "In Rachel Dolezal's Skin." *Broadly*, December 7. https://broadly.vice.com/en_us /article/rachel-dolezal-profile-interview.

Svrluga, Susan. 2015. "Genderqueer? Trans Man? UC Schools Seek to Make Applications More Inclusive." *Washington Post*, July 1. https://www.washingtonpost.com /news/grade-point/wp/2015/07/01/genderqueer-trans-man -uc-schools-seek-to-make-applications-more-inclusive/.

Swayze, Royce. 2015. "Former Belhaven Profs Recall Dolezal Student Days." *Clarion-Ledger*, June 22. http:// www.clarionledger.com/story/news/2015/06/22/former -belhaven-profs-recall-dolezal-student-days/29138167/.

Sweet, Frank W. 2005. *Legal History of the Color Line: The Rise and Triumph of the One-Drop Rule*. Palm Coast, FL: Backintyme.

Talbot, Margaret. 2013. "About a Boy: Transgender Surgery at Sixteen." *New Yorker*, March 18, pp. 56–65.

TallBear, Kimberly. 2013. *Native American DNA: Tribal Belonging and the False Promise of Genetic Science*. Minneapolis: University of Minnesota Press.

Talusan, Meredith. 2015. "There Is No Comparison between Transgender People and Rachel Dolezal." *The Guardian*, June 13. http://www.theguardian.com /commentisfree/2015/jun/12/comparison-transgender -people-rachel-dolezal.

Tamburin, Adam. "UT Removes Web Post on Gender-Neutral Pronouns." *Tennesseean*, September 4. http://www.tennessean.com/story/news/education/2015/09/04/ut-removes-web-post-gender-neutral-pronouns/71726984/.

Taylor, Paul. 2014. "The Next America." *Pew Research Center*, April 10. http://www.pewresearch.org/next-america/.

Taylor, Paul C. 2014. "Taking Postracialism Seriously." *Du Bois Review: Social Science Research on Race* 11, no. 1: 9–25.

Thanem, Torkild, and Louise Wallenberg. 2016. "Just Doing Gender? Transvestism and the Power of Underdoing Gender in Everyday Life and Work." *Organization* 23, no. 2: 250–71.

Thomas, William Isaac, and Dorothy Swaine Thomas. 1928. *The Child in America: Behavior Problems and Programs.* New York: A. A. Knopf.

Tilly, Charles. 1998. *Durable Inequality.* Berkeley: University of California Press.

Titman, Nat. 2013. "About That Often Misunderstood Asterisk." *Practical Androgyny* (blog), October 31. http://practicalandrogyny.com/2013/10/31/about-that-often-misunderstood-asterisk/.

Tobia, Jacob. 2015. "I Am Neither Mr, Mrs nor Ms but Mx." *Guardian*, August 31. http://www.theguardian.com/commentisfree/2015/aug/31/neither-mr-mrs-or-ms-but-mx.

Towle, Evan B., and Lynn Marie Morgan. 2002. "Romancing the Transgender Native: Rethinking the Use of the 'Third Gender' Concept." *GLQ: A Journal of Lesbian and Gay Studies* 8, no. 4: 469–97.

Turkle, Sherry. 1995. *Life on the Screen: Identity in the Age of the Internet.* New York: Simon & Schuster.

U.S. Court of Appeals. 2016. *Grimm v. Gloucester County School Board.* April 19. http://www.ca4.uscourts.gov/Opinions/Published/152056.P.pdf.

U.S. Census Bureau. 2012. *The American Indian and Alaska Native Population: 2010*. http://www.census.gov/prod /cen2010/briefs/c2010br-10.pdf.

U.S. Department of Education. 2015. "Settlement Reached with Palatine, Ill., Township High School District 211 to Remedy Transgender Discrimination" (press release), December 3. http://www.ed.gov/news/press-releases /settlement-reached-palatine-ill-township-high-school -district-211-remedy-transgender-discrimination.

U.S. Departments of Education and Justice. 2016. "Dear Colleague Letter on Transgender Students." http:// www2.ed.gov/about/offices/list/ocr/letters/colleague -201605-title-ix-transgender.pdf.

U.S. District Court. 2016. "Complaint for Declaratory and Injunctive Relief." https://www.texasattorneygeneral.gov /files/epress/files/2016/complaint_FM.pdf.

Vade, Dylan. 2005. "Expanding Gender and Expanding the Law: Toward a Social and Legal Conceptualization of Gender That Is More Inclusive of Transgender People." *Michigan Journal of Gender & Law* 11: 253–316.

Valentine, David. 2007. *Imagining Transgender: An Ethnography of a Category*. Durham, NC: Duke University Press.

Vertovec, Steven. 2007. "Super-Diversity and Its Implications." *Ethnic and Racial Studies* 30, no. 6: 1024–54.

———. 2010. "Towards Post-Multiculturalism? Changing Communities, Conditions and Contexts of Diversity." *International Social Science Journal* 61, no. 199: 83–95.

Vilain, Eric, and J. Michael Bailey. 2015. "What Should You Do If Your Son Says He's a Girl?" *Los Angeles Times*, May 21. http://www.latimes.com/opinion/op-ed/la-oe-vilain -transgender-parents-20150521-story.html.

Wacquant, Loïc. 1997. "For an Analytic of Racial Domination." *Political Power and Social Theory* 11: 221–34.

———. 2008. *Urban Outcasts: A Comparative Sociology of Advanced Marginality*. Cambridge: Polity.

———. 2010. "Class, Race and Hyperincarceration in Revanchist America." *Daedalus* 139, no. 3: 74–90.

Waidzunas, Tom. 2013. "Intellectual Opportunity Structures and Science-Targeted Activism: Influence of the Ex-Gay Movement on the Science of Sexual Orientation." *Mobilization* 18, no. 1: 1–18.

———. 2015. *The Straight Line: How the Fringe Science of Ex-Gay Therapy Reoriented Sexuality*. Minneapolis: University of Minnesota Press.

Wald, Gayle. 2000. *Crossing the Line: Racial Passing in Twentieth-Century U.S. Literature and Culture*. Durham, NC: Duke University Press.

Walker, Bela August. 2008. "Fractured Bonds: Policing Whiteness and Womanhood through Race-Based Marriage Annulments." *DePaul Law Review* 58: 1–50.

Walsh, Matt. 2015. "Rachel Dolezal Is Just Another Person Driven Insane by Liberalism." *The Blaze*, June 16. http://www.theblaze.com/contributions/rachel-dolezal-is-just-another-person-driven-insane-by-liberalism/.

Wang, Wendy. 2012. "The Rise of Intermarriage." Washington, DC: Pew Research Center.

———. 2015. "Interracial Marriage: Who is 'Marrying Out'?" *Pew Research Center*, June 12. http://www.pewresearch.org/fact-tank/2015/06/12/interracial-marriage-who-is-marrying-out/.

Warren, John T. 2001. "Doing Whiteness: On the Performative Dimensions of Race in the Classroom." *Communication Education* 50, no. 2: 91–108.

Waters, Mary C. 1990. *Ethnic Options: Choosing Identities in America*. Berkeley: University of California Press.

Waters, Mary C., and Philip Kasinitz. 2015. "The War on Crime and the War on Immigrants: Racial and Legal

Exclusion in 21st Century United States." In *Fear, Anxiety, and National Identity: Immigration and Belonging in North America and Western Europe*, edited by Nancy Foner and Patrick Simon, 116–43. New York: Russell Sage Foundation.

Weeks, Jeffrey. 1987. "Questions of Identity." In *The Cultural Construction of Sexuality*, edited by Pat Caplan, 31–51. London: Tavistock.

West, Candace, and Sarah Fenstermaker. 1995. "Doing Difference." *Gender & Society* 9, no. 1: 8–37.

West, Candace, and Don H. Zimmerman. 1987. "Doing Gender." *Gender & Society* 1, no. 2: 125–51.

West, Cornel. 1994. *Race Matters*. New York: Vintage Books.

Westbrook, Laurel, and Kristen Schilt. 2013. "Doing Gender, Determining Gender: Transgender People, Gender Panics, and the Maintenance of the Sex/Gender/Sexuality System." *Gender & Society* 28, no. 1: 32–57.

White, Khadijah. 2015. "Blackness Isn't Something That Can Be Acquired with a Little Bronzer." *Quartz*, June 13. http://qz.com/427519/rachel-dolezal-is-not-transracial/.

Wilchins, Riki Anne. 1997. *Read My Lips: Sexual Subversion and the End of Gender*. Ithaca, NY: Firebrand Books.

———. 2002. "It's Your Gender, Stupid." In *GenderQueer: Voices from beyond the Sexual Binary*, edited by Joan Nestle, Clare Howell, and Riki Anne Wilchins, 23–32. Los Angeles: Alyson Books.

———. 2004. *Queer Theory, Gender Theory: An Instant Primer*. Los Angeles: Alyson Books.

Wildhagen, Tina Marie. 2008. "What's Oppositional Culture Got to Do with It? Weighing the Empirical Evidence for Oppositional Culture Explanations for

Black-White Academic Achievement Gaps." PhD dissertation, University of Iowa.

Wilhelm, Maria. 1984. "Whether He's Black or White, the Voters Want Stebbins to Stay." *People*, June 11. http:// www.people.com/people/archive/article/0,,20088031,00 .html.

Wilkins, Amy C. 2008. *Wannabes, Goths, and Christians: The Boundaries of Sex, Style, and Status*. Chicago: University of Chicago Press.

Wilkinson, Will. 2015. "The Caitlyn Jenner Moment." *The Economist*, June 9. http://www.economist.com/blogs /democracyinamerica/2015/06/conservative-politics -and-american-religion.

Wilson, William Julius. 2011. "*The Declining Significance of Race*: Revisited and Revised." *Daedalus* 140, no. 2: 55–69.

———. 2012. *The Declining Significance of Race: Blacks and Changing American Institutions*. 3rd ed. (Orig. pub. 1980.) Chicago: University of Chicago Press.

Wimmer, Andreas. 2013. *Ethnic Boundary Making: Institutions, Power, Networks*. New York: Oxford University Press.

Winant, Howard. 2000. "Race and Race Theory." *Annual Review of Sociology* 26: 169–85.

Wright, Luther, Jr. 1995. "Who's Black, Who's White, and Who Cares: Reconceptualizing the United States's Definition of Race and Racial Classifications." *Vanderbilt Law Review* 48: 513–69.

Wright, Kristopher Thomas. 2010. "Queering Race." MA thesis, University of Texas, Austin.

Yang, Tseming. 2006. "Choice and Fraud in Racial Identification: The Dilemma of Policing Race in Affirmative Action, the Census, and a Color-Blind Society." *Michigan Journal of Race & Law* 11: 367–417.

Young, Cathy. 2014. "Campus Rape: The Problem with 'Yes Means Yes.'" *Time*, August 29. http://time.com/3222176/campus-rape-the-problem-with-yes-means-yes/.

Yoshino, Kenji. 2002. "Covering." *Yale Law Journal* 111, no. 4: 769–939.

———. 2006. *Covering: The Hidden Assault on Our Civil Rights*. New York: Random House.

Zhou, Zuyan. 2008. "Androgyny." In *The Oxford Encyclopedia of Women in World History*, edited by Bonnie G. Smith, 108–11. Oxford: Oxford University Press.

Zimeta, M. G. 2015. "Did It Have to Be the Hair?" *London Review of Books* (blog), June 15. http://www.lrb.co.uk/blog/2015/06/15/mg-zimeta/did-it-have-to-be-the-hair/.

Zucker, Kenneth J., and Anne A. Lawrence. 2009. "Epidemiology of Gender Identity Disorder: Recommendations for the Standards of Care of the World Professional Association for Transgender Health." *International Journal of Transgenderism* 11, no. 1: 8–18.

Index